GRAPHIC AS~~TROLOGY~~

The
ASTROLOGICAL
HOME STUDY
COURSE

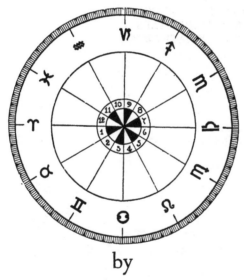

by

Ellen McCaffery, M.A.

MACOY PUBLISHING COMPANY ~ New York

By the Same Author

ASTROLOGY: ITS HISTORY AND INFLUENCE IN THE WEST-
ERN WORLD
THE SYMBOLISM OF COLOR
POETS AND THEIR STARS
THE FOUR INITIATIONS

To
MY ASTROLOGICAL FRIENDS
AND STUDENTS

PREFACE

♈ ♉ ♊ ♋ ♌ ♍ ♎ ♏ ♐ ♑ ♒ ♓

IT HAS always seemed to me that I learned astrology the hard way. I had been interested in the subject for many years, and had read a good deal about the signs and planets, finding them to be the co-ordinating factors in my extensive research into many phases of Symbolism. However, when I finally decided to settle down to the mathematics of astrology during the First World War, I found myself floundering through logarithmic corrections before I knew exactly what I was trying to correct, and also before I knew, without looking at the titles, just which of my textbooks was an Ephemeris, and which was a Table of Houses.

The logarithms were not new to me, but no one gave me any bird's-eye view of what the horoscope was supposed to show. To me, it was an enigma, because the east was where I might have expected the west. When I constructed a chart for noon, I was not told that the symbol of the Sun must assuredly be in the south. I was taught on a rule-of-thumb method, not understanding what I was doing, but blindly striving to follow a routine, and being reproved when I asked why.

When I had time to reflect upon my notes, I realized that things would have been simpler, if only some reasons had been introduced. Then and there I made up my mind that if I ever taught astrology—which did not seem likely at the time—my students should not wander through the same labyrinths. They should build fact upon fact, and they should have plenty of diagrams to help them. One diagram is often of more value when teaching than a thousand words.

In true teaching, we must proceed from the known to the unknown. As we add facts, these facts must provide the base for the next step. GRAPHIC ASTROLOGY, or THE HOME STUDY COURSE, takes you easily step by step, with only the simplest elementary-school arithmetic, into the full understanding of your horoscope. There is nothing mysterious about the subject. In fact, it is so logical that you will be amazed.

The more you study astrology, the more interesting and illuminating it becomes. Even apart from prediction, the subject has definite value in your life. It enables you to consider the events of your life in a more intelligent way, for the simple reason that it reveals the particular forces which bring about events. Because you understand cause and effect, you become less impatient with life. When you know the forces that are operating, you can to a large extent control, if not the events, then certainly most of the effects upon yourself. You are enabled to seize opportunity at the right moment. You discover that when one line of action is not propitious, another line of action may be feasible.

You should try to understand astrology as a philosophy that explains life, and not merely as a predictive science. Astrology is the searchlight that reveals your own self to you. It is more than this. It is the Awakener, for when you see clearly, you discover within yourself the reservoir of your being. In this reservoir there are many qualities that you have never used. These will be awakened. Set them into motion and your life will be more completely rounded, more purposeful, and more useful.

I hope all my readers will enjoy this textbook.

ELLEN McCAFFERY

New York
1952

CONTENTS

♈ ♉ ♊ ♋ ♌ ♍ ♎ ♏ ♐ ♑ ♒ ♓

Page

DIAGRAMS AND ILLUSTRATIONS

♈ ♉ ♊ ♋ ♌ ♍ ♎ ♏ ♐ ♑ ♒ ♓

Looking into Thomas A. Edison's Horoscope,
   by Charles H. Forbell   FRONTISPIECE

ILLUSTRATIONS

By Charles Forbell

Getting Acquainted with Astrology

♈ ♉ ♊ ♋ ♌ ♍ ♎ ♏ ♐ ♑ ♒ ♓

What is Astrology—this subject which has captured the imagination of the ages? It is man's attempt to discover the unity of the universe, to know that the infinitely distant Sun, Moon, and planets, in their motions and reactions upon one another, are symbolic of his own journey through life—they may even influence him.

Astrology was originally divided into four parts, and we still recognize the four divisions:

1. **Natural Astrology** is that which relates to the motion of the heavenly bodies, and to their physical effects upon the earth, such as are seen in weather, earthquakes, etc.
2. **Judicial Astrology** deals with nations and governments. It illumines current events and shows the trend of national policies.
3. **Genethliacal Astrology** is that which is applied to the birth data of an individual. Prenatal Astrology is that which is applied to conception. The data is calculated from the birth chart.
4. **Horary Astrology** is that which is applied to some specific question of the moment.

Natural Astrology has become our modern science of Astronomy, although weather prediction is still a highly perfected art in the hands of certain astrological specialists. Genethliacal Astrology is now termed **Natal Astrology,** while Judicial Astrology is termed **Mundane.**

All civilized nations seem to have studied astrology from quite an early date, whether in America, North Africa, the Near East, Asia, or Europe. Dr. H. J. Spenden of the Peabody Museum of Harvard, has this to say concerning the amazing knowledge of the Mayans: [1]

"Their record of eclipses from the eighth to the fifteenth century were 70 per cent correct, a record all the more wonderful considering the fact that only 10 per cent eclipses can be seen from Central America."

The evidence of the influence of the stars upon human beings was known to the Egyptians many centuries before Christ. Champollion, the great French pioneer in Egyptology, found in the tomb of Rameses V a papyrus, laid there to help the dead king on his journey through the underworld, giving the ascending stars and their influence for every hour of every day for a whole year.

Professor G. Maspero,[2] in his book *The Dawn of Civilization,* speaking of the ancient Egyptians, tells us that the priests trained their young novitiates to look at the stars so assiduously that in time the boys developed distant sight, so that they could observe stars of the fifth magnitude.

Then far away on the banks of the Euphrates and Tigris, the Babylonians developed an extraordinary civilization in which their chief science was astrology. Archeologists have discovered whole libraries of clay tablets upon which astrological knowledge had been inscribed. Chaldea, having lost its independence, became a province of Babylon, but by the eighth century before Christ, the Chaldeans had become the ruling class in Babylonia, and their very name became a synonym for astrology. Some years ago historians doubted the fact that Sargon the Agade, an ancient king of Assyria, could have flourished as early as 3,800 B.C. However, when the *Annals* of his life were discovered in a clay tablet library, Professor A. H. Sayce, a most able researcher on Assyria, took the trouble to have all the astrological data checked, and the dates corresponded to that period. **Astrology proved the date.**

The Greeks became heirs of much of the astrological knowledge of Persia, Egypt, and Assyria. When Alexander the Great set out to conquer the world, he took with him a scientist named Callisthenes, a nephew of Aristotle.[3] When the army reached Babylon, Callisthenes sent back to his uncle, Aristotle, large quantities of astronomical observations, which the Babylonians had been gathering for over nineteen hundred years before Alexander reached the city. He wrote his uncle that still earlier observations had been recorded, but that he had not been able to obtain them.

The Roman Cicero [4] in his *Divinations* says that the Assyrians and Babylonians knew so much concerning astrology because they lived on a vast plain from which they could gaze at an unbroken sweep of sky. We know that the Greeks, Romans, and Babylonians, invented certain instruments to determine the movement and position of the planets. In the palace of Sennacherib [5] at Koyunjik a portion of an astrolabe (an instrument used to determine the altitude of the stars) was discovered. It is now in the British Museum. Cicero was acquainted with all phases of divination. At one time he aspired to the high office of Chief Augur of the Romans, but he did not receive this appointment. Consequently, when he came to write his *Divinations*, much of his criticism of astrology and other forms of prediction can be put down to sour grapes.

The best textbook of Roman astrological practice that has come down to us was written by **Manilius**, who is said to have planned to dedicate it to the Emperor Augustus Caesar. It was translated into English by Thomas Creech in 1697. We shall give you a few extracts from this later. It is obvious that

Manilius knew that the world is round, and he went to some length in his book to prove it. Whatever the enemies of astrology say to the contrary, there has been no astrologer of repute since the time of Manilius who has believed in a flat earth theory. Manilius stated that the Milky Way is composed of millions of little stars, a fact which today is said to have been unknown until the discovery of the telescope.

PTOLEMY AND ASTROLOGY

In the first half of the second century after Christ, the greatest astronomer and geographer was **Ptolemy**. He was a native of Egypt and lived at Alexandria, a famous seat of learning. His works on astronomy were the main authorities until the time of **Copernicus**. He wrote a treatise on astrology called *Tetrabiblos*, which, though not used by modern astrologers to any great extent, shows many of the truths of the science. It is quite easily obtainable in English. Ptolemy also wrote a hundred aphorisms on astrology. These he called the *Centiloquy*. The book can be described as the hundred best answers to students' questions on the *Tetrabiblos*.

THE NEAR EAST AND ASTROLOGY

Although the Western part of the Roman Empire fell before the barbarians in 475 A.D., the Eastern part of the Empire with its capital at Constantinople (formerly Byzantium, and now Istanbul) remained secure for a long time, ruling for varying periods over Greece, the Balkans, the Near East, Palestine, and Egypt. In this city, books on art, science, and astrology were written and studied for many centuries. The textbook on astrology written by **Julius Firmicus Maternus** shortly after 334 A.D. seems to have been the most renowned. In it the author mentions that Julius Caesar made a translation of *The Phenomena* of the Greek **Aratus** of Soli. This was a poem dealing with astronomy. We know that Julius Caesar was elected Pontifix Maximus in 67 B.C., and that in this position he supervised the augurs. One wonders if some of the emperor's campaigns might not have owed much of their success to his use of astrology.

As the Arabs grew in power and knowledge, they obtained scientific and astrological books from the Byzantines; thus, from the eighth to the tenth centuries they developed able writers on astrology. These Arabic books were in time translated into Latin by Europeans after the latter had settled down and become more civilized. Among the translations we find astrological books and treatises by **Al Kindi** and **Albumazar**. Copies of these, and of other well-known writers of the Near East, together with those of several Persians, were found in William Lilly's library, and were later donated by Sir Elias Ashmole to the Ashmolean Library at Oxford. Arabic textbooks were the standard textbooks on astrology down to the seventeenth century. Longfellow, when translating Dante into English verse, studied Albumazar's works in order to follow the astronomical and astrological references in *The Divine Comedy*. Albumazar predicted a great social revolution in 1789. This could have been one of the earliest forecasts of the French Revolution.

ASTROLOGY IN THE MIDDLE AGES

Although the Druids [6] were great astrologers, much of their learning was apparently lost during the Dark Ages; so also was the astrological legacy left by Persian priests of Mithraism, who were displaced by Christianity. Thus, during the Middle Ages, when we find a revival of astrology, the knowledge seems to have come to Europe indirectly through the Byzantine Empire, and directly through Arabic translations. Some slight knowledge also came through those Crusaders who were interested in the learning of the Arabians. The literature of the Middle Ages teems with references to astrology. Geoffrey

Chaucer [7] wrote *A Treatise on the Astrolabe* in order to teach astrology to his young son at Oxford. He says: "Every one of the twelve signs hath respect to a certain part of the body of man, as Aries governs thy head, and Taurus thy neck and thy throat, Gemini thine armholes, and arms, and so forth as shall be shown in the five parts of this Treatise."

Thomas Aquinas [8] is said to have written and spoken against astrology, but it seems that his objection was to the charlatans of his time, and not to those who really knew and understood their astrology. Paul Choisnard in 1926 wrote an extraordinarily illuminating book entitled *St. Thomas d'Aquin et l'Influence des Astres* in order to bring out this fact. He says:

"When one speaks of eminent beings,. who in the course of centuries have adhered to this 'absurd superstition,' so to speak, one does not as a rule need to state them in any apologetic tone, nor with any embarrassment. There are: St. Thomas, Tacitus,[9] Galien,[10] Tycho Brahe, Kepler, Cardinal d'Ailly,[11] and others. What demands attention in St. Thomas, is that he is the only philosopher who has openly adopted the principles of the influence of the stars in his doctrine, and who has spoken of astrology with politeness in many parts of his discussions. I believe that in the matter of astrology the doctrine of St. Thomas has been very little understood. St. Thomas was not an astrologer in the sense of a maker of horoscopes, but he had too good sense and courage in the light of astrology to avoid its essential facts in his works, and to avoid what astrology has of truth. It is to my knowledge the only philosophy which has known how to distinguish between true and false astrology, and not confound the two in the same superstition. He has maintained with good sense, but with a shining prudence which we must admire, that a guard must be set against the abuse which people can make of astrology."

Dante: [12] The basic structure of Dante's *Divine Comedy* is astrological. Dante starts on his wanderings accompanied by

Virgil, when the Sun is in Aries, which rules new beginnings. He comes to Purgatory when the Sun is in Scorpio, the sign of regeneration. He comes to the top of Purgatory when the Sun is in Taurus, the sign of the Earthly Paradise. In the *Paradiso* he journeys through the seven planets, learning the lesson of each, and feeling the deep joys of each.

Jerome Cardan: In the very early sixteenth century the most spectacular physician, mathematician, and astrologer was Jerome Cardan, who was born in Pavia, Italy. He wrote a text-book on astrology and also *Century of Aphorisms*. His claim to mathematical fame rests upon his discoveries of the solution of cubic equations in which he transcended every mathematician of his day.

Tycho Brahe (born December 14, 1546—died 1601) was a Dane and the major astronomer of his times. The King of Denmark built and equipped for him an observatory in the Island of Hvea. This observatory was called Stellberg, or City of the Stars. There Brahe worked on what is called the Tychonic system of astronomy, which sought to reconcile some of the old findings of Ptolemy with those of Copernicus. His pupil, Kepler, however, working on some of the later findings of his master, decided to destroy all that he thought wrong in Brahe's system. Tycho Brahe was also an astrologer and wrote horoscopes for the king's family. In 1577 he made a remarkable prophecy that in Finland there would be born a warrior prince who would conquer Germany. He stated that this prince would disappear in 1632. There is no doubt that this was Gustavus Adolphus, King of Sweden, who was born in Finland, who warred with Germany, and who was finally killed in battle in 1632.

John Napier (born 1550—died 1617), Laird of Merchiston, near Edinburgh, was so interested in astrology that he invented logarithms in order to simplify some of the calculations.

John Kepler (born December 21, 1571—died 1630) was at

first assistant-astronomer to Tycho Brahe, then on the latter's death, succeeded him as Principal Mathematician to the Emperor. His three great laws on planetary motion revolutionized astronomical calculations. He was also a good astrologer, and made some valuable suggestions on progression, directions, and aspects. Kepler chose his second wife by means of astrology.

Francis Bacon (born January 22, 1561—died 1626) wrote among other things a book of *Essays*, one of which is called "Of Prophecy." In this he relates the story of the death of the French king, Henry II, who was mortally wounded in a tournament with the Comte de Montgomery. The queen, Catherine de Medici, had had Henry's horoscope calculated under an assumed name, and she had been told that the native would be killed in a duel. Since no one was allowed to challenge the king, it did not seem likely that Henry could meet his death in this way, but it happened that Henry challenged the Comte. It is said that the queen's own special astrologers—Ruggieri, Gauricus, and Nostradamus—all prophesied this event.

Although Francis Bacon seems to have been friendly to astrology, we find that the era in which he lived was one of the great periods for the hunting and burning of witches. This was largely due to the private views of James I, who had a firm belief in the evil power of witchcraft, and who wrote a book against demonology and witchcraft. The early Stuart age also witnessed a great struggle throughout Europe between the adherents of the Copernican [14] system of astronomy and those of the Ptolemaic system. Curiously enough, those who adhered to Ptolemy were the most opposed to astrology. Among these was Canon John Chamber, lecturer at Oxford on the Ptolemaic System, who wrote a book entitled *Treatise Against Judicial Astrology*, in 1601. This was ably answered by Sir Christopher Heydon, a well-known soldier of the period, whose major hobby was astrology. In spite of condemnation from many quarters, astrology took hold of the people more strongly than ever. William Lilly published the first major textbook on the subject in the English language, and many Latin textbooks were translated into English. People who were religiously inclined, stated boldly that the only kind of astrology to be condemned was "that which imposeth necessity upon our souls," that is, the kind that prevents us from exercising our free will, or rather our capacity to make free choice between good and evil.

THE MODERN AGE OF ASTROLOGY

William Lilly (born April 30, 1602 O.S.—died 1681) was prominent in his astrological practice, but his claim to fame rests upon his books. His textbook on Horary Astrology is still used by astrologers. He was a yeoman's son and had to learn Latin before he could study astrology. He therefore determined that for the future astrologers should learn their subject in their native tongue. Perhaps the best known of his prophecies were those predicting the Great Plague of London in 1663 and the Great Fire in 1666.

One of the satirists of the times, Samuel Butler (1612–1680), wrote a long poem, called *Hudibras*, for the amusement of Charles II, satirizing the Puritans, but Butler for some reason could not help ridiculing Lilly also, and astrology in general. Lilly is called Sidrophel (angel of the stars), and the hero Hudibras comes to him for a reading. The story of how the Puritan Hudibras has to conquer his religious scruples before he can interview Sidrophel, and how Sidrophel makes his servant find out in advance what the knight wishes to know, the various arguments for and against astrology, and the final free fight that develops between Sir Hudibras and the astrologer, provide some of the most delightfully humorous reading in the English language.

Modern newspapers and magazines often treat their readers

to similar arguments against astrologers, but Samuel Butler said it all much better in 1664. *And still astrology goes forward!*

One great value of *Hudibras* is that we see from a contemporary source the enormous popularity of Lilly during the English Civil War:

> Did not our great reformers use
> This Sidrophel to forbode news;
> To write of victories next year,
> And castles taken, yet i' the air?
> Of battles fought at sea, and ships
> Sunk two years hence? the last eclipse?
> A total overthrow given to the king
> In Cornwall, horse and foot next spring?

Lilly was once asked why he could not help Charles 1, since he had once given that monarch a reading. Lilly replied laconically, "I told him to go east, and he went west."

The Royal Observatory at Greenwich: One of the greatest things that Francis Bacon did was to stir up a desire for experimental science. He wanted men to tabulate the result of their findings, and from these findings to make their conclusions. In this way modern science grew into being. Under the old method men stated their beliefs, and then tried to make facts fit their theories.

Bacon did not live long enough to see the Royal Observatory built at Greenwich, a suburb of London. However, it was largely due to his insistence upon observation that such an observatory came into being.

John Flamsteed (1646–1719) was quite a noteworthy astronomer-astrologer of the period. He just missed the credit of being the discoverer of the planet Uranus by thinking, when he observed it through his telescope, that it was a fixed star. He was appointed first Astronomer Royal before the building was erected. According to the custom of the time, he calculated a horoscope for the laying of the foundation stone, and chose August 10, 1675, at 3:14 P.M. The map of this is still preserved at the observatory among his effects. The planetary positions for this date are given in *A Thousand and One Notable Nativities*. Reading the chart we find the lordly Jupiter rising, indicating that Charles II took a great interest. The king was quick to realize that the observatory would provide his sea captains with accurate nautical almanacs. Flamsteed did not know of Uranus, Neptune, and Pluto. If he had known the qualities of Neptune, he would not have allowed this planet to lie in the Second House of money. The sporadic payment of his salary made him so desperate at times that he was forced to eke out his income by clerical duties and teaching. Like Galileo, Tycho Brahe, and Kepler, he earned money by reading horoscopes.

NINETEENTH AND TWENTIETH CENTURY ASTROLOGERS

There had been astrologers in America from at least 1738 when a Welshman, Crawson Craniker, came over. Also before the Revolution were Michael Peter Jarris, Philip C. Widmer, and Hubert Johnstone. These were succeeded by others, and a great revival in astrology took place both in America and in Europe during the nineteenth century. **Dr. Luke D. Broughton** (1828–1899), a physician of New York City, in his *Elements of Astrology* gives exciting accounts of violent men and women storming his home at times, merely because he thought human beings could be helped by his astrological knowledge. His major prediction was that the United States would be at war during the early 1940's. How true that was!

In England, later, **Alan Leo** (Frederick William Allan, 1860–1917) did perhaps more than anyone else to put the subject on a philosophical basis. Through his publications he brought a number of other capable astrologers before the public. Among these was **Sepharial** (Walter Gornold, 1864–

1930). Sepharial was an astronomer and became a member of
the Royal Astronomical Society of Great Britain, being introduced to that body by H. M. Christie, then the Astronomer
Royal. Owing, however, to the objection of some of the members to his use of the letters F.R.A.S. in connection with his
astrological work, he resigned. Camille Flammarion, then the
most famous French astronomer, introduced him into the
Société Astronomique of France, and Sepharial continued as a
member of that body until his death. Sepharial was later
elected a member of the Astronomical Society of Great Britain,
and he continued as a member of that body also until his
death.

WHY IS ASTROLOGY ATTRACTING SO MUCH NOTICE?

Astrologers assign the rulership of astrology to the planet
Uranus. Uranus takes eighty-four years to move through its
orbit. It is consequently about seven years in each sign. It was
in its own sign Aquarius from 1912–1919, and a great impetus
was given to astrology about that time. When it entered the
sign Aries, which rules all dynamic beginnings, the American
people became fascinated with the subject. It was during this
period that **Evangeline Adams** made her radio broadcasts. By
the time Uranus entered Gemini, a sign which has much influence over the United States, there was hardly a person in
the country who had not read an astrological magazine.

Among the planets, Uranus is termed the Awakener. Astrology is essentially a subject that awakens the interest, the consciousness, and the forces within the mind in a way that practically no other subject can. It gives man new concepts, and a
new grasp of every subject to which he applies its principles,
whether philosophy, color, art, chemistry, agriculture, or
weather forecasting. The only warning of the "Big Snow" in
New York on December 26–27, 1947, came from an astrologer!
The proof of any science is that one can predict by it. Ulti-

mately, astrology becomes the greatest co-ordinating factor within the totality of human knowledge and experience. For this reason too it is a science—not an amusement.

ASTROLOGY AND THE CONQUEST OF FEAR

The most destructive of all our emotions individually and collectively is fear. Through fear we may lose the greatest opportunities of our lives. Through fear we make enemies. Through fear we lead narrow and compressed lives which are of very little value to ourselves or to those whom we contact. Through fear we create thoughts of trouble, anxiety, disaster, and strife. Such thoughts attract the very things we wish to avoid.

How can astrology help us to dispel fear? Rightly understood, astrology is the most valuable of all studies in this connection. It teaches us that we are all parts of the harmony and symmetry of the universe. No one is unwanted and no one is unnecessary. No one is independent of the whole. Consequently, if we study our charts seriously, we must realize that there is **a real plan in our lives.** The plan must be right, but we, through fear, mismanage the construction. We work in a perfunctory way, we grumble, and wish we had some other plan. Astrology gives us the courage to know that the plan would never have been given to us, if we could not carry it through. Sorrows and afflictions are merely the factors employed to shape, and to alter, the crude materials, to bend the iron to the right shape, and to cut the stone to the right proportions. The joys and happiness that we meet in life are the beginnings of contacts with the infinitely greater harmony of the spheres.

ASTROLOGY TEACHES US TO BE OURSELVES

Our stars rule us until we have reached the stage mentioned in the previous paragraph. While we are in process of being shaped and formed, we are unable to express our real true self, because we are under the limiting and confining influence of the planets. When, however, we are free enough to express the real purpose for which we came, and are working with our stars, then, being at one with them and the high destiny which they plan for us, we may be said to rule them in the sense that, understanding all, we desire nothing but what is planned, purposed, and desired by the Power that puts the stars in motion. We become rulers then, not by pitting our will against destiny, but by co-operating with it. Iron sinks in water, but by understanding the laws of the universe, man has discovered how to keep iron ships afloat. There are few conditions in life that cannot be improved by the application of right thought. The childish mind, however, prefers to smash things.

The charts of the greatest people are often the most sorely afflicted, but these people, by exercising their powers of knowledge, faith, and will, have made their successes quite extraordinary. They have prided themselves upon penetrating to the heart of each difficulty and discovering the adjustments that have to be made. When there is great pressure, a powerful boiler is needed to prevent the steam from bursting the boiler. So the greatest souls are often enclosed in the hardest circumstances of life, until they learn how to direct their innate powers to the specific work they came to do. They learn how to use safety valves.

ARE NOT THE SAME STARS OVER ALL?

The usual objection made by the unthinking, and by those not acquainted with the procedure of casting the horoscope, is that the same stars are over everyone and that the stars therefore cannot have anything to do with individual fate. When you have learned how to calculate the horoscope of birth, you will see that even a few minutes can make a real and vital difference in the fate. In the case of twin girls born twelve minutes apart, the difference was so vital that with one there were two marriages, while with the other there was no marriage.

HOW CAN THE SUN AFFECT US?

The Sun affects all life on this earth, including mankind, and the astrologer assigns the life force within man to the Sun. Science knows that different periods of the day bring about different effects upon vegetation. One often hears the gardener say, "This plant cannot thrive unless it has morning sunshine." The astrologer estimates the energy of the person under consideration from the sign, house, and aspects of the Sun. He can also tell the direction of the energy, whether it affects money, mind, sports, science, or the arts.

Since man derives life from his father, the astrologer states that the father is partly indicated by the Sun; he determines the kind of father and, in part, the social status of the father from the place, house, and aspects of the Sun. There are, of course, other indications which you will learn later.

CAN THE MOON AFFECT US?

The Moon affects the tides and water in particular. Since man's body is over 70 per cent water, it is reasonable to postulate that the Moon will have some effect upon man's physical body. It is interesting to note that more deaths take place at low tide than at high tide, while births are more numerous at high tide than at low. The astrologer assigns motherhood and the emotions to the Moon. In almost all the mythologies of the world there has been a Moon goddess said to preside over birth. This was because woman is peculiarly attuned to the Moon's twenty-eight-day period. We might note that the number forty in symbolism was said to be a number of endurance, or suffering. If we take forty weeks of seven days, or 280 days, this is, approximately the time of the duration of pregnancy.

WHY DOES AN ASTROLOGER SAY CERTAIN DAYS
ARE GOOD OR BAD?

When making any statement as to whether certain days are good or bad, the astrologer is wise if he will study the birth chart of the individual he is considering. A day that is good for one individual may be bad for another. Generally speaking, we call certain planets benefic and others malefic. If during a particular day a benefic planet comes to the same degree that a benefic occupies in the birth chart, then good results will follow. If a malefic comes to this benefic planet then trouble may follow, but if a malefic comes to the degree of a malefic in the birth chart, then considerable trouble may come.

"Fate is not the ruler but the servant of Providence." Astrology shows us that the planet Mercury governs the mind. We reap our reward according to the way we use our mind. If Mercury comes to the planet Mars, we can use this energy to fight people, or we can do some constructive work. If Mercury comes to Saturn, we can be melancholy and mean, or we can use the rays of Saturn to help us delve down into the structure of things. It all depends upon how we discipline our minds, just what we will do when the planets move. The more un-evolved the soul, the more it responds to adverse planetary vibration. When looking over some of the horoscopes of the dictators during World War II, one could not help but notice how malefic transits over their birth planets simply indicated the evil things they did to other people—until their own hour struck!

WHY WE USE THE PLANETS AND NOT THE FIXED STARS
IN ASTROLOGY

The answer is that occasionaly the astrologer does use the fixed stars, but he should be able to read all the main trends and events of life and character from the planets without any reference to the fixed stars. Some of William Lilly's mundane predictions were accomplished by noting fixed stars impinging upon the Ascendant of London, which is 17°54′ Gemini.

The planets are peculiarly attuned to our solar system, since they were originally thrown off the body of the sun. The distances of each of our planets from the sun are not irregular, but in proportion. This was discovered by a German astronomer, Johann Elert Bode (1747–1825). His findings are known as Bode's Law, but this law does not seem to work too well on the proportional distances of the newer planets.

THE PLANETS AND THE FIXED STARS

The name planet means a wanderer. The term was applied because the planets do not keep their places among the fixed stars. They are satellites of the sun and belong to the solar system. In early days there were said to be seven planets. This number included the Sun and the Moon, although the old astrologers knew, as well as we do, that neither of these latter bodies are planets. When we ask a student of today to be sure that he has inserted all ten planets in his horoscope, we mean eight planets plus the Sun and Moon. The phrase "seven planets," or "ten planets," is simply a convenient term of reference.

The fixed stars keep their relative places in the constellations. It is because of this "fixity" that we are able to recognize each constellation. Of course, all the stars have motion, but the term "fixed" is in general use in the sense that we cannot see any appreciable change in their relative positions from year to year. As regards the Sun, it is not in a "fixed" place in the heavens, but actually travels through space. Everything moves. The astrologer still uses the Ptolemaic System of imagining that the earth, from which he makes his calculations, is "fixed" for an instant in time; thus, he uses distances and positions as seen from the earth, as being more convenient to him. He uses what are called the **Geocentric** * positions of the planets. In

the Copernican System the astronomer imagines that the Sun
is in a "fixed" position, and he makes all his calculations from
the Sun to the planets, calling these **Heliocentric** * positions.
As regards accuracy, both methods are correct. It is the same
distance from the Earth to the Sun as it is from the Sun to
the Earth. We should add, however, that a great many astrologers have for the last hundred years, or more, experimented
with heliocentric positions of the planets, and that they have
compiled heliocentric almanacs.

Since the planets travel on their own elliptical orbits around
the Sun, it will often happen that they are much farther away
than at other times. For example, Venus can be as close as
twenty-five million miles away, but when she is at the farthest
point of her orbit, she can be a hundred and sixty-five million
miles away.

The following terms, referring to the least and greatest
distances, are in general use among astrologers:

Perihelion: refers to any planet, or the earth, at its closest distance
from the Sun.

Aphelion: refers to any planet, or the earth, at its greatest distance from the Sun.

Perigee: refers to the Moon at its closest distance to the earth.

Apogee: refers to the Moon at its farthest distance to the earth.

INFERIOR AND SUPERIOR PLANETS

Because the Moon, Mercury, and Venus lie between the
Earth and the Sun, they are said to be *Inferior Planets*, while
all the other planets are said to be *Superior*. The words *Inferior* and *Superior* in this sense refer to position, and not to
quality.

PLANETARY TRAVEL AROUND THE SUN

We do not have to memorize the rate at which the planets
travel around the Sun, but it is sometimes helpful to the as-

* These words are derived from Ge the earth and *Helios* the sun.

trologer to realize the approximate rates at which they travel:

Mercury takes	88	days to travel around the Sun						
Venus	"	224½	"	"	"	"	"	"
Earth	"	365¼	"	"	"	"	"	"
Mars	"	1	year and 322 days "		"	"		
Jupiter	"	12	years to travel	"		"	"	
Saturn	"	29½	"	"	"	"	"	"
Uranus	"	84	"	"	"	"	"	"
Neptune	"	165	"	"	"	"	"	"
Pluto	"	248	"	"	"	"	"	"

THE SIGNS VERSUS THE CONSTELLATIONS

The constellations of the heavens and the signs of the zodiac have the same names, and so are often confused. They have identical names because their positions used to coincide approximately. In round numbers this was about 2000 B.C., when the spring equinox lay in the constellation of the Ram. Now the signs and the constellations are nearly one sign apart. The spring equinox lies in the sign Aries, but in the constellation of the Fishes. *The astrologer uses the signs, and not the constellations*, when he states planetary positions. The signs are merely divisions of thirty degrees of space in the heavens, and the first sign Aries is the first thirty degrees of space that subtends the vernal equinox. The vernal equinox is the day in spring (about March 21) when day and night are equal in time. Astrologically, the equinox falls on the day when the Sun reaches the zero degree Aries. Our signs are thus calculated from what is termed by astrologers the Aries ingress which, as we said before, is now in the constellation Pisces, or one sign behind. We mention this because you may meet persons who have learned a little astronomy, and who enjoy baiting the student astrologer. You may happen to say your Sun sign is Cancer, whereat he will say with an air of finality which he hopes will ruin your confidence, "You were born in the constellation Gemini." Your best answer is to say pleasantly, "Then since we are both right, there is no need to argue."

IMPORTANCE OF THE YEAR OF BIRTH

Mercury and Venus never travel very far away from the Sun sign in any year, but the other planets may be close, or far away, according to the year of birth. Neptune may stay fourteen years in a particular sign, while Uranus may stay seven years. These more ponderous planets affect the individual, not only in his own life, but also in the historical period in which he is born.

The children born from 1915–1939 all had Neptune in Leo. Leo stands for authority and Neptune seeps at the foundation of the sign he occupies. Thus the children born during that period, part of which coincided with World War I, seemed to be more opposed to authority than those born before the war. Leo also rules kings, and Neptune in Leo disposed of a large percentage of them. Pluto in Leo (1938–1957) is also adverse to kings and to authority.

WHAT IS A HOROSCOPE?

The word *horoscope* means the hour pointer, and referred originally to the degree of the sign rising upon the eastern horizon at the time of birth. William Lilly said, "The nineteenth degree [17'54"] of Gemini is London's **horoscope**, and at the foundation of the city the Sun was in twenty-five degrees of the same sign." We see from this that the term **horoscope** was confined to the Ascendant. It now means more than this: **A horoscope is the map of the heavens erected in order to determine the destiny of a person born at a specific time and place upon the earth.** Such a map is not to be confused with the **solar horoscope,** which is not a map of the heavens at all, but merely a reading based upon the Sun sign as a possible Ascendant. Since there can be only twelve solar horoscopes, it stands to reason that these cannot account for the lives of all the millions of people in the world. A horoscope is sometimes

called a **Nativity,** and the person whose data is used is termed
the **Native.**

From our definition of a horoscope, it will be seen that it is
necessary for the astrologer to know the latitude and longitude
of the birthplace, also the time of birth, before he can erect a
correct horoscope. Such a horoscope, or chart of the heavens
related to time and place, is essential before the astrologer can
proceed to any definite interpretation and judgment.

The horoscope reveals, if read intelligently, the native's
most beneficial planets, and the departments of life in which
success is most probable.

The erection of a chart is comparatively easy for any person
who can add, subtract, and multiply. The reading of a chart,
however, calls for the faculty of judgment, that is, the ability
to deduce what is likely to happen when two or more forces are
put into action. Remember that nothing in this world is sure,
but some probabilities can be greater than others. In a horoscope we may note that some planets may be over the place of
birth, while others will be under the earth. The rays from the
planets above the earth tend to bring the native into prominence early in life, yet those below may give more enduring
fame. To determine such and other matters requires reflection,
time, and consideration.

THE ZODIAC AND ITS SIGNS

The names of the signs of the zodiac can be remembered
from the following ancient lines:

> The Ram, the Bull, the Heavenly Twins,
> And next the Crab, the Lion shines,
> The Virgin and the Scales;
> The Scorpion, Archer, and Sea-Goat,
> The Man that bears the Water-Pot;
> And Fish with glittering tails.
> —Isaac Watts

The term *zodiac* is one of the numerous Arabic terms be-
queathed to us by the Arabic astrologers. It means animals,
and has reference to the various animals mentioned above.

THE TWELVE SIGNS OF THE ZODIAC AND THE PARTS OF THE BODY

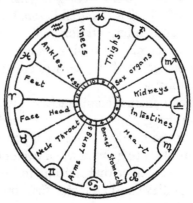

DIAGRAM 1
The Signs and Parts of the Body

The twelve signs of the Zodiac are in the following order:

1. Aries, the Ram
2. Taurus, the Bull
3. Gemini, the Twins
4. Cancer, the Crab
5. Leo, the Lion
6. Virgo, the Virgin
7. Libra, the Scales
8. Scorpio, the Scorpion
9. Sagittarius, the Archer
10. Capricorn, the Goat
11. Aquarius, the Waterman
12. Pisces, the Fishes

The twelve signs form in succession the twelve main parts of
the human body:

1. Aries, the head and face
2. Taurus, the neck and throat
3. Gemini, the arms and shoulders, hands and lungs
4. Cancer, the breast and stomach
5. Leo, the heart and spinal
marrow
6. Virgo, the intestines, bow-
els
7. Libra, loins and kidneys
8. Scorpio, the sex organs

   9. Sagittarius, the thighs   11. Aquarius, legs and ankles
10. Capicorn, the knees   12. Pisces, the feet

The signs must be learned by heart and in their correct sequence. Later, they should be learned in pairs of opposites. These opposing signs are really polarities, because there is a reflex action between them. For example, we know that when we are violently nauseated, our knees can become shaky. As soon as you begin to set up a chart, you will realize why you need facility in knowing these opposite signs. One last word of caution:

Remember that all twelve signs of the zodiac will be in your own horoscope, so start from the beginning to see the good in each sign, and despise none. Each one of you has a head, even if your Sun sign does not happen to be Aries.

LESSON TWO

The Signs and Their Symbols

♈ ♉ ♊ ♋ ♌ ♍ ♎ ♏ ♐ ♑ ♒ ♓

INTRODUCTION: The symbols of the signs are the alphabet of astrology. *It is very important that you memorize them, and that you think of each sign in terms of its symbol. As a child you had to think of the symbol 7 as number seven. It was impossible for you to learn arithmetic properly until you had mastered the symbols of the numbers. In the same way, you cannot work with any facility in astrology until you know its symbols.*

Regarding our Calendar of Birthdays, since the Sun does not always change its sign on the same calendar day each year, it is sometimes necessary to set up a whole horoscope of a person before one can determine whether the Sun is in the last few minutes of a sign, or at the beginning of the next sign. When compiling this Calendar over a period of years with several thousand dates under consideration, one might have thought that famous people would have been evenly distributed through the days. This is not so. For some days there were twenty or thirty people to list. For others days it took years to find even one famous person who had been born on that particular day. In a few cases famous people have been born on the same day and year. We have inserted a few of these astrological twins.

THE SYMBOL OF ARIES IS

*For Those Born
March 21–April 19*

The symbol of Aries looks like the horns of a ram. It also resembles the nose and eyebrows of a man. It is really composed of two half-moons joined by a straight line. The vertical line in all symbolism is emblematic of the scepter of authority of the Sun—the source of all life and vitality. It was said by ancient astrologers that the Sun symbolized the real ego of man —his individuality. The Moon is only the reflector of the light of the Sun. It has no light of itself, so it was said to represent the soul of man, which had life and consciousness only in so far as this life has been conferred by the Sun. The Moon's symbol is the crescent moon which, when on its side, looks like a bowl or cup.

In the symbol of Aries there are two moons inverted, for in this life all things appear to be in pairs of opposites or in polarity; for example, male and female, north and south, heat and cold, light and darkness, positive and negative, etc. Aries, being the first of the signs, is given a wonderful symbolism, revealing by the vertical line the descent of the life force into the brain and head of man. Note that the moons are inverted. This is because in Aries the consciousness is always turned down to inspire new beginnings. Aries is essentially the sign of beginnings, of enterprises, and of pioneer work. Aries never collects. These Arian moons are not made to retain, but to pour out. The Arian holds nothing. He conceives the plan for the building, thus making it possible for other people to build. He is acutely forceful and dynamic. He is the brains of new ideas, but he may become the rolling stone that gathers no moss. Actually, he hates moss and collections. When he has created something, he never wants to duplicate it, but prefers to create a new thing.

Aries is said to be a Fire * sign, since Fire in astrology represents ceaseless activity.

It is important to note that we cannot judge character completely from the Sun sign alone. Character implies a depth of

---

* The quality of the signs, whether of Fire, Earth, Air, or Water, is considered more fully in subsequent lessons.

experience which has been formed through modification of inner experiences encountered in the conflict of life, hence character is the result of the total horoscope. The Sun merely reveals the general type of life expression. In some signs it rushes forth. In others it circles around, and in others it holds back. One should also add that the Sun may be in any one of the thirty degrees of the sign, and every degree is different. Even if we know the degree, there are nine other planets which modify the effect of the Sun. The beginner is inclined to think that only soldiers and pioneers should be born in Aries, but we find such dissimilar characters as are listed in the biographical calendar.

When the Sun sign is known to be Aries, then we can say of such people that they are dynamic and quick, if not physically, then mentally. The Fire quality of the sign confers originality and "drive." Aries people may not drive other people, but they always drive themselves. They are inclined to start projects that other people seize and use to advantage. It has aptly been said that Aries is the lamb that is shorn in order that the world may be warm.

On page 28 is given a list of people who have their Sun sign in Aries. We hope that you will look up the lives of the people mentioned and see in what respect, or in what direction, their originality lay, how they fought for their opinions, or what new movements, ideas, or conditions, they inaugurated. As you understand the symbols of the other signs, work in the same way.

Note on Birthdays before September 3, 1752

A word of caution is necessary to students who are looking up birthdays of people born in the United States, or Great Britain, previous to September 3, 1752. On that date the British calendar was changed. September 3 (Old Style) was decreed to be September 14 (New Style). Books of reference do not always say what style calendar they are using. George Washington was born February 11 (O.S.), but February 22 (N.S.). Old Style means according to the Julian Calendar. On October 5, 1582 (Old Style Julian Calendar, abbreviated O.S.) Pope Gregory VIII decreed that this date should be called October 15 (New Style Gregorian Calendar, abbreviated N.S.). Some countries changed their calendars at that time, but some did not, hence, since that time there has been considerable uncertainty about old dates. Russia changed in 1917. Greece did not change until 1923. For the twentieth century, thirteen days must be added to Old Style dates to make them tally with our Gregorian New Style Calendar.

ARIES BIRTHDAYS

March 21, 1751   James Martineau, philosopher and divine.
March 22, 1868   Robert A. Millikan, physicist, measured the electron.
March 23, 1887   Sidney Hillman, labor leader.
March 24, 1834   William Morris, poet; John Wesley Powell, explorer.
March 25, 1867   Arturo Toscanini, conductor.
March 26, 1884   Wilhelm Backhaus, musician.
March 27, 1845   Wilhelm Röntgen, discoverer of X rays (1895).
March 28, 1878   Herbert H. Lehman, former Governor of New York.
March 29, 1790   John Tyler, President of the United States.
March 30, 1844   Paul Verlaine, poet.
March 31, 1809   Edward Fitzgerald, and Nikolai Gogol, writers.
April   1, 1873   Sergei Rachmaninoff, composer.
April   2, 1805   Hans Christian Andersen, author of fairy tales.
April   3, 1822   Edward Everett Hale, author.
April   4, 1828   Margaret Oliphant, novelist.
April   5, 1827   Joseph Lister (Baron), worked on antiseptics.
April   6, 1874   Houdini, magician.
April   7, 1770   William Wordsworth, poet laureate.
April   8, 1732   David Rittenhouse, astronomer.
April   9, 1821   Charles Baudelaire, poet.
April 10, 1868   George Arliss, actor.
April 11, 1862   Charles Evans Hughes, jurist.
April 12, 1777   Henry Clay, American statesman.
April 13, 1743   Thomas Jefferson, President of the United States.
April 14, 1889   Arnold J. Toynbee, historian.
April 15, 1831   George M. N. Yost, typewriter inventor.
April 16, 1844   Anatole France, writer.
April 17, 1837   J. P. Morgan, Sr., financier.
April 18, 1882   Leopold Stokowski, conductor (1887?).
April 19, 1905   James A. Mollison, aviator.

Aries would excel as:

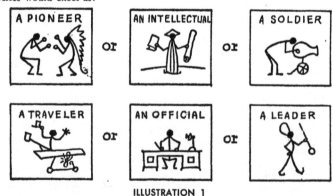

ILLUSTRATION 1

THE SYMBOL OF TAURUS IS   *For Those Born*
                                            April 20–May 20

The symbol of Taurus looks like the horns of a bull. It also resembles the chin and throat of a man with the Adam's apple showing. Note that it is made up of a crescent Moon reposing on the Sun. Here we perceive a less active looking symbol than that of Aries. The horns of the Moon point upward so that the cup can hold something, and this factor is important in helping us to understand the basic nature of Taureans. The people of this sign are not pioneers; they are settlers. They are retentive of what they have and of what they acquire, whether in worldly goods or in emotion. They do not scatter their forces but conserve them. They are more contented by nature than the restless wandering sheep of Aries, and they carry more conviction; hence we note that instead of the scepter of the Sun, they are assigned the whole round Sun in their symbol. The incisive thought and swift action of Aries is replaced by mature conviction, and by steamroller tactics.

Taurus is said to be an Earth sign, since Earth in astrology represents stability and practicality, also supply and possessions.

When studying character in a horoscope, we cannot rely entirely upon the Sun sign. With some people we find that the sign rising in the east at the time of birth can modify the Sun's expression considerably. The rising sign can only be found by means of calculations, such as we shall give you later.

TAURUS BIRTHDAYS

April 20, 1808   Napoleon III.
April 21, 1926   Queen Elizabeth II (2:42 A.M.).
April 22, 1874   Ellen Glasgow, novelist.
April 23, 1791   James Buchanan, President of the United States.
April 24, 1856   Henri Philippe Pétain, Marshal of France.
April 25, 1874   Guglielmo Marconi, inventor.
April 26, 1868   Harold F. Harmsworth, First Viscount Rothermere.
April 27, 1791   Samuel Morse, inventor telegraph system.
April 28, 1758   James Monroe, President of the United States.
April 29, 1879   Sir Thomas Beecham, conductor.
April 30, 1909   Queen Juliana (7:00 A.M.).
May 1, 1848   James Ford Rhodes, historian.
May 2, 1879   James F. Byrnes, former Secretary of State.
May 3, 1844   Richard D'Oyly Carte, musician, producer.
May 4, 1796   Horace Mann, educator; William H. Prescott, historian.
May 5, 1780   John James Audubon, naturalist and artist (1785?).
May 6, 1856   Sigmund Freud, psychoanalyst; Robert E. Peary, explorer.
May 7, 1833   Johannes Brahms, composer.
May 8, 1884   Harry S Truman, President of the United States.
May 9, 1860   James M. Barrie, playwright.
May 10, 1850   Sir Thomas Lipton, tea planter and merchant.
May 11, 1888   Irving Berlin, composer.
May 12, 1850   Henry Cabot Lodge, political leader.
May 13, 1914   Joe Louis, boxer.
May 14, 1853   Hall Caine, novelist.
May 15, 1850   R. W. Cross (Raphael VI), astrologer.
May 16, 1832   Philip D. Armour, meat packer.
May 17, 1886   Alfonso XIII of Spain.
May 18, 1872   Bertram Russell, philosopher and mathematician.
May 19, 1879   Lady Astor (Nancy), first woman Member of Parliament.
May 20, 1806   John Stuart Mill, economist.

Taurus would excel as:

A DIETICIAN   or   A SINGER   or   A BUILDER

A GARDENER   or   A SCHOLAR   or   A SCIENTIST

ILLUSTRATION 2

THE SYMBOL OF GEMINI IS   ⅠⅠ   For Those Born
                                                                 May 20–June 20
                                                                 Approximately

The sign of Gemini is made up of two staves. It is an ideograph
(picture of a thought) of the two lungs of man, and the two
arms. It exhibits more definitely than does the symbol of Aries,
the essential nature of polarity. Here is the scepter of the Sun-
god and the shadow of the scepter, the object and the idea of
an object. Here are two arms whose work has to be co-ordinated. Here are two pathways, and in the choice between the
two the Gemini person tends towards restlessness and indecision.

Gemini sees two sides to every question, and inclines to flit
from one to the other. This may be an advantage, or not. With
a highly developed skill, such as Wagner had in music, his
Gemini Sun enabled him to see the whole of a great opera as
one unit, and then write down its component parts in musical
score. Every conductor must have this Geminian ability to
know, not only what one instrument is supposed to be playing
at a particular moment, but many. Every business executive
must have a somewhat similar faculty. This does not mean that
the Sun must be in Gemini.

With most Geminians, it is essential that they cultivate
perseverance as a real habit, and strive to continue on one path
until a project is completed. The usual Geminian's work is
rarely completed because he has thought of some other thing
that will interest him more. This is why certain of the Twins
with truly wonderful mentality never accomplish anything
worth while.

Here we should distinguish Gemini restlessness from that of
Aries. Aries, as a rule, has one objective; Gemini, as a rule, has
more than one. Suppose Aries should set out with the idea of
going to San Francisco from New York. He will eventually get

there, even though he may stop at a dozen cities en route. Because he does not settle down in one city, people think he has no definite purpose, but it is because he has a purpose, possibly not revealed, that he does not settle. Gemini is restless because he lacks one central purpose, therefore, he likes to see city after city before he arrives at any decision whether to reach San Francisco, or not.

Gemini is said to be an Air sign because it is essentially mental. Air in astrology pertains to mentality. Note that when everyone is thinking or talking of a certain subject, it is said to be "in the air." Why is an Air sign said to be mental? It is because the way we breathe has a profound effect both upon the ability of the brain to function properly, and upon the general health of the body. We cannot think without air. A child with adenoids is often called a dull child, yet it may be that the only factor preventing him from being bright is his inability to get air easily into his lungs. Because Gemini is a mental sign the functions of his body are usually well co-ordinated. He uses his hands and arms with facility.

As we have seen in the last two signs, the position of the Sun is not everything in determining character. Sometimes the sign in which the Moon is placed on the day of birth will affect the personality more than the Sun sign. In later lessons you will be taught how to find the Moon sign, and how to judge if this is of extreme importance.

GEMINI BIRTHDAYS

May 21, 1884	Sir Claude Auchinlech, British general.
May 22, 1859	Sir Arthur Conan Doyle, creator of *Sherlock Holmes*.
May 23, 1883	Douglas Fairbanks, Sr., film actor.
May 24, 1819	Queen Victoria.
May 25, 1803	Ralph Waldo Emerson, Edward Bulwer-Lytton, writers.
May 26, 1868	Mary, Queen Consort of George V.
May 27, 1878	Isadora Duncan, dancer.
May 28, 1934	Dionne quintuplets.
May 29, 1736	Patrick Henry, patriot.
May 30, 1888	James A. Farley, former Postmaster General.
May 31, 1819	Walt Whitman, poet.
June 1, 1801	Brigham Young, Mormon leader.
June 2, 1857	Sir Edward Elgar, composer.
June 3, 1808	Jefferson Davis, President of the Confederacy.
June 4, 1867	Baron von Mannerheim, Finnish general against Russia.
June 5, 1819	John Couch Adams, calculated positions of Neptune.
June 6, 1875	Thomas Mann, writer.
June 7, 1843	Susan E. Blow, opened first kindergarten in U. S. A.
June 8, 1810	Robert Schumann, composer.
June 9, 1781	George Stephenson, of steam locomotive fame.
June 10, 1832	Sir Edwin Arnold, author *Light of Asia*.
June 11, 1864	Richard Strauss, composer.
June 12, 1819	Charles Kingsley, churchman and novelist.
June 13, 1865	W. B. Yeats, poet.
June 14, 1811	Harriet Beecher Stowe, novelist.
June 15, 1843	Edvard Grieg, composer.
June 16, 1880	Alice Bailey, occult leader.
June 17, 1867	John Robert Gregg, inventor of a shorthand system.
June 18, 1881	James J. Walker, Mayor of New York City (1925–32).
June 19, 1896	Wallis, Duchess of Windsor.
June 20, 1913	Prince Juan of Spain.
June 21, 1819	Jacques Offenbach, composer.

Gemini would excel as:

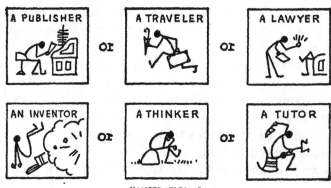

A PUBLISHER or A TRAVELER or A LAWYER

AN INVENTOR or A THINKER or A TUTOR

ILLUSTRATION 3

THE SYMBOL OF CANCER IS

The symbol of Cancer is a pictograph (writing in picture form) of the human breasts; hence of all signs it is most significant of the mother and the home. The symbol is made up of two small suns, each connected with a crescent moon, which looks like a cup, container, or bowl. The cup which holds water (emotion) is indicative of the mother principle, which desires to gather and store things for the child. The inverted cup which pours out, but cannot hold, water, signifies the quality of giving. The true mother will give up everything she possesses for the child.

We find the Cancerian has a somewhat dual nature. At times he can be shrewd and grasping, but if he likes you, there is nothing he will not do for you—shelter you, house you, and give you of his possessions. He is a very sensitive and emotional being. Just as the crab is all soft meat inside but surrounded by a hard shell, so the Cancerian sometimes presents a hard exterior to the world, but do not be discouraged by this. He does it only to hide the fact that he is tenderhearted and the world might take advantage of him.

The emotional nature of the Cancerian tends to make him highly dramatic, and you will find him glorying at times in posing as the center of many dramas which lie largely in his own imagination.

Cancer is said to be a Water sign. Water in astrology represents anything that is fluid, emotional, or psychic. The tendency of water is to flow downwards. To raise it one needs a pump, or some force. It flows to its own level as soon as the force is released. It moves around objects and does not attack them until forced to do so.

As we have noted in the last three signs, the character cannot be fully determined by the astrologer from the Sun sign alone. It will sometimes happen that three, or four, or more planets are grouped in a sign, making this latter sign more spectacular than that of the Sun. It is, therefore, very important that one should not try to delineate the character too exactly, until one has discovered all the prominent factors within a horoscope.

CANCER BIRTHDAYS

June 22, 1856   H. Rider Haggard, novelist.
June 23, 1894   Edward, Duke of Windsor.
June 24, 1813   Henry Ward Beecher, clergyman.
June 25, 1900   Lord Louis Mountbatten, naval and military leader.
June 26, 1824   William Thomson, Lord Kelvin, physicist.
June 27, 1880   Helen Keller, blind writer ("about 4:00 A.M.").
June 28, 1712   Jean Jacques Rousseau, writer.
June 29, 1901   Nelson Eddy, singer.
June 30, 1819   William Almon Wheeler, Vice President with Hayes.
July 1, 1872   Louis Blériot, first to fly English Channel (July 25, 1909).
July 2, 1714   Christolph Willibald Glück, composer.
July 3, 1908   Mary F. K. Fisher, author (How to Cook a Wolf).
July 4, 1872   Calvin Coolidge, President of the United States.
July 5, 1810   Phineas T. Barnum, showman.
July 6, 1832   Maximilian, Emperor of Mexico.
July 7, 1888   Arthur T. Vanderbilt, lawyer and educator.
July 8, 1838   Count Ferdinand von Zeppelin, airship designer.
July 9, 1819   Elias Howe, sewing-machine inventor.
July 10, 1834   James A. McNeill Whistler, painter.
July 11, 1767   John Quincy Adams, President of the United States.
July 12, 1730   Josiah Wedgwood, china manufacturer.
July 13, 1527   Dr. John Dee, mathematician and alchemist.
July 14, 1868   Gertrude Bell, traveler and writer (soon after sunset).
July 15, 1865   Alfred Harmsworth, Viscount Northcliffe, publisher.
July 16, 1821   Mary Baker Eddy, founder of Christian Science.
July 17, 1876   M. M. Litvinov, former U. S. S. R. ambassador.
July 18, 1811   William Makepeace Thackeray, novelist.
July 19, 1834   Edgard Degas, French impressionist painter.
July 20, 1890   George II of Greece (died 1947).
July 21, 1898   Ernest Hemingway, writer.
July 22, 1898   Stephen Vincent Benét, poet and writer.
Cancer would excel as:

ILLUSTRATION 4

THE SYMBOL OF LEO IS

For Those Born
July 23–August 22
Approximately

The symbol of Leo is an ideograph of the human heart with its two valves. If we look at it carefully, we find it is very much like that of Cancer, that is. it has two small suns and two crescent moons. But whereas in Cancer the moons are separated, in Leo the moons face each other and are joined at the top, while the circles of the two suns are not quite completed.

The ancient astrologers, being in most cases priests and philosophers, intended by this symbol to convey the fact that the Sun-god has a link with the human soul. When this link was perfected, the great energy of the Sun could circulate through man's life in all its fullness. One Sun is of power from above; the other is the life within man. For this reason, Leo was said to be King of the Zodiac. He is so *en rapport* with the power of the Sun that everyone immediately feels his radiance and vitality, and rarely questions his authority. If we study the Leo man we find that he seems to have some innate faith in himself, and perhaps this is the real secret of his power.

Like Aries, Leo is a Fire sign, that is, one having activity, power, and drive. There is, however, a great difference between the activity of Aries and that of Leo. In Aries it rushes out towards the object, whereas in Leo it draws everything to a center, focus, or heart. Therefore, we call the Arian activity, centrifugal (fleeing from the center), and the Leo activity, centripetal (seeking the center).

As we have seen from the previous four signs, astrology is not quite as simple as some books that talk merely about the Sun sign would have us believe. If this were so, then all persons born in Leo or in any other sign would be alike, and this is not the case. The Sun may be aspected, or not aspected at all. It may be well aspected, or it may be aspected by malefics.

LEO BIRTHDAYS

July 23, 1783   Simon Bolivar, South American liberator.
July 24, 1802   Alexandre Dumas (Père), novelist (1803?).
July 25, 1854   David Belasco, playwright and producer.
July 26, 1856   George Bernard Shaw, playwright.
July 27, 1870   Hilaire Belloc, writer.
July 28, 1898   Dr. Charles Mayo, surgeon.
July 29, 1869   Booth Tarkington, novelist.
July 30, 1863   Henry Ford, automobile manufacturer.
July 31, 1850   Robert Planquette, composer (1848?).
Aug. 1, 1819   Herman Melville, creator of *Moby Dick.*
Aug. 2, 1854   F. Marion Crawford, novelist.
Aug. 3, 1900   Ernie Pyle, newspaper correspondent.
Aug. 4, 1870   Sir Harry Lauder. singer, entertainer.
Aug. 5, 1850   Guy de Maupassant, writer.
Aug. 6, 1809   Alfred, Lord Tennyson, Poet Laureate.
Aug. 7, 1881   Admiral Jean Darlan.
Aug. 8, 1819   Charles A. Dana, newspaper editor.
Aug. 9, 1913   Herman E. Talmadge, Georgia politician.
Aug. 10, 1874   Herbert C. Hoover, President of the United States.
Aug. 11. 1833   Robert G. Ingersoll, lawyer and lecturer.
Aug. 12, 1881   Cecil B. de Mille, motion picture producer.
Aug. 13, 1818   Lucy Stone, reformer.
Aug. 14, 1867   John Galsworthy, novelist and playwright.
Aug. 15, 1879   Ethel Barrymore, actress.
Aug. 16, 1890   Sir Carl Berendsen, New Zealand statesman.
Aug. 17, 1868   Gene Stratton Porter, novelist.
Aug. 18, 1835   Marshall Field. merchant.
Aug. 19, 1878   Manuel Quezon, First President of Philippines (died 1944).
Aug. 20, 1833   Benjamin Harrison, President of the United States.
Aug. 21, 1930   Princess Margaret Rose.
Aug. 22, 1862   Claude Achille Debussy, composer.
Aug. 23, 1869   Edgar Lee Masters, poet and satirist.

Leo would excel as:

ILLUSTRATION 5

THE SYMBOL OF VIRGO IS   *For Those Born*
August 23–September 22
Approximately

The symbol of Virgo is an ideograph of the generative organs of a female, closed, as in virginity. Before marriage, the consciousness tends to search, weigh, and consider all people in the light of possible mates. We find that in Virgo there is always this tendency to weigh, consider, and discriminate. It is ever seeking the perfect form, and rejecting what it considers faulty or imperfect. It is sometimes said that all old maids' children and husbands are perfect.

We must remember that Virgo is basically an idealist expecting to find the ideal in the physical world, and never content until this ideal is discovered. It is, therefore, of all signs inclined to be the most discontented, because the ideal is so rarely found in this world. There is at times a marked tendency to be too exacting and too "picky." In highly developed Virgoans, however, we find the greatest facility in handling all the details of a huge organization with marked success.

Among great artists Virgo is often strongly marked, for then they are equipped to present their ideals through some specific medium, whether paint, marble, or music, with perfect execution. This does not necessarily mean we shall find artists having the Sun in Virgo, for Virgo of itself is not a creative sign, but Virgo can certainly give finesse. Chopin could not have taught the world a new pianoforte technique without his Virgo ascendant. You will understand better what is meant by the accentuation of a sign when you have learned to erect a chart for for yourself. The sign Virgo is the greatest gift to us all, for without it nothing could be patterned in shape or form. It is a sign of matter in specific form, crystallized and not amorphous.

Like Taurus, Virgo is an Earth sign; that is, it stands for practicality, and the ability to enter into some phase of work connected with man's material world. The better the brain, the greater the skill, and the execution.

As we have seen in the previous five signs, the astrologer can say certain things which can be true in general for all those born under a certain sign, but he must beware of trying to say too much until he knows the whole horoscope. The Sun rising will act very differently from the Sun setting. In the former case, it irradiates the whole personality; in the latter case, other people reflect the radiance.

VIRGO BIRTHDAYS

Aug. 24, 1810   Theodore Parker, preacher, social reformer.
Aug. 25, 1839   Francis Bret Harte, writer (1836?).
Aug. 26, 1819   Albert, Prince Consort.
Aug. 27, 1871   Theodore Dreiser, novelist.
Aug. 28, 1833   Sir Edward Burne-Jones, painter.
Aug. 29, 1862   Maurice Maeterlinck, poet, dramatist.
Aug. 30, 1871   Ernest Rutherford (Baron), first to disintegrate atom.
Aug. 31, 1880   Former Queen Wilhelmina.
Sept. 1, 1907   Walter Reuther, labor union leader.
Sept. 2, 1839   Henry George, economist.
Sept. 3, 1905   Carl D. Anderson, discovered the positron.
Sept. 4, 1801   Count Alfred d'Orsay, famous dandy of Paris.
Sept. 5, 1826   Thomas Sterry Hunt, American geologist, surveyed Canada.
Sept. 6, 1757   Marquis de Lafayette, aided American Revolution.
Sept. 7, 1867   J. Pierpont Morgan, II, financier.
Sept. 8, 1889   Robert A. Taft, Senator.
Sept. 9, 1828   Count Leon Tolstoi, writer. (New Style Calendar).
Sept. 10, 1885   Carl Van Doren, writer.
Sept. 11, 1877   Sir James Jeans, physicist and astronomer.
Sept. 12, 1880   Henry L. Mencken, editor and satirist.
Sept. 13, 1851   Walter Reed, surgeon, discovered connection between yellow fever and a certain kind of mosquito.
Sept. 14, 1883   Margaret Sanger, exponent of birth control.
Sept. 15, 1857   William H. Taft, President of the United States.
Sept. 16, 1823   Francis Parkman, historian.
Sept. 17, 1871   Leo Stanton Rowe, Director-General Pan-American Union.
Sept. 18, 1709   Dr. Samuel Johnson, writer.
Sept. 19, 1802   Lajos Kossuth, Hungarian patriot.
Sept. 20, 1878   Upton Sinclair, writer and politician.
Sept. 21, 1866   H. G. Wells, writer.
Sept. 22, 1791   Michael Faraday, physicist, electro-magnetic induction.

Virgo would excel as:

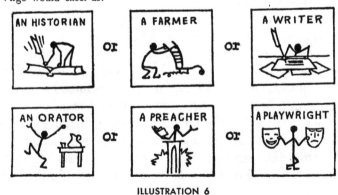

AN HISTORIAN or A FARMER or A WRITER

AN ORATOR or A PREACHER or A PLAYWRIGHT

ILLUSTRATION 6

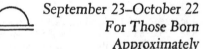

September 23–October 22
For Those Born
Approximately

The symbol of Libra is that of the setting sun which has just sunk halfway below the horizon, half seen and half unseen. It thus becomes a symbol of the halves of one unit, and is pre-eminently the symbol of partnership and marriage. Since the halves are equal, Libra is said to be the sign of balance, equipoise and peace. In order to keep peace between one individual and another, man has instituted codes of law and justice. Law, as between individuals, comes under the sign Libra.

The beginner is inclined to think that Libra is like Gemini because two ideas, lines of argument, or work, come to him at the same time, but whereas Gemini usually decides on one in preference to another, Libra seems to want both. He tries to see the good in both, and wants to unite the two in one. Gemini halts momentarily between two activities. Libra seizes both. If he really has to make up his mind which to.keep, he exasperates the whole world by making them wait while he considers. It is impossible to obtain a decided opinion from him on any subject. Today he sides with you; tomorrow he sides with the other person, and so we have the ancient expression "the law's delays."

Libra is an Air sign; thus like Gemini, mental in outlook. Charming as Libra is, do not expect him to be too emotional. In fact, his sense of mental balance prevents him from being "too anything." He perceives differentiations from the normal just as quickly as does Virgo, but he is inclined to be more gracious in telling you where you are out of line.

When considering the previous six signs of the zodiac, we have noted that the astrologer cannot judge character accurately from the Sun sign alone. To all the reasons previously given as to why this cannot be done, we must add the house position of the Sun. We divide our wheel of the horoscope into twelve sectors, each one referring to some specific department of life. The Sun may be in any one of these segments, or houses, according to the time of day when the native was born. (See Diagrams 4–7.)

LIBRA BIRTHDAYS

Sept. 23, 1889   Walter Lippmann, editor, publicist.
Sept. 24, 1755   John Marshall, American jurist.
Sept. 25, 1793   Felicia Hemans, poet.
Sept. 26, 1898   George Gershwin, musician, composer.
Sept. 27, 1904   Frieda B. Hennock, first woman in F.C.C.
Sept. 28, 1839   Frances E. Willard, temperance lecturer.
Sept. 29, 1758   Admiral Horatio Nelson (Viscount).
Sept. 30, 1867   Charles Henry Hawes, anthropologist, excavated in Crete.
Oct.   1, 1847   Annie Besant, theosophical leader.
Oct.   2, 1869   Mohandas K. Gandhi, Indian leader.
Oct.   3, 1873   Emily Post, adviser on etiquette.
Oct.   4, 1822   Rutherford B. Hayes, President of the United States.
Oct.   5, 1830   Chester A. Arthur, President of the United States.
Oct.   6, 1887   Maria Jeritza, opera singer. .
Oct.   7, 1888   Henry A. Wallace, former Vice President.
Oct.   8, 1838   John Hay, American statesman.
Oct.   9, 1863   Edward Bok, editor; Gamaliel Bradford, biographer.
Oct. 10, 1813   Guiseppe Verdi, composer.
Oct. 11, 1884   Eleanor Roosevelt.
Oct. 12, 1803   A. T. Stewart, merchant.
Oct. 13, 1919   Marion Hargrove, author (See Here, Private Hargrove!)
Oct. 14, 1890   Dwight D. Eisenhower.
Oct. 15, 1844   Frederich Wilhelm Nietzsche, philosopher.
Oct. 16, 1888   Eugene O'Neill, playwright.
Oct. 17, 1760   Claude Henri, Comte de Saint Simon, French socialist.
Oct. 18, 1859   Henri Bergson, author (Creative Evolution).
Oct. 19, 1822   Louis Nicolas Ménard, poet, chemist, discovered collodion.
Oct. 20, 1891   Sir James Chadwick, discoverer of the neutron.
Oct. 21, 1772   Samuel Taylor Coleridge, poet.
Oct. 22, 1811   Franz Liszt, composer (early morning).

Libra would excel as:

ILLUSTRATION 7

THE SYMBOL
OF SCORPIO IS   ♏ or ♏⚲   *For Those Born October 23–November 21 Approximately*

The first symbol of Scorpio is a pictograph of the sex organs of the female. The scorpion is usually associated with this sign, but two birds also have been assigned to it by artists and sculptors—the eagle [1] and the dove. All three emblems can characterize the three main types born under Scorpio. First, there is the sarcastic Scorpio, who, like the scorpion, carries a death-dealing sting. He may be coarse and passionate. Second, there is the highy evolved type, who, like the eagle, leaves the ground, or crude passions, and soars upward into the mental realms, giving to mankind some of his most brilliant thoughts. Third, there is the type who, like the gentle dove, is contented, and soars into the air carrying a message of love.

Scorpio is said to be the sign of death, but sometimes that of regeneration. The Scorpio person may kill many a noble thought by his sarcasm, but, if he leaves his stinging words aside, and lives in his eagle consciousness, he has power to take hold of ideas, and an ability to present them to people in such a fascinating way that few can resist. When he has gone a step farther, and starts to live in his dove consciousness, then only is he liked by the other signs. Until this time, they fear him.

Scorpio is a Water sign, that is, highly emotional and psychic, but whereas with Cancer the emotions are never hidden, with Scorpio one might never know that emotion exists until it is released with compelling power.

As we have seen when dealing with the previous seven signs, one cannot be sure that character is being delineated accurately when the Sun sign only is known. We shall discover later that each sign has a planetary ruler, and one has to know in what sign and in what house this ruler is situated, before one can state in what direction the power of the Sun will be revealed.

* NOTE: The second symbol of Scorpio is used only in written horoscopes.

SCORPIO BIRTHDAYS

Oct. 23, 1844   Sarah Bernhardt, actress; Robert Bridges, Poet Laureate.
Oct. 24, 1804   Wilhelm Eduard Weber, measured electrical quantities.
Oct. 25, 1888   Rear-Admiral Richard E. Byrd.
Oct. 26, 1800   Helmuth von Moltke, Prussian general.
Oct. 27, 1858   Theodore Roosevelt, President of the United States.
Oct. 28, 1836   Homer Dodge Martin, American painter.
Oct. 29, 1740   James Boswell, biographer.
Oct. 30, 1735   John Adams, President of the United States.
Oct. 31, 1795   John Keats, poet.
Nov. 1, 1880   Sholem Asch, novelist and playwright.
Nov. 2, 1795   James Knox Polk, President of the United States.
" " 1865   Warren G. Harding, President of the United States.
Nov. 3, 1901   Ex-King of the Belgians, Leopold III.
Nov. 4, 1879   Will Rogers, actor, lecturer and humorist.
Nov. 5, 1853   Ella Wheeler Wilcox, poet and lecturer (1850?).
Nov. 6, 1901   Martin Dies, Congressman.
Nov. 7, 1867   Marie Skladowska Curie, discoverer of radium.
Nov. 8, 1831   Earl of Lytton, Viceroy India (1876–1880).
Nov. 9, 1841   Edward VII.
Nov. 10, 1801   Samuel Gridley Howe, philanthropist for the blind.
Nov. 11, 1885   George S. Patton, United States general.
Nov. 12, 1877   Warren R. Austin, chief delegate for America at the UN.
Nov. 13, 1850   Robert Louis Stevenson, writer.
Nov. 14, 1889   Jawaharlal Nehru, Indian leader.
Nov. 15, 1738   Sir William Herschel, astronomer, discovered Uranus.
Nov. 16, 1895   Michael Arlen, novelist; Paul Hindemuth, composer.
Nov. 17, 1794   George Grote, historian.
Nov. 18, 1836   W. S. Gilbert, of Gilbert and Sullivan opera fame.
Nov. 19, 1831   James A. Garfield, President of the United States.
Nov. 20, 1884   Norman Thomas, Socialist leader.
Nov. 21, 1787   Sir Samuel Cunard, founder of Cunard Line.

Scorpio would excel as:

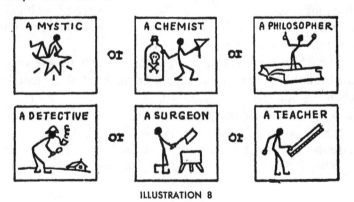

ILLUSTRATION 8

THE SYMBOL OF
SAGITTARIUS IS

For Those Born
November 22–December 21
Approximately

The symbol of Sagittarius looks like an arrow, but it is a pictograph of the leg from the thigh down to the knee. The arrowhead seems to take cognizance of the fact that we have two thigh bones.. In the symbol of Gemini we had two lines to represent the two arms, indicating that Gemini was dual in nature. Sagittarius has a certain amount of duality, but it has a singleness of thrust, hence the two potential legs are condensed into one.

It is characteristic of Sagittarians that when they are euthusiastic, they immediately get out their arrows and try to shoot their ideas into everyone they meet, until their whole circle of friends has received an arrow of thought. They are the great propagandists of ideas and opinions. They are ambassadors of new thoughts.

The legs help us to travel in the physical world, hence it is said that the Sagittarian is fond of travel, outdoor sports, and exercise. When the Sagittarian is an evolved type, he travels far in the world of thought and ideas. Generally speaking, he is quick to understand abstract ideas and the principles upon which things are constructed, hence he becomes interested in religion, philosophy, and law. While Libra is interested in law as between individuals, Sagittarius is more interested in jurisprudence, or the science of law.

Sagittarius is a Fire sign, ceaselessly active, with great driving power, more talkative than the Arian, and not quite so naïve and genial as the Leonian.

As we have discovered when dealing with previous signs, there is no certainty of knowing from just the Sun sign, whether we shall find a philosopher born under Sagittarius, an athlete, a great traveler, or a too insistent talker. It is necessary to know the horoscope in detail before we can specify such matters. Something about the professional life, or a man's standing in public, can be obtained only by knowing what sign of the zodiac is overhead at the time of birth. We are inclined to forget that the stars are affecting us even in the day-time when we cannot see them, and that they are just as important when unseen. We can only determine the sign over-head by learning to cast the horoscope.

SAGITTARIUS BIRTHDAYS

Nov. 22, 1808	Thomas Cook, founded Cook's Tourist Agency.
Nov. 23, 1804	Franklin Pierce, President of the United States.
Nov. 24, 1784	Zachary Taylor, President of the United States.
Nov. 25, 1862	Ethelbert Nevin, composer *The Rosary.*
Nov. 26, 1810	William George Armstrong (Baron of Cragside), inventor.
Nov. 27, 1874	Chaim Weizmann, First President of Israel.
" " "	Charles A. Beard, American historian and educator.
Nov. 28, 1831	John William Mackay, founder Postal Telegraph.
Nov. 29, 1832	Louisa M. Alcott, author of *Little Women.*
Nov. 30, 1874	Winston Churchill.
Dec. 1, 1844	Alexandra, Queen Consort of Edward VII.
Dec. 2, 1899	John Barbirolli, conductor.
Dec. 3, 1795	Sir Rowland Hill, started penny postage in Great Britain.
Dec. 4, 1795	Thomas Carlyle, historian; Joseph T. Reinaud, orientalist.
Dec. 5, 1782	Martin Van Buren, President of the United States.
Dec. 6, 1732	Warren Hastings, Governor General of India.
Dec. 7, 1888	Heywood Broun, writer; Hamilton Fish, Congressman.
Dec. 8, 1886	Diego Rivera, Mexican painter.
Dec. 9, 1909	Douglas Fairbanks, Jr., film actor.
Dec. 10, 1805	William Lloyd Garrison, abolitionist.
Dec. 11, 1882	Fiorello La Guardia, Mayor of New York.
Dec. 12, 1821	Gustave Flaubert, author *Madame Bovary.*
Dec. 13, 1797	Heinrich Heine, poet.
Dec. 14, 1859	Lazarus Zamenhof, inventor of Esperanto.
Dec. 15, 1852	Antoine Henri Becquerel, discoverer of radio-activity.
Dec. 16, 1863	George Santayana, writer and philosopher.
Dec. 17, 1807	John Greenleaf Whittier, poet.
Dec. 18, 1859	Francis Thompson, poet.
Dec. 19, 1608	John Milton, poet (date in New Style Calendar).
Dec. 20, 1902	George, Duke of Kent, killed 1942 in airplane crash.
Dec. 21, 1804	Benjamin Disraeli, statesman.

Sagittarius would excel as:

A PHILOSOPHER   or   A PROPHET   or   A PROFESSOR

AN ATHELETE   or   A COUNSELOR   or   A MARKSMAN

ILLUSTRATION 9

The symbol of Capricorn is a pictograph of the knee. Many interpreters of symbolism run on wrong tracks. We consider that those who imagine that the astrological symbols were derived from Greek letters are incorrect. *The astrological symbols are one and all derived from the parts of the human body.* They were in effect in their present form among nations whose civilization antedated that of the Greeks. Capricorn is very definitely a stylized representation of the knee, the little rounded enclosure at the end being that of the kneecap. The symbol is made like an r with an s at the end.

The knee is a highly important part of the human anatomy, since it enables man to stand upright, and to climb. The Capricornian is essentially fitted by his organizing capacity to take executive positions. The symbol is partly patterned on the horns of the mountain goat, an animal which climbs easily to the most inaccessible places without fear.

Capricorn, like Taurus and Virgo, is an Earth sign. It is practical and able to function well in the material world, but other things being equal, it will have more ambition.

It would be foolish to think that by reading a book on Sun signs, anyone could understand the whole character of any man. Astrology is an art based upon a scientifically constructed horoscope. The more we study, weave, and collate the factors within this horoscope, the more we find the truth. We know that every Capricornian is not an executive. He may in fact be a very timid creature, and quite incapable of giving orders to anyone. A good executive needs a good mind; hence, the planet Mercury will have to be well placed in his chart. We can only discover the place of Mercury by learning how to set up a horoscope on scientific principles.

CAPRICORN BIRTHDAYS

Dec. 22, 1831   Charles Stuart Calverley, poet.
Dec. 23, 1790   Jean François Champollion, founder of Egyptology.
Dec. 24, 1905   Howard Hughes, motion-picture producer and aviator.
Dec. 25, 1876   Mohammed Ali Jinnah, Pakistan statesman.
Dec. 26, 1837   Admiral George Dewey.
Dec. 27, 1822   Louis Pasteur, chemist.
Dec. 28, 1856   Woodrow Wilson, President of the United States.
Dec. 29, 1808   Andrew Johnson, President of the United States.
Dec. 30, 1865   Rudyard Kipling, author.
Dec. 31, 1869   Henri Matisse, French artist.
Jan.   1, 1892   Manuel Roxas, President of the Philippines, died 1948.
Jan.   2, 1895   Count Folke Bernadotte, U.N. mediator, killed 1948.
Jan.   3, 1883   Clement R. Atlee, British Labor leader.
Jan.   4, 1813   Sir Isaac Pitman, inventor of a shorthand system.
Jan.   5, 1642   Sir Isaac Newton, astronomer (date in New Style).
Jan.   6, 1822   Heinrich S. Schliemann, discoverer of site of ancient Troy.
Jan.   7, 1800   Millard Fillmore, President of the United States.
Jan.   8, 1836   Sir Lawrence Alma-Tadema, painter.
Jan.   9, 1859   Carrie Chapman Catt, woman suffrage leader.
Jan. 10, 1739   Ethan Allen, American soldier.
Jan. 11, 1864   Harry Gordon Selfridge, American and British merchant.
Jan. 12, 1856   John Singer Sargent, painter.
Jan. 13, 1890   Elmer Davis, columnist, news analyst.
Jan. 14, 1882   Henrik Van Loon, writer.
Jan. 15, 1870   Pierre Samuel Du Pont, industrialist.
Jan. 16, 1770   Ludwig van Beethoven, composer.
Jan. 17, 1706   Benjamin Franklin, printer, diplomat, and scientist.
Jan. 18, 1782   Daniel Webster, American statesman.
Jan. 19, 1813   Sir Harry Bessemer, inventor of Bessemer steel process.
Jan. 20, 1804   Eugene Sue, French novelist.

Capricorn should excel as:

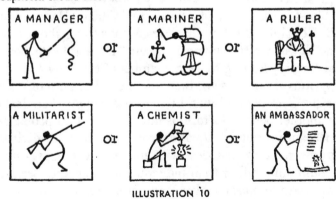

A MANAGER   or   A MARINER   or   A RULER

A MILITARIST   or   A CHEMIST   or   AN AMBASSADOR

ILLUSTRATION 10

For Those Born
January 19–February 18
Approximately

The symbol of Aquarius has been a puzzle to many astrologers. Does it represent the waves of water which Aquarius pours out of his urn, or, since Aquarius is an Air sign, and not a Water sign, does it represent the wind which disturbs the water?

Aquarius governs the ankles and the legs below the knees. The ankle is the part of the body by means of which man raises himself when walking, and so can move forward. The wavy lines are really a pictograph of the rise and fall of the ankles when in motion. Progress advances in waves. There is a crest to each wave, as there is also a trough. Apparently, the trough is just as necessary as the crest.

Aquarius is the sign farthest away from Leo, the heart sign. Aquarians are apparently more altruistic than Leo types. Leo gives to those he loves, but Aquarius can give to all humanity. His love is more impersonal, hence less understood. He likes to circulate around his friends and to join groups. The sign rules the circulation of the blood and its capillary action. The wavy lines represent the flow of the blood to and from the heart. Ancient astrologers evidently knew of the circulation of the blood, a discovery attributed to William Harvey about 1628. Certainly, the Egyptians knew something about it, for in the Edwin Smith Papyrus it states: "There is in the heart a canal (artery) leading to every member of the body."

Aquarius is an Air sign, therefore mental in outlook, as are the signs Gemini and Libra. Libra is most happy when dealing with another person. Gemini is interested both in people and in mechanism, but in Aquarius, the mind tries to reach out to grasp problems that deal with masses and groups—life in the community rather than individual life. Aquarius seems to understand the hopes, wishes, and objectives of mankind.

There are many facts which the astrologer must learn before he can judge character. We have mentioned before that he should know the position of the Moon, but here we might add that he should also know whether the Moon is increasing or decreasing in light. A person born during the fourteen days after new moon is more positive, as a rule, than one born during the fourteen days after full moon. The psychologist would term the former an extrovert, and the latter an introvert. Just how extroverted or introverted a person may be cannot, however, be told merely by knowing the phase of the Moon. Generally speaking, if an extrovert is learning to dance he plunges into a dance and tries to learn in action. An introvert under the same necessity of learning to dance, would like to think out in his mind where to put his feet before he makes any trial.

AQUARIUS BIRTHDAYS

Jan.	21, 1824	Thomas Jonathan (Stonewall) Jackson, Confederate general.
Jan.	22, 1861	Maurice Hewlett, author.
Jan.	23, 1832	Edouard Manet, impressionist artist.
Jan.	24, 1832	Joseph H. Choate, American lawyer and ambassador.
Jan.	25, 1759	Robert Burns, poet.
Jan.	26, 1880	General Douglas MacArthur.
Jan.	27, 1832	Lewis Carroll (Charles L. Dodgson) author.
Jan.	28, 1893	Rabbi Abba Hillel Silver.
Jan.	29, 1843	William McKinley, President of the United States.
Jan.	30, 1882	Franklin Delano Roosevelt, President of the United States.
Jan.	31, 1797	Franz Peter Schubert, composer.
Feb.	1, 1901	Clark Gable, film actor.
Feb.	2, 1875	Fritz Kreisler, violinist.
Feb.	3, 1811	Horace Greeley, founder New York *Tribune*.
Feb.	4, 1902	Charles A. Lindbergh, aviator.
Feb.	5, 1840	Sir Hiram Maxim, inventor of Maxim gun.
Feb.	6, 1838	Sir Henry Irving, actor.
Feb.	7, 1812	Charles Dickens, novelist.
Feb.	8, 1819	John Ruskin, writer and art critic.
Feb.	9, 1773	William H. Harrison, President of the United States.
Feb.	10, 1883	Andrei Vishinsky, Soviet official.
Feb.	11, 1847	Thomas A. Edison, inventor.
Feb.	12, 1809	Abraham Lincoln, President of the United States.
"	" "	Charles R. Darwin, researcher on evolution.
Feb.	13, 1885	Mrs. Harry S Truman.
Feb.	14, 1894	Jack Benny, radio and film actor.
Feb.	15, 1882	John Barrymore, actor.
Feb.	16, 1838	Henry Adams, lecturer and writer.
Feb.	17, 1888	Dorothy Kenyon, lawyer.
Feb.	18, 1882	Wendell Willkie, presidential candidate.

Aquarius would excel as:

AN ORATOR   or   AN AUTHOR   or   A MUSICIAN

A SCIENTIST   or   AN OCCULTIST   or   A PHILOSOPHER

ILLUSTRATION 11

THE SYMBOL OF PISCES IS ⟩─(For Those Born
February 19–March 20
Approximately

The symbol of Pisces is that of two fishes tied together with a band. It consists of two crescent moons placed back to back and securely riveted by the horizontal line which denotes the material world. As we said in the section under Aries, the Moon represents the consciousness. The two moons of Pisces represent man's finite consciousness linked, during his earth life, with an infinitely greater cosmic consciousness. For this reason, Pisces inclines to be the most psychic of all the signs.

The symbol also represents the two feet of man, the parts of the body which sustain the weight of the whole. If the feet are not strong, the rest of the body is thrown out of alignment. If the feet are not beautiful, then the rest of the bodily beauty counts for little. If the consciousness of man is not beautiful, there is little beauty in his actions. The consciousness is not beautiful until there is harmony between the subconscious and the super-conscious. When this harmony does not exist, we find maladjustment and unhappiness. When it does, then we find the most gracious of human beings. Do not think that Pisces is a weak sign. Any fisherman can tell you of the strength of some fish. *Litheness is never a result of weakness.*

Pisces is a Water sign, hence linked to emotion. The emotion of Pisces is never as obvious as is that of Cancer. It is never as repressed as is that of Scorpio, but its causes are often hidden like underground rivers.

There are endless reasons why a character delineation based merely on the Sun sign requires modification, so that it is well for all people to accept any such readings with a grain of salt. What the Sun, however, does reveal to the astrologer is the inner activity of the life expression, and how this manifests itself. A Piscean never acts like a Taurean, and a Taurean never acts like an Arian. The motivation is different. The more we try to understand the symbols of the signs, the more they will reveal this innerspring of action. Just how man is helped or hindered when trying to manifest the great Sun-life within his soul, will be shown by the rest of his horoscope. In some horoscopes the Sun is tucked away in such an insignificant place that it is only during a crisis or emergency that it seems to shine forth.

PISCES BIRTHDAYS

Feb. 19, 1865   Sven Hedin, Swedish explorer.
Feb. 20, 1820   Elisha Kane, American surgeon and Arctic explorer.
Feb. 21, 1937   Prince Harold of Norway.
Feb. 22, 1732   George Washington, President of the United States.
Feb. 23, 1817   George Frederick Watts, painter and sculptor.
Feb. 24, 1814   Henry Kirke Brown, American sculptor.
Feb. 25, 1842   Camille Flammarion, astronomer.
Feb. 26, 1846   William F. Cody, "Buffalo Bill."
Feb. 27, 1807   Henry Wadsworth Longfellow, poet and professor.
Feb. 28, 1533   Michel de Montaigne ("between 11:00 A.M. and noon").
Feb. 29, 1896   George E. Allen, Director, Reconstruction Finance Corp.
Mar. 1, 1848   Augustus Saint-Gaudens, sculptor.
Mar. 2, 1876   Pope Pius XII.
Mar. 3, 1869   Sir Henry Wood, conductor.
Mar. 4, 1829   Samuel R. Gardiner, historian.
Mar. 5, 1908   Rex Harrison, actor.
Mar. 6, 1806   Elizabeth Barrett Browning, poet (not 1809).
Mar. 7, 1802   Sir Edwin Landseer, painter.
Mar. 8, 1841   Oliver Wendell Holmes, Judge of Supreme Court.
Mar. 9, 1884   Ernest Bevin, British labor leader.
Mar. 10, 1845   Czar Alexander III.
Mar. 11, 1890   Vannevar Bush, atomic scientist.
Mar. 12, 1863   Gabriele d'Annunzio, author and soldier.
Mar. 13, 1813   Lorenzo Delmonico, restaurateur.
Mar. 14, 1879   Albert Einstein, theoretical physicist.
Mar. 15, 1767   Andrew Jackson, President of the United States.
Mar. 16, 1751   James Madison, President of the United States.
Mar. 17, 1846   Kate Greenaway, painter.
Mar. 18, 1837   Grover Cleveland, President of the United States.
Mar. 19, 1813   David Livingstone, missionary and explorer.
Mar. 20, 1828   Henrik Ibsen, playwright.

Pisces would excel as:

ILLUSTRATION 12

MASCULINE AND FEMININE SIGNS

The signs are divided into two main types—masculine and feminine. The masculine, or positive, signs have greater power in action. The feminine, or negative, signs have greater endurance. The masculine signs go out and get what they desire, while the feminine ones wait for the things they desire to come to them. Masculine signs are dynamic; feminine signs are receptive. Do not interpret the word *negative* as meaning, lazy, uninterested, or worthless. Think of it as the necessary negative pole in electricity. The masculine and feminine signs follow one another alternately around the zodiac.

1. **Masculine Signs**
   Aries, Gemini, Leo, Libra, Sagittarius, Aquarius.

2. **Feminine Signs**
   Taurus, Cancer, Virgo, Scorpio, Capricorn, Pisces.

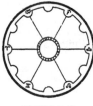

DIAGRAM 2

DIAGRAM 3

THE CARDINAL POINTS

It is essential for the student to note at the start that the astrologer always places the eastern horizon at the left of his wheel. The southern, or noon, place of the Sun is at the uppermost part of the wheel. This is because early Sun-worshiping astrologers faced south when making their maps. Our present day map-makers face north. Actually, there is no basic disagreement in the resultant maps, as you will see should you turn the diagrams that follow upside down.

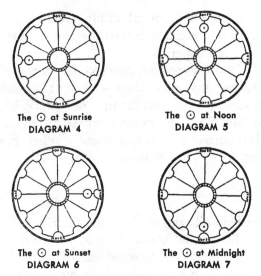

The ⊙ at Sunrise
DIAGRAM 4

The ⊙ at Noon
DIAGRAM 5

The ⊙ at Sunset
DIAGRAM 6

The ⊙ at Midnight
DIAGRAM 7

Note: The symbol of the Sun in these diagrams is ⊙.

IMPORTANCE OF THE HOUR OF BIRTH

The exact time of birth is important because of the movement of the Sun and planets in relation to the cardinal points. For example, if a child is born at dawn, the Sun must be near the eastern horizon. If a child is born at noon, the Sun must be in the south; if born at sunset the Sun must be in the west; and if born at midnight, the Sun will be north, though unseen.

THE TWELVE HOUSES OF THE HOROSCOPE

The astrologer divides every horoscope into twelve sections, which are called houses. Each house is assigned to some department of life. (See Diagram 12.)

These departments are not arbitrary, nor assigned in any haphazard way. They are related to the signs, as you will perceive, but houses and signs are two very different things. **The signs are fields of potential energy and influence which act** upon the houses, or departments of life. The signs are heavenly influences; the houses are merely convenient allotments of our earthly assets and experiences.

The First House always lies between the Ascendant and the second cusp, but any one of the twelve signs may rest upon it and influence it, according to the time of birth. Whatever sign is over the First House is succeeded by the rest of the zodiacal signs in their correct unbroken sequence. When Pisces ends, Aries begins, for the zodiac is an unbroken circle.

HOUSE I

The First House begins at the eastern horizon, the place of sunrise. It is the natural house of Aries, which rules all beginnings. This house rules the face and head in particular and the body in general. To it is assigned all commencements, and this includes childhood years. The house rules the general appearance of the native, and his characteristic actions, such as are expressed when walking, or when using his hands.

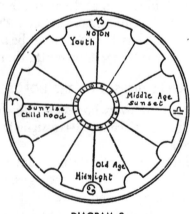

DIAGRAM 8

HOUSE II

The Second House is the natural house of Taurus, the sign which conserves and builds. This house is assigned to the money you earn, and to all tangible assets. Since your liberty depends largely upon your financial standing, this is the house of liberty.

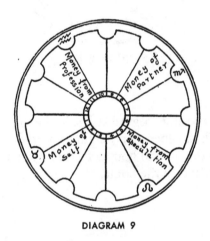

DIAGRAM 9

HOUSE III

The Third House is the natural house of Gemini, a mental sign, which links people together through like thought or experience. This house is assigned to relatives, general acquaintances, neighbors, letters, telephones, telegraphs, roads, and short journeys. It is also assigned to newspapers, and to magazines of an ephemeral nature.

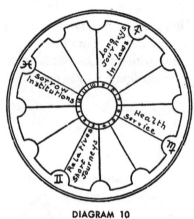

DIAGRAM 10

HOUSE IV

The **Fourth House** begins at the point of midnight. For this reason it is assigned to all endings, to old age, and to old people. Being the natural house of Cancer it is assigned to one of the parents, and to the home.

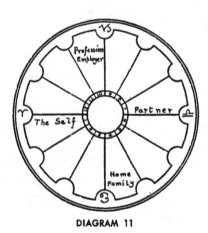

DIAGRAM 11

HOUSE V

The Fifth House is the natural house of Leo which governs the heart. This house is assigned to love and to children, also to things that cause thrills and excitement, such as theaters, entertainment, gambling, and speculation.

HOUSE VI

The Sixth House is the natural house of Virgo. It, therefore, rules work, service, servants, and subordinates. This house is also said to rule small animals and pets. It describes the general health of the native, and the type of sicknesses to which he is prone.

HOUSE VII

The Seventh House begins at the point of sunset. This house, therefore, rules, not the self, as does the First House, but the other people with whom you associate, or ally yourself. It is the natural house of Libra, ruling all partners with whom you have a contract. It, therefore, includes business partners as well as the marriage partner. The conditions of this house indicate how you act in public, and the type of public you attract. It shows the public's reaction to you.

HOUSE VIII

The Eighth House is the natural house of Scorpio. This house rules sex, death, legacies, insurance policies, and regeneration. The term legacies must be broadened to include, not merely money, but equipment, educational help, etc., received from the parents, or others, during their lifetime. It is the house of the partner's money, because it follows the Seventh House.

HOUSE IX

The Ninth House is the natural house of Sagittarius. This house rules law, religion, philosophy, and long journeys. A long journey in astrology seems to mean one of over twenty-four hours. Someday no journey need take that long. Possibly the Ninth House should rule change of states (with consequent change of laws), foreign travel, or even visits to places totally unknown to you previously. The house is assigned to in-laws, as being the Third House from the Seventh. For this reason, the old idea of long journeys might have been to one's in-laws instead of to one's own relatives, which are under the Third House. The Ninth House is also the house of publications, particularly bound books, and treatises that are meant to be lasting.

HOUSE X

The Tenth House begins at the point of noon. This house is assigned to all such things as reveal you clearly to the world, such as parentage, social status, and profession. It is the natural house of Capricorn, the climbing goat.

HOUSE XI

The Eleventh House is the natural house of Aquarius. This house rules the friends you have made for yourself and among whom you circulate; also the groups to which you belong. It rules your hopes and wishes, and your main objective, or goal, in life. It has some rule over the money you earn from any profession, since it is the Second House from the Tenth.

HOUSE XII

The Twelfth House is the natural house of Pisces. This house rules your foundations, together with the subconscious, and all that hampers and restricts your power of expression. It denotes the basic strength or weakness of your body and soul. Hereditary weaknesses lie rather in the Fourth and Sixth Houses than in the Twelfth. This house rules institutions of all kinds, hospitals, limiting circumstances, secrets of all kinds, and also secret enemies. It is the house of large animals.

SUMMARY OF THE HOUSES

A little later in the lessons much more will have to be learned about the nature of the signs and the houses. The above is enough at present for you to realize that there are reasons for what at first sight may have seemed irrational in astrology. Study the following diagram, and remember that **house positions never change.**

The signs move around them. Note that as the Sun moves towards its noon position from the Ascendant on any morning, it will remain in its own sign, but the sign plus the Sun will be moving in the direction of the Midheaven (south). In this way a new sign will arise upon the Ascendant. The signs move from east to west, while the planets increase in longitude as they move through the signs from west to east.

The lines that separate the houses are termed *cusps*. This

term has also been applied in comparatively recent years to
the end and beginnings of signs, and it must not be confused
with house cusps.

DIAGRAM 12
Summary of the Houses

LESSON THREE

The Planets and Their Symbols

♈ ♉ ♊ ♋ ♌ ♍ ♎ ♏ ♐ ♑ ♒ ♓

INTRODUCTION: *In this lesson you continue with the fascinating study of symbolism, but in this case it is directed to the study of the planets. The more you meditate upon the symbols, the greater depth will be given to your understanding. You tend to root the subject in your subconscious. Without firm roots no tree can flourish for long.*

Many students ask if the discovery of new planets * does not upset the principles of astrology. The answer is no. The chemist knows from the color pattern in the spectrum that new metals are still to be discovered. In the same way, the astrologer knows that eventually two planets beyond Pluto will be discovered, providing twelve rulers, one for each sign. The astrologer needs one of the new planets as part ruler of Gemini. Study Diagram 13 and Diagram 14 carefully, and you will understand how we know which signs will be assigned to the new planets. We have designated the new planets in Diagram 14 as Venus P(lus) and Mercury P(lus), and placed them in the center line between the old rulers of the signs. We should note that the right-hand signs are still ruled by the old planets, while the left-hand signs seem to respond more specifically to the influence of the new rulers. We shall deal with this question in greater detail later.

---

* Uranus discovered March 13, 1781; Neptune, September 24, 1846; and Pluto, March 13, 1930.

The basic pattern of the natural zodiac tells us where the planets belong before they are discovered. The discovery of Uranus and Neptune simplified the reading of charts considerably. Researchers are still working on the influence of Pluto. They will continue to do so until they learn still more about this most recently discovered planet.

WHAT IS A SYMBOL?

A symbol is an object or form which is taken as representative of some mental, moral, or spiritual thing. In a symbol there is always an inner meaning, for example, a circle which has no beginning and no end, represents what is infinite. A triangle represents spirit in three modes of expression—will, wisdom, and activity. A horizontal line represents matter. A vertical line represents spirit. A cross or square represents the material world influenced by spirit. A ram typifies the instinct of pugnacity, a lamb that of meekness, while a lion indicates courage and strength.

· It is impossible to understand astrology unless you cultivate the habit of studying a symbol and then digging down into its basic meaning. The more you ponder over the symbols of the signs of the zodiac, and of the planets, the more light will dawn in your consciousness, and deeper meanings will unfold. You will find yourself hailing each discovery with joy and pride, and you will become equipped to make judgments in keeping with the true nature of the planet and sign. In a symbol there is concealment and there is revelation. For example, it may be difficult at first sight to understand why a circle with a dot in it can mean, not only the Sun, but a father, a husband, or an employer. But as you study the symbol in its fundamental meaning, the extended meanings will gradually become clear.

THE SYMBOL OF THE SUN IS ☉

The circle represents what is infinite and boundless, without beginning and without end. It is, therefore, a good symbol for the source of man's life—the Sun. The dot in the circle is important. It represents the seed, or germ, of a lesser light contained within the larger. The whole symbol is typical of the Sun which personifies man's life and spirit given to him by the All-Spirit. As above, so below. Even the atom has a nucleus.

The symbol also depicts the heart of man, the central dynamo of the body. In a horoscope the Sun reveals, in whatever sign it is placed, the main expression of the individual. Just as the Sun has a varying effect upon vegetation during certain months, so it has a different effect upon the people born in particular months. According to the sign and house of the Sun, we are able to judge the general vitality and physique, the qualities of leadership and command, the dignity of a person, and his success.

Since the Sun indicates the source of vital supply, it comes to mean the person who provides this supply; hence in a horoscope it can refer to the father first and then employer. In a woman's chart the Sun may represent first the father and then the husband. If a man works for himself, the Sun will define the general well-being and success he obtains in such work.

The Sun portrays the real self within man—the man stripped of all his acquired habits and mannerisms, and of all the trappings of education and civilization. It denotes the man behind every mask that he can make for himself. Just as the Sun can be hidden by tall buildings or clouds, so the real source of a man's strength can be hidden. The true student of astrology knows that the Sun lies within each human being, and he should help that man uncover its glory.

The Sun in astrology represents life, not only in the heart, but in each cell. And in all life, according to the ancient astrologers, there is consciousness—not necessarily self-consciousness (see symbolism of the Moon), but a consciousness which is aware of the presence and need of other living entities.

The philosophy of the Victorian Age tended somewhat to consider consciousness as having its seat in the brain. A more modern group of thinkers, for example, Henri Bergson, states that consciousness is part of life, and in every phase of it. Medical men are coming to the same conclusion.

The Sun is a Fire planet. It is said to be masculine or positive, that is, it seeks to give rather than to receive. It is the natural ruler of the sign Leo and of the Fifth House.

THE SYMBOL OF THE MOON IS ☽

The crescent Moon being shaped like a cup, pictures all that is receptive in your nature. It governs the instincts, the emotions, and the imagination. It discloses the subconscious mind, that great storehouse of everything that has happened to you. The Moon is the storehouse of memory. If your Moon is strongly placed, you will be able to remember with little effort the events of your childhood days; or you may be fascinated by history, or by antiques.

In the Moon, as we said before, lie the instincts—the paternal and maternal instincts, the desire to touch, the desire to collect, the instinct to run away at the approach of a stranger, curiosity, anger, and so forth. All these instincts are just as natural to animals as to human beings. With man, as he learns to use his mind (Mercury), and as the rays from other planets single out and work upon these primary instincts, they become in time emotions. These may be bad, or beautiful and greatly to be desired. The desire to fight becomes courage; the parental instinct grows into the tenderness and devotion that civilizes the world; the desire to collect becomes the beginning of our great museums and art galleries; the instinct of curiosity develops into a power that gives us new inventions, radio, television, radar, jet planes, etc.

Just as the Moon by its magnetism affects the tides, so in a horoscope the Moon draws out of other planets their special qualities. The Moon in your chart declares your ability, or lack of it, to draw large masses of people to you, whether in the home, the business world, or on the stage, or in government.

The Moon causes growth and rules fecundity; hence, the Moon in your horoscope describes the matter, state, quality, or phase of consciousness within you which has the most chance of growth. It is the planet especially of the mother. It confers the ability to nurture a child, and also to take care of a business. *Caring* is an attribute of the maternal principle. The Sun is the giver of life. The Moon is the soul that takes care of the life; thus, according to the quality of your soul, you will be able to present to the world some carefully nurtured product.

When we say that the Moon in a horoscope defines the personality, we have to understand what the personality means to the astrologer. To the astrologer (not to the psychoanalyst) it is the sum total of our make-up. It gives us the power to know that we as personalities are separate and distinct from others. It will, therefore, include memory, reason to a certain extent, reflection, our likes and dislikes, our feelings, emotions, and qualities. By means of all these we are conscious that we are ourselves and not some other person—unless, of course, something happens to our memory of the self, causing us to become a dual personality, as in the famous story of Dr. Jekyll and Mr. Hyde. Such a pathological lapse of memory must not be confused with the fact that we all feel and act differently on certain days, or even in certain years of our lives, when different aspects of the Moon are forming, or when different transits are at work.

It used to be thought that our personality was made up of

our instincts and mental qualities, but our physical body plays
as large a part as do our mental capacities. The glands have a
very powerful effect upon our emotions and upon our mental
reactions.

The Moon is said to be a Water planet, that is, it deals with
the emotions. It is said to be feminine, or negative. By this we
mean that it receives and holds rather than creates. It is the
ruler of the sign Cancer and of the natural Fourth House.

THE SYMBOL OF MERCURY IS ☿

Mercury is the planet of mind, reason, and intellect. Its
symbol is made up of the cross of matter, the circle of the Sun,
and the cup of the Moon. Mind gets its first start through
receiving an impact from the physical world. This impact sets
up an emotion in the consciousness (Moon). The emotion is
then transmuted in the fire of the life of the Sun into action;
the total result is called Mind.

When Mercury, or the mind, begins to play upon the instincts of man, progress starts. For example, when it plays upon
the nutritive instinct, it begins to find new ways and means of
cooking food. When it plays upon the instinct of flight, it
thinks out the best means of escape; then, as reason runs from
cause to effect, a means is found to make conditions safe. Mind
makes fire, steam, and electricity serve the needs of mankind
instead of destroying him. When Mercury plays on the instinct
of pugnacity, man begins to make clubs, swords, and armor—
and from these has "progressed" to the terrifying weapons of
today. Mercury of itself is neither moral nor unmoral. It is
amoral.

Mercury is the planet of intellectual movement, and of
progress. The god Mercury was pictured as having wings because of this progress by means of thought. Mind sets the
human species apart from the animal, which acts from instinct.

It separates the progressive man from the unprogressive, who can do only what he has been trained to do in his youth. Instinct is an inborn gift and comes under the Moon.

Mercury rules the nervous system, for the nerve system is intimately connected with the mind and brain. Most of the nervous troubles in human beings are not strictly diseases of the nerves, but are due to wrong, or misplaced, interests and thoughts. These, conversely, may be due to wrong functioning of the glands, the senses, and the emotions. When we note that Mercury is the natural ruler of the Sixth House of health, we see that the ancient astrologers knew that mind is the cause of many of our diseases. Modern psychosomatic medicine is apparently a revival of ancient astrological belief.

Mercury rules two signs and two houses. It rules Gemini and the Third House, also Virgo and the Sixth House. It is said to be sexless, nevertheless, some astrologers say it is masculine when ruling Gemini, and feminine when ruling Virgo.

THE SYMBOL OF VENUS IS ♀

The symbol of Venus is made of two well-known symbols, that of the circle of the Sun, and cross of matter. These two are put together with the circle at the top. The whole portrays the Sun energizing the earth and causing vegetation and animal life.

Venus manifests all the things of the world glorified under the radiance of the Sun. It betokens the principle of love on earth, of attraction, joy, gifts, and benefits.

Venus plays on the primary instinct of acquisition and hoarding, and transmutes them into a desire to make possessions beautiful, and to store them in art galleries and museums. It can transmute the reproductive instinct into the emotion of love in all its beauty.

Venus confers the power of cohesion, the force that draws

things and people together. It signifies at its best harmony, sweetness, gentleness, and spirit of refinement, and of good taste. It encourages man to make his surroundings beautiful, and so governs the arts. In music it rules melody rather than harmony, the latter being more under the mental Mercury.

Venus rules two signs and two houses. It rules Taurus and the Second House, also Libra and the Seventh House. It is said to be a Water planet and feminine.

THE SYMBOL OF MARS IS ♂ OR ANCIENTLY ♂

The symbol of Mars, like that of Venus, is composed of the circle and the cross, but in this case the cross is at the top. The whole symbol describes matter emerging from the Sun, or the creation of matter through solar activity. For this reason Mars is said to rule creativeness, new outpourings of energy, construction, invention, ceaseless activity, force, power, work, strife, war, and death. It declares the ceaseless, ever-new stream of energy which brings about new forms; hence it is said to rule the sex energies.

When the rays of Mars play upon the Moon, they single out the instinct of pugnacity, anger, and self-assertiveness. Mars can make these into very destructive forces, or it can exalt them into the noblest virtues—courage, strength of character, self-confidence, and power. The very symbol of Mars in its ancient form is that of the orb of power given to kings at their coronation. In pictures made for the Church during the Middle Ages, God the Father-Creator is distinguished from the other members of the Trinity by the fact that He carries the orb—the symbol of Mars—denoting power and creation.

Mars is a Fire planet, that is, it displays ceaseless activity, zeal and fervor. It is positive or masculine. It rules two signs and two houses, Aries and the First House; Scorpio and the Eighth House. Pluto is now given part rulership of Aries, but undoubtedly this planet has some rule over Scorpio too. The Fire of Mars usually results in heat, whereas the Fire of the Sun should result in light.

THE SYMBOL OF JUPITER IS ♃

The symbol of Jupiter is composed of the crescent Moon of the soul consciousness and the cross of matter. The Moon elevated signifies the instinctive consciousness. It also signifies a consciousness which has learned all its lessons and is now perfected. It has become a moon, or soul, of what we might term the super-conscious rather than the subconscious. The emotions have been purified and become beautiful through the play of the imaginative faculty which, having seen a vision of something lovely, has worked to attain it.

The emotions can become beautiful under Jupiter, but they are always expanded in scope. The Moon and Venus may express tenderness to one, but Jupiter may express benevolence, kindness, and generosity to everyone.

The imagination of the Moon becomes vision and ideality in Jupiter. Jupiter seeks the cause and basis of actions. Instinct is left behind. Because the planet inquires into motives and purposes, it is essentially the planet of the judge and the lawmaker. Under its rays the moral qualities within man begin to develop. Largeness of outlook is cultivated. There is nothing petty or small about Jupiter. It stands for soul growth, expansion, and magnanimity.

Jupiter is said to be a Fire planet. It is masculine or positive. This planet rules two signs and two houses—Sagittarius and the Ninth House, and Pisces and the Twelfth House. Neptune, however, has some rule over Pisces and the Twelfth House. The Romans described Jupiter by two of his activities—Jupiter Pluvius, and Jupiter Tonnans. The first indicated Jupiter as the Rainmaker (Pisces), the second described him hurling the thunderbolt (Sagittarius).

THE SYMBOL OF SATURN IS ♄

The symbol of Saturn is composed of the same cross and crescent we have in Jupiter, but in this case the cross of matter is at the top. Saturn is the scientist, whereas Jupiter is the exponent of theories. Saturn is the recluse, whereas Jupiter is the man of affairs, whether as magistrate, politician, or business magnate. Saturn creates theories and states scientific laws. Jupiter makes these laws and facts known to the world. Facts and material things weigh down upon the soul of the Saturnian, and from these he evolves theories. Jupiter accepts these theories, and uses them to accelerate the social or economic progress of the world. The symbol of Saturn portrays the material facts that are churned over in the consciousness until man arrives at some inner understanding, and can give utterance to a statement, rule, law, or reason for the facts being as they are. Saturn is said to rule all that is highly organized, or in formulae—that which is condensed into, so to speak, capsule form.

Saturn is the principle of contraction, the principle of solidification. We can have water as fluid, vapor, ice, and snow. Snow crystals in all their exquisite beauty and form come under Saturn—matter in specialized form. Saturn governs form, whether the walls of a house, the shell of an egg, or the skin of the body. Saturn governs organization and, therefore, is said to rule the governments of nations, and the executive bodies of large corporations. It rules church organizations, whereas Jupiter rules the ideas upon which churches are founded.

Saturn gives depth to the character and firmness of conviction. He confers sobriety, prudence, good sense, dependability, and patience. Saturn is the builder, whereas Jupiter is the architect. If you use cheap materials and scamp the construction of the home, beware when the storms of Saturn fall upon you, for

Saturn is Lord of Time; but if you have built the foundation, walls, and roof secure, then Saturn will do you little harm.

Saturn is said to be a masculine or positive planet. It rules two signs and two houses—Capricorn and the Tenth House, also Aquarius and the Eleventh House. In modern days Aquarius is also said to be ruled by Uranus. We must remember that some of the old astrologers made some amazing prophecies without the use of the newer planets.

THE SYMBOL OF URANUS IS ⯓ OR ♅ OR ♅

Uranus is symbolized by three forms. The last one, comparable to Mars with a dot in the circle, is used by astronomers, and by European astrologers, except the British. American and British astrologers use either the first or second. The first is composed of two moons, one of the human nature, and one of the divine. The two pillars in the second symbol represent much the same idea. These two moons, or two uprights, are joined together by the cross of matter with a small circle of the Sun appended. All forms of the symbol of Uranus signify the energy of the spirit playing upon matter, and conversely, all investigation of matter resulting in some form of dynamic energy.

Uranus is peculiarly the planet of insight into the laws of nature. This insight seems to come in flashes, which reveal just how and when material things can be made more useful. It is the planet of the inventor, and is original and scientific, almost never emotional.

Uranus is said to govern astrology, because it gives insight into the whole of the laws that concern man and the solar system. Uranus is the planet of electricity. It is sometimes said to be malefic, for when it strikes, it can cause the whole efforts of a lifetime to tumble down and be destroyed. This is usually because the plan of life has been wrong. The old has to be

destroyed before something new can enter. Some of our greatest men have had to start over again in middle life, and it has
been the new profession which has brought enduring fame.

As man progressed in civilization he put lightning conduc-
tors on his buildings, so that the lightning ran harmlessly down
to earth. In the same way when man is evolved, he learns by
insight and self-control how to manage the effects of Uranus
in his chart, and how to make use of its illumination without
being destroyed. It is sometimes said to be the planet of revo-
lutionaries, for it is never content to allow old institutions to
continue without change. For this reason Saturn and Uranus
are ever in mortal conflict. Perhaps we should define the word
revolutionary in a not-too-political sense, e.g., the use of electricity in the home has revolutionized housework. The Uranian seems to act from motives and reasons that ordinary
humanity cannot understand. He is considered peculiar, and is
often disliked, because people usually dislike what they do not
understand.

Uranus is masculine, positive, and electric. It is part ruler
of the sign Aquarius.

THE SYMBOL OF NEPTUNE IS Ψ OR Ƴ

The symbol of Neptune is the trident, which was said to
confer power over the sea, and its inhabitants. The symbol is
composed of the cup of the Moon pierced by the staff of the
Sun. From the staff is appended the circle of the Sun. Spirit
penetrates swiftly and surely into man's consciousness and,
when man is worthy of it, confers the gift of prophecy.

Neptune is the most peculiar of all the planets in its effects.
Like the Uranian, the Neptunian does not seem to act from any
reason or motive that can be understood by people in general.
The Uranian has flashes of illumination that penetrate into the
laws of matter, but the Neptunian has rather a vision of a

complete whole. When highly evolved, he seeks to bring his vision into reality. Neptune makes mystics, whereas Uranus makes occultists. Neptune is concerned with beauty, whereas Uranus is concerned with forces. Neptune's vibrations can give the composer in one moment the whole of an opera. It will depend upon the rest of the chart whether this will be written in musical score, for Neptune of itself does not contribute any love of active hard work. The Neptunian inclines to be the dreamer.

Neptune bestows poetry, prophecy, and fragrance, whereas Uranus, like the Sun, gives light. Uranus is concerned with the mechanism of the radio. Neptune gives the ability to distribute the voices and music from the radio over the whole earth. Neptune rules all things that are widely distributed, whether rumors, or chain-store businesses. Uranus rules the actual act of advertising, but the carrying of the information to wide areas of people comes under Neptune.

Neptune is sometimes thought to be too elusive to help the businessman, but it is a fact that the biggest businessmen often have Neptune strongly accentuated in their horoscopes. These men have the uncanny knack of knowing what to do in their business, and the right moment when to do it. They work on "hunches," which are Neptunian rays.

Neptune, like Venus, rules music. In olden days mothers and teachers knew that what a child learned through song, and singsong rhymes, entered the subconscious, and welled up in the conscious later in life when it was needed. Modern educators threw out the "silly rhymes and singsong." Now the last few years radio and television advertisers use "singing ads" with great success, and the children love it! In the education of a child, the more the child learns beautiful and helpful ideas, the better he is equipped in later life to face difficulties, for at critical moments these early words and songs arise from apparently nowhere, and provide a fountain of help.

Neptune gives second sight, mediumistic power, and the knowledge of past and future. After denying for centuries that there were such gifts, several of our large universities are now studying these matters. In certain charts Neptune gives a great dislike of facing reality, and a strong contentment with building castles in Spain. In this case the vision and the idea are present, but there is a lack of practicality which has to be overcome. Uranus is often too positive in insisting upon his ideas being put into action prematurely. Neptune is often too negative ever to put his ideas into action. Uranus in incisive. Neptune is diffuse.

Neptune is a Water planet, that is, emotional. It is part ruler of Pisces and the Twelfth House.

THE SYMBOL OF PLUTO IS ♀ OR ♂ OR ♇

The first symbol of Pluto is composed of the Sun, Moon, and the cross of matter, or spirit, soul, and body. The second symbol appears to have been made to show the link with Mars, while the third is formed of the letter *L* plus *P*, standing for Lowell-Pluto.

Pluto marks the epochal periods of life when we suddenly become aware that changes have been going on unnoticed for some time. The caterpillar changes into the butterfly. We perceive the day when the butterfly arrives, but it takes long observation on caterpillars to know that this radical change is part of its destiny. What has taken place? We can give technical names, but actually we don't know. We know it has happened, and we know that every caterpillar, if it lives long enough, will make the change. The change is manifest, and we ascribe it to Pluto. It is not a sudden change because it is innate in the caterpillar to build towards this change. The suddenness lies in our consciousness, which becomes aware that the caterpillar has become something we did not expect. The pattern is innate, but we find it hard to conceive that a creeping thing can suddenly be made to fly.

Pluto marks the stages in our lives when action, or activities, which have been going along more or less subconsciously, suddenly become a basis for active consideration. We say to ourselves, "Why didn't I notice this in myself before?" We awake to facts, and our reflection upon these facts seems to become a turning point in our lives, for good or ill. With certain people, a Pluto aspect leads to a fuller, more constructive life, and to a more mature consciousness. With other people, it marks a period when laziness, resentment, loose morals, evil, and even crime, can become the order of the day.

Saturn in a chart represents the main factor of destiny in a life—destiny in toto—but the little marked events along the path of destiny leading to the culmination of destiny, are the events of Pluto.

Pluto marks the transformations which took place at various points of our lives that have made us today what we are. How often do we hear people say, "If I had acted differently at such-and-such a period of my life, how changed would life be today!" Check up on such a person's life, and you will find the change was due to a strong progression or transit of Pluto at that time.

Pluto aspects often mark the time when the mind sees quite clearly and vividly matters which have previously lain dormant in the subconscious. A condition may have been fermenting for quite a long time before a person realizes that anything unusual has been taking place. Pluto seems to rule the end of one phase of existence and the beginning of another. It rules the ending that leads to a new beginning—the end of the caterpillar and the start of the butterfly. For this reason it has some rule over Scorpio, the sign of transmutation and death. The planet also has rule over Aries, the sign of new beginnings. Pluto rules such things as the enzymes, which apparently cannot be seen until food that requires their work is put into the stomach.

Pluto seems to rule atomic power. It seems to be connected with the factor that transmutes the element Uranium into the unstable element Neptunium, and the latter into Plutonium. In the world of philosophy and religion Pluto rules the factor that causes radical transformations in human lives. such as have completely changed certain people, notable for laziness, selfishness, or drunkenness, into happy, radiant, constructive forces for righteousness. Under Pluto the change is real. Under Neptune such a change might be only a temporary appearance. However, the vision of Neptune may have to appear before Pluto can step in to make the change.

It is too early to say for certain whether Pluto belongs to Fire, Earth, Air, or Water, or whether it is masculine or feminine. However, it is probably a Fire planet and masculine.

SUMMARY

The Meanings of the Planets

THE SUN stands for life, vitality, health, the real self, and spiritual consciousness.

In a personal chart it represents:

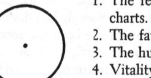

1. The real self, in both male and female charts.
2. The father.
3. The husband, in a woman's chart.
4. Vitality, energy, radiation of life and love.
5. The heart, authority, driving power, zeal.

THE MOON stands for personality, desire, mind, emotion, imagination, soul growth, consciousness.

In a personal chart it represents:

1. The personality, in both male and female charts.

2. The subconscious mind.
3. The mother.
4. The wife, in a man's chart.
5. Emotional capacity, dramatic expression.
6. Psychic power, instinctive consciousness.
7. One's interests and desires.
8. Personal magnetism.
9. Growth.
10. Physiological changes, including seven-year changes.
11. Group consciousness. Mob wisdom.
12. The stomach, digestive absorption. The breasts.

MERCURY stands for the reasoning mind, mental activity, harmony, statistical facts, power of interpretation.

In a personal chart it represents:

1. Mind, reason, logic.
2. Educational capacity, technique.
3. Everyday acquaintances, conversational ability.
4. Brothers and sisters. Near relatives.
5. Short journeys, under twenty-four hours.
6. A young man, a young friend.
7. Music (harmony rather than melody).
8. Nerve force.
9. Lungs, shoulders, arms, and hands.

VENUS stands for desire, attraction, cohesion, love, beauty, song.

In a personal chart it represents:

1. The loved one. Capacity for love.
2. A beloved child.
3. Women in general.

4. Marriage, attractions, unions, desire.
5. Art, and artistic goods. Vanity and fine clothes.
6. Melody and song.
7. Sugar and sweet foods.
8. Selfishness, laziness.
9. The venous blood.

MARS stands for dynamic energy, desire, war, creative capacity.

In a personal chart it represents:

1. Power for work or other activities.
2. Creative and constructive capacity.
3. Desire.

4. Iron, weapons, war, an enemy, strife, a soldier.
5. An active helper.
6. An engineer, a worker in metals.
7. A man in the prime of life.
8. An accident, operation, death.
9. The muscular system, blood fibrin, the red corpuscles, temperature (increasing).

JUPITER stands for the abstract mind, justice, law, aspiration, wealth, expansion.

In a personal chart it represents:

1. The aspirational mind.
2. Ability for abstract thought, religion, justice.
3. Interpretation.

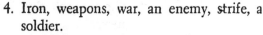

4. Jurisprudence, a judge, a lawyer, a clergyman.
5. A rich man, an important man, a magnate.
6. A man of about fifty or sixty years of age.
7. A person who helps.

       8. Prosperity, expansiveness, geniality.

       9. Cell growth, the arterial blood.

SATURN stands for crystallization, contraction, organization, ambition, science. It is the Sifter and Tester of life.

In a personal chart it represents:

1. Ambition, capacity for a public career.
2. Substance organized. Civilization and its products.
3. The Church as an organization, wisdom, conscience.
4. An executive, responsibility, government office.
5. An old person.
6. Sorrow, limitation, delay. The person who causes such matters.
7. Science, the necessity for application in order to know. The Teacher, Initiator, Guardian.
8. Depth (in contrast to Jupiter which rules height).
9. Bony structure of the body, skin, the hair.

URANUS stands for light, the lightning stroke, sudden illumination, inspiration, invention, genius, sudden destruction, revolution.

In a personal chart it represents:

1. Insight, originality, illumination, invention.
2. Conditions and persons one cannot understand.
3. The unexpected. All that is eccentric.
4. Electricity, the thunderbolt. X rays.
5. A genius, and inventor. The mechanism of airplanes.
6. Nervous spasms. Growths.

NEPTUNE stands for **immateriality,** intangibility, fermentation, psychism, spirituality, music, the movies, shadows, television, the flight of the airplane.

In a personal chart it represents:

1. Psychic and spiritual capacity, reveries, music.
2. Dreams, unreality, shadows, movies, television, flight by airplane, alcohol, drugs, volatile oils.
3. Confusion, inability to see straight.
4. Deceit, deceitful persons. Abnormal persons.
5. Distillation and fermentation. The sapping of foundations.
6. Dissolution, putrefaction, poison and malice.
7. Cosmic consciousness, freedom.
8. Business mergers, chain stores.
9. In matters of health Neptune seems to rule all that devitalizes the system.

PLUTO stands for **change,** mutation, and transformation. Atomic power is undoubtedly a product of Pluto.

We must beware of thinking that Pluto causes life to be bizarre, abnormal or unnatural. Such cannot be the case unless the rest of the chart points to this. It is necessary for the student, particularly when considering progressions or transits of Pluto, to be sure he is interpreting in terms of what is promised radically; otherwise, he will be making gangsters out of noble men, promising abortions to barren women, and generally making himself ridiculous. In most cases Pluto merely throws people out of routine, so that adjustments have to be made. It is too early in the study of Pluto to list all the matters under its control.

There is no particular reason for saying it rules dictators. Dictatorship is not any new phase of government. It has existed from remote centuries. Apparently, Uranus is far more dictatorial than is Pluto.

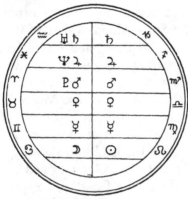

DIAGRAM 13
Sign Rulership

DIAGRAM 14
The Ladder of the Planets

Note: If you study Diagram 13, you will realize that all the new planets may have some rule over two signs. Neptune may have some rule over Sagittarius, particularly over the newer, more abstruse phases of science. It has rule over sea travel and airplane travel. Uranus may have some rule over Capricorn, particularly over the newer professions made possible through scientific research.

SEQUENCE OF PLANETS AND SIGNS

When learning the rulership of the signs, you will understand matters more clearly if you start with the Sun and Moon, and then list the planets in their correct astronomical order of distance from the Sun—Moon, Mercury, Venus, Mars, Jupiter, Saturn, Uranus, Neptune, and Pluto. Study Diagram 13 and Diagram 14 carefully, then note that if we cross the chart from the Sun-Moon signs, we arrive at Saturn, which is the true polarity of the Sun and of the Moon. Saturn was once thought to be the goal of concrete experience. The intervening steps constituted the "ladder of the planets." The old poets and artists often used the ladder to show experience. In Lesson One we spoke of Dante, who imagined himself going on a journey until finally in the *Paradiso*, he speaks of mounting the ladder of the planets. In the art of Egypt and Babylon we find the same symbolism.

In Diagram 14 the artist, by widening the outline of his central form, portrays the accumulation of experience gained on the journey from the Sun-Moon signs to Saturn. He uses the spiral line to show the slow tortuous upward path wherein man tries to understand his environment, and use the innate powers given to him by the planets. The last Saturnine rung was called by the old philosophers *The Bridge of Saturn*. It represented the stage from which one could go no farther, hence it was a place for meditation. Then having absorbed the experience, the soul would make a sure and swift return to spirit. The swift return is marked by the artist as a straight line. Of course, there was a doubt whether everyone returned, or was fit to return to the source. Saturn was sometimes called the Sifter, or the Winnower, because we are either *good grain* or chaff. After the sifting of Saturn we should show grain. If we do, then we are ready once again to be quickened in the life of the Sun, and able to produce new grain next year.

ANCIENT POSITIVE AND NEGATIVE HALVES OF THE ZODIAC

You have already learned the positive and negative signs, and you have noticed that they follow one another in alternate succession. Now think of the zodiac as a unit, and then divide it into halves, so that the signs from the beginning of Leo to the end of Capricorn inclusive are on the right of the wheel, while the signs from zero Aquarius to the last degree of Cancer are on the left (Diagram 15). Since the Sun rules Leo, the ancient astrologers termed the half on which the Sun was placed, the Solar half of the zodiac, and they called the houses on that half, Day, Positive, or Masculine. Then, because the Moon rules Cancer, they termed the half on which the Moon ruled, the Lunar half of the Zodiac, calling the houses on that half, Night, Negative, or Feminine.

It was thought that the motivating action of the Sun and the planets was at its greatest when in the Solar half. In the Lunar half one received the action. The Solar half was Causative, and the Lunar half showed Effect. The terms Day and Night Houses are very confusing, since they have nothing to do with Day and Night, except as these terms may be poetical expressions for positive and negative. However, because in old textbooks you will sometimes come across such phrases as, "Scorpio is the Day House of Mars," or

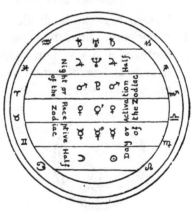

DIAGRAM 15
Ancient Day and Night Homes

"Aries is the Night House of Mars," you will want to know exactly what such phrases mean.

The new planets from Uranus outward have rule over this Night half of the zodiac. In a sense these new planets are specialized expressions of the effects of the old planets. For example, a deep and thoughtful Saturn is necessary before the illumination of Uranus can be much more than a flash in the pan. A philosophical and devout Jupiter is essential before the vision of Neptune can be anything but chaotic. A disciplined Mars is most important, or the changes brought about by Pluto may result in disaster. The planet beyond Pluto will rule Taurus, and the next one beyond that will rule Gemini.

Some modern astrologers object to the word *House* being used in connection with this ancient division of the signs. They suggest we speak of Day and Night Homes of the planets. You will appreciate the need for some change in nomenclature when you read the section below on the modern divisions of the horoscope.

MODERN DIVISIONS OF THE HOROSCOPE

A Horoscope can be divided into two parts by:

1. A horizontal line, the equator, dividing the horoscope into northern and southern sections. (See Diagram 16.)
2. A vertical line, the meridian, dividing the horoscope into eastern and western sections. (See Diagram 17.)

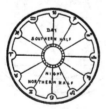   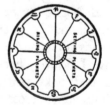

DIAGRAM 16   DIAGRAM 17
Modern Day and Night Divisions   Rising and Setting Divisions

Northern and Southern Halves: This division of the horoscope by the equator into day and night is a real division founded on fact. The southern half contains the houses from sunrise to sunset, while the northern half contains the houses from sunset to sunrise.

Many planets in the northern half tend to make the native an extrovert, that is, he will tend to plunge immediately into action. Many planets in the southern half tend to make the native an introvert, that is, he will like to consider before acting.

Eastern and Western Halves: Planets in the eastern half, that is, from midnight to noon, are said to be "rising," and rising planets have more power than planets in the western half, where they are said to be "setting," that is, going from noon to midnight.

The eastern half represents self, and planets here give freedom of action, and more apparent free will. If there are more rising than setting planets in a horoscope, then the course of life seems to be under the personal control of the native. He inclines to call himself a self-made man.

The western half is connected with other people, and an excess of planets in this half seems to bind up the life with the activities and destinies of other people.

SPECIAL KINDS OF SIGNS

Tropical Signs:

The two signs, Cancer and Capricorn, are said to be Tropical. This is because they are signs of the Tropics. Cancer is the sign where the Sun reaches farthest north each year. Capricorn is the sign where the Sun reaches farthest south each year.

Equinoctial Signs:

The two signs, Aries, and Libra, are said to be Equinoctial. When the Sun enters either Aries or Libra, the days and nights are equal.

Double-bodied Signs:

Gemini, Pisces, and the first half of Sagittarius are said to be double-bodied.

Fruitful Signs:

Cancer, Scorpio, and Pisces are said to be fruitful.

Barren Signs:

Gemini, Leo, and Virgo are said to be barren.

Mute Signs:

Cancer, Scorpio, and Pisces are said to be mute, that is, not great talkers.

Human Signs:

Gemini, Virgo, and Aquarius are said to be human, since their symbols are human figures. Libra is included in this group.

Bestial Signs:

Taurus and Capricorn are said to be bestial signs, since their symbols are the bull and the goat.

Quadrupedian, or four-footed Signs:

Aries, Taurus, Leo, and Capricorn are sometimes called quadrupedian. At other times they are included as bestial.

The Northern Signs are those from Aries to Virgo inclusive.

The Southern Signs are those from Libra to Pisces inclusive.

Spring Signs are Aries, Taurus, and Gemini.

Summer Signs are Cancer, Leo, and Virgo.

Autumn Signs are Libra, Scorpio, and Sagittarius.

Winter Signs are Capricorn, Aquarius, and Pisces.

LESSON FOUR

Why Time Is Important

♈ ♉ ♊ ♋ ♌ ♍ ♎ ♏ ♐ ♑ ♒ ♓

INTRODUCTION: *We have spoken of the fact that some people reject astrology because they argue that the stars are over us all and, if they influence us, it is en masse and not individually. Lesson Four shows you how the moment of birth makes one person's horoscope differ from another's. The time factor prevents one person's life running in the same groove as another's. This difference can extend to all departments of life, but in this lesson, we have confined it largely to partnership and marriage factors.*

In this lesson we give you a rough mental-arithmetic method of finding an approximate Ascendant. In later lessons we shall introduce you to the mathematical method; however, the present one will enable you to understand the process. When you know the Ascendant, you also know the Descendant. This is always the sign opposite the Ascendant.

THE ANGLES OF THE CHART

The **Ascendant** is the term given to the degree of the sign that is rising on the eastern horizon at the time of birth. It is a very important factor in the judgment of a chart, for whatever sign is rising has a profound effect upon the physical body, its actions, carriage and disposition. The Ascendant (abbreviated Asc.) is the cusp of the First House, and should not be applied to the whole of the First House.

The Descendant is the term given to the degree of the sign that is setting on the western horizon at the time of birth. It is the sign opposite that of the Ascendant. It puts its stamp upon the type of person, or persons, with whom you will be brought into partnership, whether through business, or through marriage. The Descendant (abbreviated Desc.) forms the cusp of the Seventh House, and is the same degree as the Ascendant.

The Midheaven is the point "overhead" at the time of birth. We say "overhead," but we know that the Sun cannot be perpendicularly overhead in our latitudes at any time. That can only happen in the tropics. The astrologer has always faced south when making his observations, hence the Midheaven indicates the south.

The term Midheaven is abbreviated M.C., since these are the first two letters of the Latin term for Midheaven, i.e. *Medium Coeli*. The Midheaven sets its stamp upon the profession, type of employer, one of the parents, the social standing, reputation, etc.—that is, on all things by means of which the public recognizes your status in the community. The Midheaven is the meridian of your birthplace, that is, it represents distance east or west of Greenwich. It forms the cusp of the Tenth House, and can be found only by calculation.

The Nadir is the term loosely given by astrologers to the cusp of the Fourth House. It represents the lowest part of the heavens (under the earth) at the time of birth—what is north of the birthplace. It is always the sign opposite the Midheaven, and carries the same degree. It is abbreviated I.C., which are the first letters of *Imum Coeli*, or lowest part of the heavens.

The four points just mentioned—Ascendant, Descendant, Midheaven, and Nadir—are termed the four angles of the horoscope. They form the Cardinal points respectively—east, west, south, and north. Later, we shall find that if planets are near these cusps, and posited in the First, Seventh, Tenth, and

Fourth Houses, they become important through position. Many planets in angles tend towards dynamic power and expression.

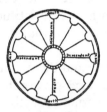

DIAGRAM 18
The Angles of the Chart

HOW TO FIND AN APPROXIMATE ASCENDANT

The signs move upwards from the Ascendant, or in clock wise motion, according to the time of day, but the houses never move. The houses are considered as fixed in the atmosphere of the earth, while the signs are thought of as traveling around the earth in the direction of the hands of a clock.

You will find it helpful as you try to understand this matter, to cut two circles from paper, one a little larger than the other. On the smaller one insert the twelve signs of the zodiac, and on the larger insert the twelve mundane houses. Next, put a pin through the center of each wheel, so that the inner can revolve within the outer one. Insert the Sun symbol on the smaller wheel in the sign of the person under consideration.

If the person is born at noon, move your smaller wheel, so that the Sun is at the top of the chart. Note what sign lies to your left, that is, on the Ascendant. Then imagine a person in the same Sun sign, but born at sunset. In this case the Sun will be at your right, and the sign opposite to the Sun will have become your Ascendant. Now suppose a person born in the same Sun sign, but at midnight. You will find the Sun at the bottom of the wheel, and again a new sign rising.

From the above you see that it is easy to estimate the house sign of the Sun, and also the ascending sign, when a person is born at sunrise, sunset, noon, and midnight. However, do not be too dogmatic about an Ascendant obtained by this method when the person is born in high latitudes. We merely want you to realize for yourself how the Ascendant depends upon the Sun's position.

Our next problem is to find the Ascendant when a person is not born at one of the times previously mentioned. Suppose, for example, you were born on March 21 at 10:00 A.M., with the Sun in Aries. In New York on that date the Sun rises at approximately 6:00 A.M., hence there are six hours to go before noon. Divide this time by three * in order to obtain the approximate time the Sun will take to move through each of the three houses above the Ascendant. It will take approximately two hours to travel through each house, so add two hours to 6:00 A.M. giving 8:00 A.M. as marking the twelfth cusp; then add four hours to 6:00 A.M., or 10:00 A.M., as marking the eleventh cusp. Your Aries Sun will be on the eleventh cusp, and this cusp will be Aries. Taurus will be on the twelfth cusp, and Gemini will be your Ascendant.

You will have the Sun in Aries modified by the characteristics of Gemini. Which will predominate? Remember that the Aries Sun is the real underlying self, yet you will present to the world Gemini characteristics. Gemini will mark your physical appearance, and describe some of your actions, such as the way you move your hands, the way you walk, and the way you talk.

The Ascendant—the physical body—is the factor which makes you obvious to people. It also indicates your mannerisms. It is your shop window. Through the window people imagine what is in the store. Through the window you look

* Later, you will find that the house cusps are not in even thirds of time between sunrise and noon.

out and see part of the world. If your window is rose-colored, everything will look rosy.

You have now discovered for yourself how the signs move around the houses. The Sun or any planet is a dynamo causing action. The sign is the medium through which the action takes place. **The sign is the field of action. The planet is the motivating power.**

SUPPOSE YOU DO NOT KNOW THE TIME WHEN YOU WERE BORN

If you cannot find out the time when you were born, it is wise for the time being to set up your chart for sunrise. Many teachers advocate setting it up for noon, but the noon positions mean very little. When the Sun rises on a particular day, it seems to put its mark on the whole day, and also on the children born that day. Thus, a chart for sunrise really does mean something, and it can give you quite a good reading.

SUNRISE AND SUNSET FOR VARIOUS CITIES

	LATITUDE 51½° N. LONDON	LATITUDE 40½° N. NEW YORK	LATITUDE 38° N. CHARLESTON, W. VA.
	A.M. P.M.	A.M. P.M.	A.M. P.M.
Dec. 21	8.03—3.53	7.21—4.35	6.58—4.58
Jan. 21	7.55—4.28	7.20—5.03	7.01—5.22
Feb. 21	7.04—5.24	6.47—5.40	6.37—5.50
Mar. 21	6.03—6.13	6.03—6.12	6.04—6.12
Apr. 21	4.54—7.05	6.03—6.12	5.25—6.34
May 21	4.01—7.53	5.12—6.45	4.58—6.55
June 21	3.42—8.21	4.37—7.16	4.52—7.10
July 21	4.06—8.06	4.28—7.35	5.06—7.06
Aug. 21	4.53—7.13	5.14—6.51	5.27—6.39
Sep. 21	5.42—6.03	5.46—6.00	5.47—5.59
Oct. 21	6.32—4.57	6.17—5.17	6.08—5.21
Nov. 21	7.26—4.04	6.54—4.38	6.35—4.57

UNEQUAL DIVISION OF DAY AND NIGHT

When finding the Ascendant, note that the Sun does not rise and set every day at the same time. It varies with the latitude, or distance north and south of the equator. *The World Almanac* for any year will give you the time of sunrise and sunset in many of the important American cities. Also, most newspapers give the time of sunrise and sunset daily in their locality.

HOW LATITUDE AFFECTS YOUR ASCENDANT

Applying the above information to your horoscope, you find that in winter the Sun may not rise until eight o'clock in temperate latitudes, therefore, there will be only four hours between sunrise and noon. Thus, there are only four hours between your Ascendant and Midheaven; but, between the Ascendant and the Nadir there will be eight hours.

LATITUDE AND LONGITUDE LINES

On almost every map you will find lines drawn north and south. These are longitude lines, or meridians. The lines from east to west are called latitude lines. Any city or place is located by:

1. The number of degrees east or west of London, or rather east and west of the Greenwich Observatory, which is the starting place of the zero degree of longitude. (Diagram 19.)

2. The number of degrees north and south of the equator, which is the zero degree of latitude. (See Diagram 20.)

Both latitude and longitude are important factors when studying time.

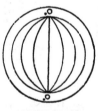

DIAGRAM 19
Longitude Lines

DIAGRAM 20
Latitude Lines

If a person is born at 10:00 A.M. during January (latitude 52 degrees North) he will have the Sun in Capricorn in the middle of the Eleventh House; one born at 4:00 A.M. will have the Sun in Capricorn in the middle of the Second House. If born at 1:00 P.M. the Sun in Capricorn will lie in the Ninth House. If born at 11:00 P.M. the Sun in Capricorn will lie in the Fourth House.

You will now begin to understand why an astrologer cannot find the Ascendant until he has some clue as to the time factor.

Example 1. Warren G. Harding was born in Ohio (Lat. 40°N., Long. 83°W.) on November 2, 1865 at about 2:30 P.M. In what sign and house was his Sun?

On November 2 the Sun is in Scorpio. In Ohio it sets at about 5:00 P.M. This gives us five hours between noon and sunset, that is, between the Midheaven and Descendant, so that the Sun at 2:30 P.M. will be halfway, that is, in the Eighth House. This gives us Scorpio on the Ninth House, Sagittarius on the Midheaven, Capricorn on the Eleventh House, Aquarius on the Twelfth House, and Pisces on the Ascendant. This will mean that in estimating his character we shall have to combine the influence of Scorpio with that of Pisces. The reserve, which is characteristic of Scorpio, would be modified by Pisces, and enable him to mix more freely and easily in company.

Example 2. George Washington was born on February 22, 1732, at Wakefield, Virginia, at 10:00 A.M. In what sign and house is his Sun? (Wakefield is 38°N., 77°W.)

On February 22 the Sun is just entering Pisces. The Sun near Washington's birthplace rose about 6:30 A.M. Thus, on his birth date there would be about five and a half hours between sunrise and noon, that is, between the Ascendant and Midheaven. Ten o'clock in the morning will, therefore, be near the eleventh cusp, hence Pisces will be on the eleventh cusp, Aries on the twelfth, and Taurus will be the Ascendant. In this case we have to combine the influence of Pisces with that of Taurus. Taurus, being an Earth sign, will bring the vision of Pisces down to earth, render the person more practical, and render him less obviously emotional.

Having found the Ascendant, we note that the seventh cusp, the Descendant, will be the sign opposite the Ascendant. Warren Harding will have a Virgo Descendant, while George Washington will have a Scorpio Descendant.

The Seventh House rules marriage and partnerships, so that the horoscope reveals, whether we like it or not, the sign conditioning our house of marriage and partnership. It is always the sign opposite the Ascendant. We do not say you have to marry a person born under the sign opposite your Sun sign, but as the Descendant is the farthest point away from your ascending sign, it is the sign you know least about. The Ascendant is your own sign, physically and mentally, but the conditions governing the house of the partner will be under the sign you know and understand least.

These opposite signs should be called Complementary Signs, that is, not necessarily antagonistic, but able to supply what the other lacks. Below are the complementary signs and their rulers:

COMPLEMENTARY SIGNS AND THEIR RULERS

The positive or masculine signs lie opposite to positive and masculine signs. The feminine or negative signs lie opposite the feminine or negative signs.

1. **Aries,** the positive masculine sign of Mars, is opposite Libra, the positive masculine sign of Venus.

2. **Taurus,** the negative feminine sign of Venus, is opposite Scorpio, the negative feminine sign of Mars.

3. **Gemini,** the positive masculine sign of Mercury, is opposite Sagittarius, the positive masculine sign of Jupiter.

4. **Cancer,** the negative feminine sign of the Moon, is opposite Capricorn, the negative feminine sign of Saturn.

5. **Leo,** the positive masculine sign of the Sun, is opposite Aquarius, the positive masculine sign of Saturn.

6. **Virgo,** the negative feminine sign of Mercury, is opposite Pisces, the negative feminine sign of Jupiter.

THE PLANETS COMPLEMENT ONE ANOTHER

The planets are in four sets of complementary opposites. To recognize these opposites instantly is helpful. Note that Saturn is the complementary opposite of both the Sun and the Moon.

1. **Mars is the complementary opposite of Venus and vice versa.** You will recollect that the planets Venus and Mars had similar symbols, the symbol of Venus being that of Mars reversed. Mars is masculine, positive, and dynamic; Venus is feminine, receptive, and static. Venus does not, like Mars, go rushing to the ends of the earth to get what she wants, but she gets it just the same. She will not fight openly for it. Her desires are just as strong as those of Mars, but she tries to draw people and things to her by her own powers of attraction. Mars expresses himself best in work and things that require ceaseless action, whereas Venus tries to avoid any violent action. Rhythmic motion suits her at all times, not great effort. The more beautiful her surroundings the better she is pleased.

2. **Jupiter is the complementary opposite of Mercury and vice versa.** Mercury and Jupiter are both planets of the mind. The mind of Mercury is that of reason, logic, and collections of facts, whereas the mind of Jupiter is that of aspiration, inspiration, and abstract ideas. Mercury excels at perception, interpretation, and exposition of the use to which ideas can be put, but the actual ideas come from Jupiter. Mercury gives the ability to reason, but Jupiter has to step in to arrive at a judgment based on morality.

3. **Saturn is the complementary opposite of the Moon and vice versa.** The Moon rules growth. Saturn rules crystallization, contraction, and what is completed, rather than what is in process of becoming. Saturn rules old people. The Moon rules water and everything that is fluid, or subject to change and alteration. Saturn rules everything that is highly organized and permanent. Since Cancer rules motherhood, the element of responsibility enters with the Moon, manifesting mainly as the desire to provide for the young, but in Saturn this is rather the sense of duty, together with ambition. The Moon is always experiencing something new, always in a state of transition and change, whereas Saturn weeds out and cuts down the things of which he does not approve. He is, therefore, often represented as a man with a scythe—Father Time.

4. **Saturn is the complementary opposite of the Sun and vice versa.** The Sun rules life and vitality, while Saturn rules old age and death. The Sun rules spirit, whereas Saturn rules matter and material things. The Sun is life at the innermost center. Saturn is said to be the Lord of the Outermost Limit, that is, he rules the things that are farthest away from the spirit. He rules all that wraps, and encloses, and keeps things together. He rules the skin, the walls of a house, the organization of a business, the government of a country. Saturn is Lord of Time. The Sun is ruler of eternity.

SIGNS CAN COMPLEMENT ONE ANOTHER

1. **Aries is the complementary opposite of Libra.** Aries is the eastern sign, the sign of sunrise, of all that is new and full of opportunity. Libra is the sign of sunset, of the ending of the day. Aries represents the beginning of self, the start of the day alone. Libra betokens the end of the day's journey, the meeting and contact with others when one's work is done. Thus, nothing could be more opposite in nature than these two signs. If Aries is on the Ascendant, we shall have a person who is quite happy when he can move about when he pleases, be alone when he wants, enthusiastic about anything new, but never wanting to do anything twice the same way. Such a person will have Libra on his Seventh House cusp. Libra will want company. He is not particularly enthusiastic about anything until he has thought all around the subject. Libra is tolerant of people, but Aries tends to become impatient with them.

Aries is inclined to be irresponsible—at least he does not willingly seek responsibility. Libra delights in taking on responsibilities, even if he soon tires of them. Aries cares little about home and fine surroundings. Libra is never happy without them.

Suppose Libra happens to be on the Ascendant, then our carefree Arian would be on the Descendant, and matters would be reversed. Libra believes in law and order, at least to the extent that peaceful relations between human beings shall be maintained. Aries is east and Libra is west and, apparently, the twain never meet. However, in true love there is neither east nor west.

How then, we ask, can marriage ever be harmonious? Is it not a wonder that under the circumstances that any marriages can be happy, since the cosmic order decrees that opposite signs must occupy the first and seventh cusps? The Descendant, being the sign of which you have least understanding, represents what you have to learn from others. It is the complement of yourself, and a complement by definition presupposes a whole, or a unit, that has been divided into two parts. The complement is that part which, added to the other, completes the whole. The partner has to help in rounding out your onesided nature, teaching you the lessons that you cannot, or will not, learn for yourself, doing the work that you do not know how to do. Conversely, you have to do for the partner the work that the partner does not know how to do. Most marriages split up through pride in not recognizing complementary action, and one or both partners expecting to "boss" the other.

We sometimes speak of marriage as two becoming one, and this is thought by some people to be merely a poetical view of the case. Nonetheless, it is the cosmic view, and it is cosmically intended that from two opposites there shall be created a power that can interpret not merely one half of life, but the whole, or both halves of life.

No individual finds himself—that is, becomes able to comprehend his full powers—until he fuses with, and understands, his opposite. Aries goes too far to the east, while Libra goes too far to the west, but if they continue around the circle of the earth, they will meet at their starting places. Each will have gone the same distance, and each will have encountered the same things, but each will have gained experience by a different means of approach. When each has made the circle, and can compare experiences, each will find that the first step necessary in partnership is to allow the other person to work in the way that is most natural, and not be continually insisting that something shall be done in the other's way.

2. **Taurus is the complementary opposite of Scorpio.** Taurus is the natural field of Venus and Second House affairs, while Scorpio is the natural field of Mars and the Eighth House. We have to consider these two signs as occupying the Ascendant

and Descendant, and, therefore, as affecting personality and partnership. Even so, we shall find that the question of money has to enter in some way or other.

Taurus is substance, form, and mass. Scorpio is power. Taurus loves things for themselves, and likes them to stay in a settled place. Scorpio likes to change and move things, and see how they work. He is an investigator. Taurus looks for ease and comfort, whereas Scorpio expects martyrdom—and usually achieves it. Taurus is continually collecting, and becoming involved in material possessions. Scorpio's final aim is to get rid of materiality and to make himself anew. Taurus is a sign of contentment, whereas Scorpio tears himself to shreds. Taurus can bear a burden patiently to the end of life, whereas Scorpio tries to get rid of the burden—not in the irresponsible way in which Aries would throw away a burden, but rather as an engineer uses cranes and machinery to supplement man's power. On the whole, we might say that Taurus prefers to carry a burden rather than go through life empty-handed. Scorpio will carry a burden only if he feels it is necessary.

Thus, if Taurus is your Ascendant, your Descendant is Scorpio, and your partner will act towards you with the characteristics of Scorpio. These two signs are much more difficult to polarize than are Aries and Libra, because Taurus and Scorpio have much more will power. Another factor is that their feelings are much more intense, Taurus because of the love nature conferred by Venus, and Scorpio because of the steam engendered by Mars in a Water sign. There is also one more factor that can cause trouble between these two signs before they can unite as one. Both are money signs, and each partner has his or her own specific theory on the spending of money.

3. **Gemini is the complementary opposite of Sagittarius.** Gemini is the natural field of Mercury in the natural Third House, while Sagittarius is the natural field of Jupiter in the

natural Ninth House. Here we put them on the Ascendant and Descendant as partners.

Gemini rules the hands, arms, and lungs. It, therefore, represents all that can be contacted in the immediate environment. Sagittarius rules the thighs, therefore, it represents the beginning of locomotion and walking, the ability to contact what is far away. Gemini is interested in the people he meets every day. Sagittarius likes to meet people from distant places. Gemini meets people very readily, and is soon acquainted with them, but he does not often know more than what is on the surface. Sagittarius also meets people easily, but he wants to know the mainspring of their actions. He therefore becomes a diplomat, because people do not so quickly reveal their mainspring. Gemini bargains with and sells commodities quite readily, but Sagittarius is a propagandist, who always has to state why one should buy his commodities. Sagittarius is a better ambassador than a salesman. He tends to create interest, whereupon Gemini can follow and sell the goods.

Gemini rules common sense, the practical and reasonable view of life, while Sagittarius, at his best, says there is something greater than reason, and this is intuition. Gemini is continually turning things around in his mind, continually flitting from one set of facts to the next, often without digesting them or arriving at any real conclusion. Sagittarius progresses upwards and forwards because he tries to understand the basic principles and laws that underlie everything in the universe. In so far as he learns to do this, he develops theories of religion and of law—national and international.

Gemini collects facts and data, but Sagittarius puts these into a theory, system, or law. He is able to transform facts into basic truths.

Gemini quickly discovers the various parts of an automobile or machine, but Sagittarius discovers why they are in their particular places. Gemini quickly knows how a business is run, but Sagittarius wants to know why it is run on particular lines. Gemini and Sagittarius are quite unlike in some ways, but both being mental signs they are adaptable. They rarely make scenes, but each goes his or her own way. Gemini can visit relatives and Sagittarius can go abroad. Signs connected with mind rather than emotion do not quarrel so violently. They may waste their lives, however, in interminable argument.

4. **Cancer is the complementary opposite of Capricorn.** Cancer is the natural field of the Moon in the natural Fourth House. Capricorn is the natural field of Saturn in the natural Tenth House. Hence, when these two signs are placed on the Ascendant and Descendant, they tend to bring Fourth and Tenth House matters into all partnerships.

Cancer governs the northern part of the chart and the time of midnight. Capricorn governs the southern part of the chart and noon. Cancer governs what is hidden in the depths of nature. Capricorn rules what is open and apparent to all. Cancer looks within to get his knowledge. It is an introspective sign. Capricorn looks to externals and is ambitious. Cancer governs the home and family. Capricorn governs the professional and public life. Cancer feels and senses if conditions are right. Capricorn demands facts.

It would seem as if these two signs are quite difficult to polarize, but as a matter of fact they are not so hard as some of the others. Cancer may get hurt in the process of readjustment, for he cannot understand the harshness of Capricorn. Capricorn becomes exasperated with anyone continually crying for emotion and affection. He demands efficiency.

Both signs, however, are alike in one respect. They are acquisitive. They like to collect—of course, in different ways and for different purposes—nevertheless, each desires material things. Cancer scrapes and saves for the home and for the family. He holds on tightly, like a crab, for sentiment's sake, whereas Capricorn seizes and holds things because they increase his value in the eyes of the world. Therefore, when a thing is worn out, Capricorn would replace it with something finer and better, whereas Cancer will cling to it in the hope that it will come in useful some day.

Cancer likes variety and change. Cancer likes new clothes, but will not give away the old. Capricorn prefers one or two good dresses or suits that have been well cut and are correct in every detail.

Cancer will always spend money on food, whereas Capricorn will starve himself to death to live in a fine house.

Cancer is always looking for someone to take care of him— not always financially. Capricorn is self-sufficient. He does not want, nor ask, help, but he is ever seeking people of higher social standing so that he can use them. Cancerians want you to be emotionally interested in every detail of their lives. They have vivid imaginations, and they weave wonderful dreams about themselves, their family, their ancestry, homes, and children. Capricorn is more reticent unless there is some foundation for bragging.

5. **Leo is the complementary opposite of Aquarius.** Leo is the natural field of the Sun in the Fifth House, while Aquarius is the natural field of Saturn, or Uranus, in the Eleventh House. Hence, in the partnership of Leo and Aquarius the affairs of these two houses are important.

Leo radiates warmth and sunshine on all things, causing them to glow with, and to partake of, the gift of life. It is the sign of happiness, romance, love, and children (though, curiously enough Leo rarely has many children). Leo understands life by living it. Aquarius, being mental, tries to understand life through studying the forms in which life is expressed, or by studying groups of people rather than individuals. Leo is interested in the theater as a source of pleasure, or as an outlet for his dramatic capacity. Aquarius becomes interested in the theater as an organization, studying its effect upon masses of people, criticizing it, and always desiring to adapt it to special needs, or even to propaganda.

Leo is interested in children because he loves them. Aquarius is interested because he wishes to educate them and watch over the process of education. Leo loves and does not question love, but Aquarius wants to analyze and dissect it, usually coming to the conclusion that friendship is saner and more valuable. If we analyze friendship there is mutual help, but Leo loves children who can offer him no return, except perhaps a smile or a squeal of delight.

Leo has faith and confidence in himself, therefore he believes that he can guide and rule others. Aquarius lacks the implicit faith of Leo. He studies the principles of rulership and government. He believes that all men are capable of participating in government. This to the lordly Leo is either rank heresy or food for laughter.

Leo is childlike in nature, enthusiastic, never trying to hide his feelings. He takes chances and loves strong drama. He partakes of the nature of the Sun, shining on all, and never caring about—sometimes never noticing—people's reactions to him. Aquarius partakes of the old age of Saturn, or the nervousness of Uranus. Having studied most things, he rarely gets much joy out of them. However, Saturn may help him to be patient and serve others, but Uranus may be strong enough to make him discard all the old teachings.

Few people except Aquarians questions the authority of the Sun. On the other hand, the rule of Saturn is always resented. Aquarius seems incapable of understanding that the small simple things of life are more interesting to the rest of humanity than the great, soulless, lifeless structures which he builds. Leo understands that one living puppy is of much greater value to a child than large quantities of mechanical toys. The work of Aquarius is extremely valuable because it tends to distribute first the blood through the body, and second, to distribute the benefits of civilization through the people of the world.

If Leo is your Ascendant then Aquarius must be your Seventh House sign. Each partner has to learn the lesson of the other. Without Aquarius, Leo would never see beyond the center. Without Leo, Aquarius would never come to a center. Leo will only consider one person—the one he loves. Aquarius wants to study everyone, but he inclines to forget that he must study one in particular in order to find the key to others.

6. **Virgo is the complementary opposite of Pisces.** Virgo is the natural field of Mercury in the natural Six House, while Pisces is the natural field of Jupiter, or Neptune, in the Twelfth House. For this reason when they become the Ascendant or Descendant of a chart, the affairs of these two houses enter into relationship.

In Virgo we learn how things should be done. It is the sign of discrimination, the ability to know the exact weight, size, shape, and texture of materials. Virgo gives the exactness of touch necessary to the artist to get the right effect. Virgo sees life in its minutest details. Pisces, however, sees the oneness of life, and he cares very little for details. He desires to be free from every restriction, but he usually is restricted. Every time he frees himself, he ties another chain around himself.

Virgo likes to be on time. Pisces thinks time was made for slaves. Virgo is practical, since it is an Earth sign. Pisces is emotional, since it is a Water sign. Virgo loves service and work. Pisces loves freedom and laughter, though he is often in tears. He can laugh and cry at almost the same moment.

Virgo is inclined to see only the present and to make that good, but Pisces with his psychic powers sees the past and the future. Because he senses the future, nothing of the present contents him for long. He seems to know that the present is not everything, and that however beautiful existing things are, they will some day be destroyed, or not wanted. This often gives him a pessimistic turn of mind, making him grieve about something that is intangible and indefinite. This mood can annoy Virgo who thinks things that are obvious need attention, rather than things that may never happen. Pisces is often called the sign of self-undoing, because he persists in taking incomprehensible views of life. He is called the sign of sorrow, whereas he never seeks sorrow. It is rather that he creates an atmosphere of "sweetest songs that tell of saddest thought." At times Pisces loves sociability and pleasure, but he will occasionally slip away and let the company entertain itself.

If Virgo is the Ascendant then Pisces must be the Descendant, and of all the various sets of complementary opposites, these two find it hardest to understand each other.

CIRCULAR MEASURE

If we divide any circle into four equal parts, the space between the two lines forming one quarter division is termed a right angle.

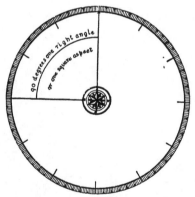

DIAGRAM 21
Degrees and the Squares

If we divide the right angle into 90 equal parts, each part is said to be one degree. There are 360 degrees in any circle, however large. The symbol for a degree is a very small circle.

One degree is written 1°. Although a degree seems very small, yet on the circle of the earth it covers about 60 miles. The degree is subdivided into lesser parts termed minutes, and seconds of arc. Do not confuse these minutes and seconds of arc with minutes and seconds of time.

Minutes of arc have as their symbol one short stroke ('). Seconds of arc have as their symbol 2 short strokes ("). The table of circular measure is as follows:

$$60'' = 1'$$
$$60' = 1°$$
$$90° = 1 \text{ right angle}$$
$$4 \text{ right angles, or } 360° = 1 \text{ circle}$$

or, in a form better suited to astrological practice:

$$60'' = 1'$$
$$60' = 1°$$
$$30° = 1 \text{ sign of the zodiac}$$
$$12 \text{ signs} = 1 \text{ circle of the zodiac}$$

LESSON FIVE

The Kinds of Houses and Signs

♈ ♉ ♊ ♋ ♌ ♍ ♎ ♏ ♐ ♑ ♒ ♓

INTRODUCTION: *In the study of music every student recognizes various patterns within the musical scale—thirds, fifths, etc. In the same way, the astrological student needs to know the basic patterns within the natural horoscope. Everything in nature has its pattern. Remember that the penetration of the atom has revealed the most beautiful patterns. Jacob Boehme called the intrinsic patterns within nature Signatures. This lesson lays the foundation for the analysis of a horoscope.*

There Are Three Kinds of Houses:

1. The first group of houses—the first, fourth, seventh, and tenth—are called **Angular Houses** because they occupy the angles of the chart. These angles indicate east, north, west, and south respectively. Planets in angular houses have greater scope for dynamic action than planets in other houses.

2. The second group of houses—the second, fifth, eighth, and eleventh—are called **Succedent Houses** because they succeed, or come after, the angular houses. Planets in any of these four houses tend towards stability, will power, and fixity of purpose, rather than towards any great activity.

3. The third group of houses—the third, sixth, ninth, and twelfth—are called **Cadent Houses.** Planets in these houses do not have much opportunity for action. They do not confer great stability, but they tend towards adaptability of

thought, communication of ideas, and the ability to get along with people.

The house position of the planet tends to modify the nature of the sign in which the planet is placed. For example, suppose we have a person with the Sun in Taurus, an obstinate sign. If this should be placed in a cadent house, this Taurean will be more adaptable and not quite so obstinate as one whose Sun lies in a succedent house. Again, suppose the Sun should be in Gemini in a succedent house, this Geminian will be more stable than one whose Sun lies in a cadent or angular house. We therefore discover that house position is very revealing. When reading a horoscope it is necessary to make a list of the houses in which the ten planets are placed, and to estimate modifications due to position.

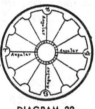 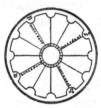 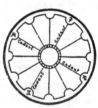

DIAGRAM 22   DIAGRAM 23   DIAGRAM 24
Angular Houses   Succedent Houses   Cadent Houses

HOUSES OF FUNCTION

There is a fourfold division of houses, known to astrologers, but not often recognized in textbooks on astrology.

1. **The Houses of Life**—the first, fifth, and ninth. These are houses of dynamic energy, enthusiasm, motivating power, and religious conviction. (See Diagram 25.)

2. **The Houses of Endings**—the fourth, eighth, and twelfth. The Fourth House refers to the end of life, the eighth to death, and the twelfth to the results of our course of life, particularly in regard to health, or wrong-doing. (See Diagram 26.)

3. **The Houses of Substance**—the second, sixth, and tenth. The Second House describes the accumulated money and possessions of the native; the sixth shows his ability to work; and the tenth describes his employer, or profession. (See Diagram 27.)

4. **The Houses of Relationships**—the third, seventh, and eleventh. These houses describe the native in relation to the community. The third describes his relatives and neighbors, the seventh his partner or partners, and the eleventh describes the friends he chooses for himself. (See Diagram 28.)

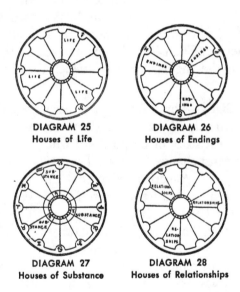

DIAGRAM 25
Houses of Life

DIAGRAM 26
Houses of Endings

DIAGRAM 27
Houses of Substance

DIAGRAM 28
Houses of Relationships

CARDINAL, FIXED, AND MUTABLE SIGNS
Sometimes Called the Quaternaries

Much in the same way that we divide the houses of the horoscope into three kinds—Angular, Succedent, and Cadent—we divide the signs of the zodiac into three kinds—Cardinal,

Fixed, and Mutable. Each group consists of four signs, and each group is called a **Quaternary**, or a **Quadruplicity**.

1. **Cardinal Signs**—The Cardinal Quaternary comprises those signs which in the natural, or usual chart, start with Aries as the Ascendant and form the four cardinal

points. They are all signs of great activity, and consist of Aries, Cancer, Libra, and Capricorn. Note that the four rulers are Mars, Moon, Venus, and Saturn. It would seem as if the fitful changing Moon, acting upon the desires innate in these three planets—

DIAGRAM 29
Cardinal Signs

Saturn for position, Mars for self, and Venus for the mate—causes all four signs to be as restless as herself. The cardinal signs have much the same active nature as the angular houses to which they naturally belong.

2. **Fixed Signs**—The Fixed Quaternary comprises those signs which in a natural chart, lie in the succedent houses. They are signs of great fixity of purpose and will power. They resist change. They are Taurus, Leo, Scorpio, and Aquárius. Note that in this group the rulers are Venus, Sun, Mars, and Saturn (or Uranus). It would seem as if the unchanging Sun acting upon the three above planets—Venus for money and possessions, Mars for reproduction, and Saturn for hopes and wishes—causes all four signs

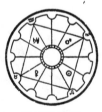

DIAGRAM 30
Fixed Signs

to hold on to their desires. Uranus seems, however, to be the one planet that prevents the world staying in a rut. The fixed signs are of the same fixed nature as the succedent houses to which they naturally belong.

3. **Mutable Signs**—The Mutable Quaternary comprises those signs which in a natural chart lie in the cadent houses.

Some astrologers designate these signs as **Common.** They are Gemini, Virgo, Sagittarius, and Pisces—signs of adaptability, thought, and intercommunication of ideas. Their rulers are Mercury and Jupiter (also Neptune). Gemini with its powers of observation, ability to collect facts, and desire for change and movement, seems to be the motivating sign. Mercury plays upon Virgo making matter express the ideas of the mind, making Sagittarius consider legislation and religion, and making Pisces consider the whole gamut of cause and effect. Because the mutable signs desire less than the other signs, they are able to adapt themselves to other people.

DIAGRAM 31
Mutable Signs

We probe these Cardinal, Fixed, and Mutable signs later, but we have to analyze the **Elements** first. There are three signs in each element.

THE ELEMENTS OF FIRE, EARTH, AIR, AND WATER
Sometimes Called the Triplicities *

Knowing the elements is of considerable significance when judging a chart, for **according to the predominating element, so is the person.** The elements assume momentous value when we try to discover whether two persons will be in harmony.

All twelve signs are distributed among the four elements of Fire, Earth, Air, and Water. We call them "elements" for want of a better name. Astrologers do not use the word with the same connotation as do scientists, who are inclined to think that we do not know what they mean by an element.

1. **The Element of Fire**—The three Fire signs are Aries, Leo, and Sagittarius. Fire signs, like fire, impart action, light,

* The keynote in any group of elements is the cardinal sign, and the cardinal sign of any triplicity provides the keynote of the group.

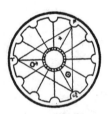

DIAGRAM 32
Fire Signs

and radiance. They are, therefore, related to the qualities of enthusiasm, zeal, love, eagerness, passion, courage, enterprise, individuality, faith, and spirituality. Note that this triplicity has its beginning in the cardinal sign Aries, ruling the east or sunrise, the beginning of self. The keynote of the Fire signs is SELF. The word self may call to mind a vain egotistical person, but it also can refer to one much greater, sometimes very fine. We can mean a person who has developed his innate powers to such an extent that he stands out as being highly individualized. He is not conceited, nor anxious to show off, but he knows within himself that he has certain powers. For example, a man like Professor Millikan knows so much that when he says he has something to offer to the world, it is not conceit that makes him say so, but a sure knowledge of his own powers. Robert A. Millikan, physicist who measured the electron, is an Arian.

2. **The Element of Earth**—The three Earth signs are Taurus, Virgo, and Capricorn. Earth signs, like earth, give stability, solidarity, dependability, reliability, power to gather and collect, to discriminate, and to build. They form the basis of supply. This triplicity has its beginning in Capricorn, which is the life as seen by others, the knowledge that the public has concerning public activities. The keynote of this triplicity is that of possessions—materials, property, goods, information, tools, and servants.

DIAGRAM 33
Earth Signs

These are the things by means of which the average person knows you.

3. **The Element of Air**—The three Air signs are Libra, Aquarius, and Gemini. Air signs, like air, give the ability to circulate and move freely in and around people and

things. The Air signs are associated with thought, adaptability, and the gift of meeting people with ease. This triplicity has its beginning in the sign Libra—the west, sunset, and other people. The keynote struck in the Air triplicity is *other people*—partners, friends, relatives, and nearby acquaintances. The Air signs adapt themselves to other people. They shine in company.

DIAGRAM 34
Air Signs

4. **The Element of Water**—The three Water signs are Cancer, Scorpio, and Pisces. Water signs, like water, impart the

DIAGRAM 35
Water Signs

ability to flow smoothly, or possibly with great power according to the terrain, or the wind. They can be conspicuous for grace, or for power. They are signs of emotion, psychic power, and soul development. The Water triplicity starts with the cardinal sign Cancer, hence emotion is the keynote. In Cancer emotion is directed towards the home and children, in Scorpio towards the partner, and in Pisces towards all people, particularly those in distress. In Cancer this emotion helps to provide a home, and provide (that is, see in advance) the needs of a home. In Scorpio emotion results in a desire to probe life itself. It may also express itself in spiritual longings.

The Water triplicity is intimately connected with the Houses of Ending, for Cancer governs old age, Scorpio death, and Pisces the sorrows or rewards that result from our actions.

THE ELEMENTS ARE ALWAYS IN SQUARE

A square, or cross, is said by some astrologers to be evil, but this is misleading. The word evil means wicked. Squares may be troublesome, but they do not necessarily make people evil or wicked. Many thousands of children are born each day, hence many must be born on some particular day when the planets are in square aspect, yet statistics prove that most of these children will be good, and only a few be bad. Charts cannot be read properly until erroneous ideas about the squares and oppositions are discarded. Most of the great people of the world have had many of these in their horoscopes. A square causes intense activity, which can polish the rough diamond into the gleaming, glittering object that catches and reflects the most brilliant light. If squares were fundamentally evil, they would not be built into the very fabric of the horoscope which, as we have said before, is simply a pattern or plan of man, or Cosmic Man, in manifestation. We find that certain signs are basically in square, or opposition to others, and nothing can prevent them being so. We have to look upon these aspects as causes of activity, motion, or power.

The elements of Fire, Earth, Air, and Water will always be involved in square, or opposition. Cosmically, one can never have Air square to Air, or Earth square to Earth. It must always be some other element. This war of the elements is the beginning of manifestation in a cosmic sense, and the beginning of events in a personal chart. Look over your chart and you will find that some of the most profound turning points of your whole life started on a square or on an opposition. *

COMMENTS ON THE ELEMENTS

Fire tends to move upwards. Unlike water, it does not come down to its own level again. Fire signs always seem to be trying to reach the unobtainable. Earth sign people consider them dangerous, because enthusiastic people are not careful of material objects that stand in their way. Just as fire can be put out by water, so Fire signs are often dampened by the presence

* Water and Earth can be polarized. Fire and Water cannot. Air and Fire can be polarized. Air and Earth cannot. Fire, Earth, Air, and Water are all acting and interacting upon one another. They smooth the corners of the personality.

of Water signs, which are square to them. However, if the fire is hot enough steam is engendered, and at a greater heat water is vaporized.

Earth is our source of supply. Just as the earth cannot produce vegetation or animal life, nor maintain life, without water, so Earth signs seem to need the presence of Water signs in order to function properly. Too much water, however, causes floods and destruction. Air is also necessary to all life upon the earth; hence we do not find the Earth-Air squares inimical. The Earth-Fire squares are as dangerous as forest fires to those who have not learned to control themselves.

Air tends to be in constant motion. Like the air, Air signs are never rooted. They argue that reason and understanding are more important than material things. Just as air is necessary before fire can burn, so Air signs act as a great stimulus to Fire signs. Conversely the enthusiasm of the Fire signs sharpens the reasoning faculties of the Air signs, and brings new mental concepts and even genius. However, in order to make these concepts usable by mankind, a horoscope should show some Earth sign planets. Earth, however, lies in square to Air tending to make conflict between thought and practice. In order to inspire humanity, ideas have to be linked to emotion, but emotion is despised by reason. For this reason the square of Air to Water is difficult to harmonize.

Water tends to run down to its own level, back to the level whence it came. Water signs go up in emotional outbursts, but they always come down again to placidity. They are without desire, as a rule, for leverage. They are content with themselves and tend to go around difficulties rather than fight them. In this way they may run into ruts from which they seem unable to extricate themselves without the help of either Fire or Earth people. However, if the latter are dominant types who insist upon handling the problems too efficiently, Water signs grow moody. They may even grow violent.

THE SQUARE OR CROSS OF PROGRESS

1. **The Cardinal Cross**—Aries, Cancer, Libra, and Capricorn. This is the cross of activity, progress, pioneering, disregard of the status quo, and of sameness.

DIAGRAM 36
Cross of Progress

Watch for people with the majority of their planets in cardinal signs, and you will observe that they are the ones who take up lost or unpopular causes and make a success of them. They are not afraid of hard knocks, and they do not turn back because the pathway is difficult. They focus their attention on the vision of the new. Even cautious Capricorn can become a powerful factor in building up new businesses. Aries is the start and shows the strength of the brain, and the initial driving power. It is acted upon by squares from Cancer the home, and from Capricorn the necessity of the profession. Libra shows the reaction of the public, and cooperation, or otherwise, from partners and close associates. It represents the fight for place. The goal or height is found in Capricorn, and the result is found in Cancer.

THE SQUARE OR CROSS OF MATTER

2. **The Fixed Cross**—Taurus, Leo, Scorpio, and Aquarius. This is sometimes called the square of gain, or the square of matter. In its desire to possess it employs will power. The Cardinal signs are like jeeps, because they have excessive mobility. The Fixed signs are like the heavy tanks which make their way through the greatest of obstacles. Just as each is good for certain types of work, so we find the Cardinal signs are useful for some kinds of work, and the Fixed sign people good for others.

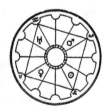

DIAGRAM 37
Cross of Matter

When you study the charts of people who have a preponderance of planets in Fixed signs, you find people who have made their way in spite of almost overwhelming obstacles, or, in some cases, people who are tragedies because they cannot, or will not, alter themselves to meet new circumstances. They have become to deeply attached to their own opinions.

The second sign, Taurus, sets the keynote of gain. It represents the money earned by the person of the First House. On what can one spend one's money? There are three basic things represented by the houses of Leo, Scorpio, and Aquarius. By its square to Leo money will be spent on pleasures, entertainment, and children. By its square to Aquarius money will be spent on friends and also on the achievement of one's objective in life. The opposition to Scorpio indicates money spent on sex, death, and funerals.

Taurus represents money earned by the self; Leo the money coming from the home or family, since it is the Second House from the Fourth. Scorpio represents money from the partner, since it is the Second House from the Seventh; Aquarius can represent money obtained from the profession, since it is the Second House from the Tenth.

THE SQUARE OR CROSS OF REASON

3. **The Mutable Cross**—Gemini, Virgo, Sagittarius, and Pisces. This is called the square of thought, or of reason. The keynote of the square is given by Gemini, which represents mind acting upon circumstances. The Third House reveals the general circumstances into which the child is born, and his ability to change or modify them. He begins by moving around, walking, and talking. As he does this, he learns about his environment and he starts to modify it by his actions—at first somewhat

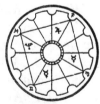

DIAGRAM 38
Cross of Thought

destructively. He learns to modify the relatives or neighbors by either his smiles or his cries. If he is adaptable, he learns what he can accomplish by means of action or conversation.

The child is later acted upon by the Sixth House of service, health and work. He may also be acted upon by the affairs of Pisces, those of confinement, troubles, the necessity for silence, and even secrets. As he absorbs the lessons from these two signs which are square to him, he will later be able to consider abstract things, such as religion or justice. He may also desire to travel to distant places. In other words, he begins to partake of the affairs of his polarity, Sagittarius.

If you study the charts of people who have many Mutable planets, you will find that they have had to adjust themselves to the people they have met in business and society. They may have had experience either in serving or in employing others. They like change and travel, and hearing what other people have to say. Generally speaking, the Gemini mind, which is that of reason, dislikes contacting sickness and sick people. It is distressing to it to do so, until it is polarized with the Sagittarian mind, which reaches out to cause and effect. After this, Gemini can consider trouble and sickness as a necessity making for ultimate justice, and not as a factor in an external fate punishing the just and the unjust for inexplicable reasons.

SYNTHESIS OF THE ELEMENTS

When we read any horoscope we should count the planets in the various elements of Fire, Earth, Air, and Water. Next, we should count them according to their qualities—Cardinal, Fixed, and Mutable. We then have to appraise them and group them as follows:

1. CARDINAL

    Fire   —expressing excessive enterprise, enthusiasm in new ideals or work.

Earth —expressing enterprise, but still practical.

Air —expressing mental originality.

Water—expressing feeling and dramatic power.

2. FIXED

Fire —expressing changeless zeal and driving power.

Earth —expressing stability of purpose. Nonprogressive, unless the remainder of the chart indicates otherwise.

Air —expressing changeless ideals, or purpose.

Water—expressing changeless emotions.

3. MUTABLE

Fire —expressing mental enthusiasm, but subject to change.

Earth —expressing mental ability to guide work, and to consider supply.

Air —expressing mind and giving the ability to analyze the concepts of thought.

Water—expressing mind in its ability to analyze emotion and imagination.

The Cardinal, Fixed, and Mutable signs enter into modern theories of Time, Space, and Motion, with their extensions:

Motion represented by Cardinal signs

Time " " Fixed "

Space " " Mutable "

We can parallel this thought into the three types of houses:

Motion represented by Augular houses

Time " " Succedent "

Space " " Cadent "

We should beware of thinking of Motion, Time, and Space, as three rigidly separated phases of life. We realize this when we consider that Motion can only occur in Time and Space. If human action starts in the sign or house of Aries, it must

also affect both Taurus and Gemini. Within a motor lies the
power to move a car, and when in time it acts, the car can
travel on the road through space. The type of action started in
Cancer must affect Leo and Virgo—motherhood affects children and causes work, and so on.

MANILIUS ON THE TWELVE SIGNS

In order to show you the antiquity of astrology, we quote
below from Manilius who wrote a poem in five books about
the time of the Emperor Augustus entitled *Astronomica*. It
was translated into English by Thomas Creech in 1697.
Note how he calls Water and Earth signs, Sea and Land signs:

> Some Signs for Sea, and other Signs for Land:
> Thus watery Pisces, and the Crab retain
> Their proper nature, and respect the main:
> The Bull and Ram possess their old command,
> They lead the herds, and still they love the land,
> Tho' there the Lion's force their rest invades,
> And poisonous Scorpio lurks in gloomy shades;
> The danger is despised, the Ram and Bull
> Keep land, so powerful is the lust of rule:
> The Twins, the Centaur, and the Scales dispose
> In the same rank; and join the Maid with those.
>
> Of middle nature some with both agree, .
> One part respects the Land, and one the Sea:
> The double Goat is such, whose wild command
> Now Sea affects, and now enjoys the Land:
> And young Aquarius pouring out his stream
> Here spreads a watery, there an earthly beam.
>
> How small these things, yet they reward thy pain,
> Reason's in all, and nothing framed in vain. . . .
>
> And now if you will know what signs dispose
> To Leagues and Peace, and friendly thoughts disclose:

THE FIRE TRIPLICITY

The Ram's bright births you may securely join
As friends to the production of his trine:
But the Ram's births are more fiercely plain,
They give more love than they receive again
From thy fierce Leo, or than his can show
That strides through heaven, and draws the Cretan bow
(Sagittarius).
For (Aries) 'tis a sign of thoughtless innocence,
Exposed to harms, unpracticed in defence;
Unused to fraud or wrong, but gentle, kind,
And not more soft in body than in mind.
The others (Leo and Sagittarius) carry fierceness
in their rays.
Their nature's brutish, and intent on prey;
Ungrateful still, nor can they long retain
A sense of kindness. They are unjust for gain:
And though by nature these are both inclined
To frequent quarrel, yet expect to find
More force in that which is of double kind (Sagittarius).

THE EARTH TRIPLICITY

The Bull, the Goat are equally inclined
To mutual friendship; both alike are kind;
The Bull's productions love fair Virgo's race,
Yet frequent jars disjoin their close embrace.

THE AIR TRIPLICITY

The Scales and Urn one friendly soul inspire,
Their love is settled, and their faith entire;
To both their births the Twins productions prove
The surest friends, and meet an equal love.

THE WATER TRIPLICITY

The Crab and Scorpion to their births impart
A friendly temper, and an open heart;
Yet Scorpios (fraud among the stars is found)
Though friends they seem, yet give a secret wound.
But those whom Pisces' watery rays create,

Are constant neither in their love, nor hate;
They change their minds, now quarrel, now embrace,
And treachery lurks behind their fawning face.

The student will readily discern from the above which signs
Manilius liked and those he did not like. True judgment requires that an astrologer divest himself of partiality and preju-
dice. When he compares signs he should balance the ideals of
one sign with the ideals of the other, or the faults of one sign
with the faults of the other. Never should he compare the
faults of one sign with the ideals of another, or vice versa. Such
is not even logic. Each sign is part of the human anatomy, so
when you start diatribes against any particular sign, just pull
up short, and ask yourself whether you would like to be deprived of that particular part of your body.

PLANETARY DIGNITIES

When a planet is in the sign it rules naturally, it is said to
be **dignified**; as when we find Saturn in Capricorn, its own
sign.

When a planet is in the sign exactly opposite to the one
which it rules, it loses some of its power, because its nature is
not in harmony with the nature of the opposite sign. It is then
said to be in its **detriment.**

Libra and Taurus are the detriment of Mars
Scorpio and Aries are the detriment of Venus
Sagittarius and Pisces are the detriment of Mercury
Capricorn is the detriment of the Moon
Aquarius is the detriment of the Sun
Gemini and Virgo are the detriment of Jupiter
Leo and Cancer are the detriment of Saturn
Leo is the detriment of Uranus
Virgo is the detriment of Neptune
Libra is the detriment of Pluto

Every planet has one particular sign, apart from the one it

normally rules, in which it seems able to express its nature harmoniously. This is the sign of its **exaltation.**

If, however, planets are placed in the signs opposite their exaltations, they are said to be on their **fall,** for in these they cannot express their real nature.

> ☉ is in its exaltation in ♈   in its fall in ♎
> ☽ is in its exaltation in ♉   in its fall in ♏
> ☿ is in its exaltation in ♊   in its fall in ♐
> ♀ is in its exaltation in ♓   in its fall in ♍
> ♂ is in its exaltation in ♑   in its fall in ♋
> ♃ is in its exaltation in ♋   in its fall in ♑
> ♄ is in its exaltation in ♎   in its fall in ♈
> ♅ is in its exaltation in ♏   in its fall in ♉
> ♆ is in its exaltation in ♌   in its fall in ♒
> ♇ is in its exaltation in ♒   in its fall in ♌

If we think seriously about the nature of the signs and planets, we shall discover the reason for these exaltations and falls. It is expedient for you to ponder well Diagrams 39 and 40, which are given later in this chapter.

EXALTATIONS AND FALLS

Sun Exalted in Aries—The Sun gives life and motive power. Its energy keeps us alive. Aries is active and quick, so that the Sun in Aries can work with facility in a sign that has qualities similar to its own. Libra is quiet, never wants to hurry, and has the ideal of poise. When the Sun would rush forth, the nature of Libra is to hold back and consider. Hence the Sun is in constant limitation in Libra, and is said to be in its fall there.

Moon Exalted in Taurus—The Moon is the sign of motherhood, fecundation, and growth. Taurus is the sign of supply, so that in Taurus the Moon has great help. Taurus is, so to speak, a storehouse of food and good things for the Moon. In Scorpio, however, we have a field of action adapted to the hot, fiery, energetic Mars, but most inimical to the dreamy watery Moon. The Moon is a planet of growth, while Scorpio is the sign of change, destruction, and death. For this reason the Moon is in its fall in Scorpio.

Mercury Exalted in Gemini—The planet Mercury can best express its intelligence in weighing, measuring, and adapting the things needed for material progress. It can carry supplies to the place where they are needed. Mercury knows how or why a thing should be done. He gives finesse and exactness to concrete thought and action. In Sagittarius, Mercury is working in a sign which does not necessarily love what is practical, nor deal with concrete thought. The ideas of Sagittarius are often too abstract for practical Mercury, hence Mercury is in its fall in Sagittarius. In a good chart, however, Mercury in this position gives the ability to interpret religion and law to the masses.

Venus Exalted in Pisces—This exaltation seems wrong to many students at first sight, for they think of Venus as merely pleasure-loving and interested in the indulgence of self. Venus is the principle of attraction, coagulation, and harmony. However, when Venus really falls in love, she is not deterred by the poverty, illness, or misfortune of the loved one.

In Pisces, Venus betokens the beautiful feet, without which no person can become a great dancer, since they hold the whole body in delicate but perfect balance. Again Pisces is the sign of poetry, and Venus in Pisces confers rhythm, so that poetry can partake of music. Visions of other-world beauty can be captured and revealed to humanity. Venus is in its fall in Virgo, a sign which ever seeks exactness in form, but is inclined to miss the soul of beauty, which is more than form and mathematical exactitude.

Mars Exalted in Capricorn—Mars gives creative energy, while Capricorn has the patience to organize and construct material things with this energy. Some of the best known construction engineers have Mars in Capricorn. The great bridges, tunnels, and dams need the organized supplies of this Earth sign combined with the creative thought of Mars. They need too the caution of Capricorn to ensure safety. Mars is in its fall in Cancer. Its fire and enthusiasm are not welcome to the watery Moon, which likes to dream and grow as it wishes.

Jupiter Exalted in Cancer—Jupiter rules the principle of expansion, hence it is helpful to Cancer which desires growth and increase. Jupiter is the planet of lofty ideas, and when these ideas are placed in the sign Cancer, they are nurtured and cherished in the mother-sign, until they can become large enough to change the whole destiny of civilizations. Jupiter is in its fall in Capricorn, for in this cautious limiting sign, expansion is hindered.

Saturn Exalted in Libra—Saturn is the principle of contraction, the ability to crystallize thought into its simplest terms without any frills. Saturn makes the scientist who weighs and considers every statement, hence the planet is perfectly at home in the sign of the Balance. Libra, however, being a sign of Venus, takes away some of the coldness of Saturn. In the Middle Ages when philosophers understood astrology, we often find great praise of Saturn in Libra hidden under the term *Melancholy*, but we must remember that the word is one that has changed its meaning somewhat since that time. Today Melancholy means cheerless, despondent, and soul-sick. In former days it meant merely pensive, with the ability to take joy in reflective thought. For this reason we find many of the old poets writing poems in praise of "The goddess sage and holy, divinest Melancholy." Again, the great artist Dürer [1] makes a famous etching which he called **Melencolia,** in which we can find all the symbols of Saturn exalted in Libra. [2] Saturn is in its fall in Aries, for the patient reflective Saturn has little in common with the impetuous Arian.

Uranus Exalted in Scorpio—Uranus gives insight. The

planet works in flashes like the lightning, and makes everything plain. It is well placed in the powerful sign Scorpio,
which is essentially that of new changes of consciousness, and
the ability to penetrate the secrets of nature. Uranus, however,
is much too disturbing for the placid Taurean who wants
everything to stay where it is put. For this reason, Uranus is
in its fall in Taurus.

Neptune Exalted in Leo—Neptune has often been considered as exalted in Cancer, but Diagram 40 will explain to
you why Leo is its exaltation sign. Neptune aids in the illusion
of love, and in the delusion of power. Who can dream and
forget even his food like the lover? If he doesn't, he is not in
love. Neptune weaves visions around the loved one, and calls
forth ideality. In Leo Neptune's clouds are rose-tinted. Facts
are lost to sight, and reason goes to the four winds. (Love call
forth the self-sacrifice of the Neptune-ruled Pisces.) Neptune
is very much out of place in Aquarius, for though one's hopes
and wishes may be at first nebulous, yet they can become very
fixed. When they have become fixed they are certainly not to
be considered illusionary. Aquarius is ruled by both Saturn and
Uranus, and neither of these planets is interested in what is
misty or indefinite. Hence Aquarius is the fall of Neptune.

Pluto Exalted in Aquarius—Although Aquarius is a Fixed
sign, it is the least fixed of the Fixed signs, for it loves change,
and all that is new. Monsoons can be ascribed to Aquarius—
change recurring with regularity. Pluto, which is ever making
changes, can work very efficiently in Aquarius. In Leo it is in
its fall, for neither love nor power seeks change.

THE ANCIENT EXALTATION PATTERN

Students often ask if the exaltation signs were chosen by
chance or by observation. Certainly, they were not chosen by
chance as we have just tried to show you. Many students in the
past have desired to change them, but when they discover that

everything in the natural horoscope is founded upon patterns, they seem more content to accept them as they are. The exaltation pattern is quite ancient.

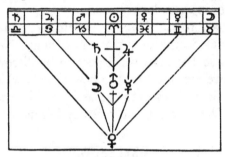

DIAGRAM 39
Exaltation of Seven Planets

In Diagram 39 the seven planets are placed upon the top line in what is called Planetary Hour sequence, with the Sun in the center. On the second line, we place the signs in which the planets have always said to have been exalted.

1. On the top line we find the Sun in the center and Aries below.

2. Below Aries we place its ruler Mars on the center vertical line. Below this we place Venus, because it rules the signs in which the outer planets, Saturn and the Moon, are exalted.

3. Note that the Sun is flanked by Mars and Venus, the two planets of desire. Underneath Mars is Capricorn, while underneath Venus is Pisces. Since Saturn rules Capricorn, and Jupiter rules Pisces, we put Saturn on a slanting line to our left, and Jupiter on a slanting line to our right.

4. Now note we have formed a six-pointed figure with six of our planets, while the seventh, Mars, lies within the hexagon. Mars and Venus lie on the center vertical line as polarities. Saturn and the Moon lie on our left as

polarities. Jupiter and Mercury lie on our right as polarities.

By following this ancient pattern of exaltations, we see that everything lies in some logical order.

We next have to see if we can obtain a reasonable pattern which will include the new planets—Uranus, Neptune, and Pluto—and also the ones we expect to be discovered. As in Diagram 15 we are inserting the new planets which will rule Taurus and Gemini respectively, as Venus P(lus) and Mercury P(lus). We now ask you to study Diagram 40.

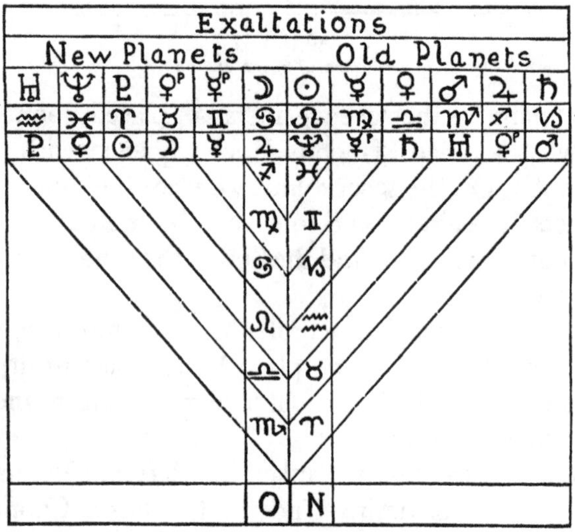

DIAGRAM 40
Exaltation of Twelve Planets

In this new exaltation pattern we allow the Sun and the Moon to occupy the center. Our original five planets lie to the right, while to the left lie all the new planets.

1. On the top line we place all twelve planets.
2. On line two we place the signs ruled by the twelve planets,

counting Pluto as ruler of Aries, Mercury P(lus) as ruler of Gemini, and Venus P(lus) as ruler of Taurus.

3. On line three we first inserted all the exaltations of the seven planets as known to the ancients. Then we started to draw a pattern and discovered that if we were to hold to the pattern:

> Neptune must be exalted in Leo
> Uranus must be exalted in Scorpio
> Pluto must be exalted in Aquarius
> Mercury P(lus) must be exalted in Virgo
> Venus P(lus) must be exalted in Sagittarius

4. In the vertical spaces below Jupiter and Neptune, the signs make a pattern in which we have:

> Sagittarius and Pisces ruled by Jupiter and Neptune
> Virgo and Gemini ruled by Mercury and Mercury P(lus)
> Cancer and Capricorn ruled by the Moon and Saturn
> Leo and Aquarius ruled by the Sun and Uranus
> Libra and Taurus ruled by Venus and Venus P(lus)
> Scorpio and Aries ruled by Mars and Pluto

5. From #4 note on our left (in the vertical spaces) the signs ruled by the old planets (marked O). On our right are the signs ruled by the new planets (marked N).

6. From #5 we discover that Mercury must be exalted in Gemini, and not in Virgo. Mercury P(lus) will be exalted in Virgo, while Venus P(lus) will be exalted in Sagittarius (spiritual love).

7. Also from #4, if we take two rows of vertical signs successively, we have polarity planets ruling them:

a. Jupiter and Neptune	Mercury and Mercury P(lus)
b. Moon and Saturn	Sun and Uranus
c. Venus and Venus P(lus)	Mars and Pluto

PTOLEMY ON EXALTATIONS

The great Ptolemy in his *Tetrabiblos*, written in the Second
Century, gives us the following clues regarding exaltations:

"The Sun on his entrance into Aries is then passing into
the higher and more northern semicircle; but on his entrance into Libra, into the more northern or lower one;
his exaltation, therefore, is determined to be in Aries, as,
when present in that sign, he begins to lengthen the days,
and the influence of his heating increases at the same time.
His fall is placed in Libra for the converse reason. . . .

"Saturn obtains his exaltation in Libra, and his fall in
Aries; since, in all cases, the increase of heat must be at-
tended by a diminution of cold, and the increase in cold
by a diminution of heat.

"Mars possesses a fiery nature, which receives its greatest
intensity in Capricorn, in which sign this planet is most
southerly."

Needless to say, Ptolemy's arguments would not suit astrologers born in the southern latitudes below the equator.

THOUGHTS ON PLANETS IN THEIR FALL

Saturn in Aries	—Speed (Aries) is hampered by the obstacles of Saturn
Uranus in Taurus	—Possessions (Taurus) are ruined by the drastic actions of Uranus
Mars in Cancer	—The home (Cancer) is no place for strife
Pluto in Leo	—Love and power (Leo) dislike change
Venus in Virgo	—Work (Virgo) is no place for the finery of Venus

Sun in Libra	—The Balance (Libra) is disturbed by dynamic action
Moon in Scorpio	—Death (Scorpio) arrests growth
Jupiter in Capricorn	—Crystallization (Capricorn) is ruined by expansion
Neptune in Aquarius	—The objective in life (Aquarius) cannot thrive under nebulous thought
Mercury in Sagittarius	—Ideas (Sagittarius) dislike being checked at times by cold facts

We have not presumed to interpret the characteristics of the planets that have not yet been discovered, although we might say briefly that Venus P(lus) will cause the science of heredity to make great progress. Under Mercury P(lus) our whole system of communications will be revolutionized.

ACCIDENTAL DIGNITY

When a planet is placed in an angle—that is, near the cusp of the First, Tenth, Fourth, and Seventh Houses—it becomes very important. Hence, because of place, and not because of sign, it is said to be **Accidentally Dignified.**

The Various Kinds of Time

♈ ♉ ♊ ♋ ♌ ♍ ♎ ♏ ♐ ♑ ♒ ♓

INTRODUCTION: *No horoscope can be erected until you have mastered several basic factors concerning time. You will discover in Lesson Six that when governments have tried to simplify man's relation to time, they have often created endless difficulties for the astrologer. When in doubt about zoning laws, Time Zone maps or charts must be consulted.*

Before we can calculate a horoscope we need to understand the various kinds of time—Local Mean Time, Standard Time, Daylight Saving Time, Greenwich Mean Time, and Sidereal Time. **Local Mean Time** (abbreviated L.M.T.) gives us exactly noon when the Sun is directly overhead, or, rather, at its highest place in the heavens. Since the Sun apparently moves in relationship to the earth, it stands to reason that the actual time of noon will vary as we happen to live in various places, for example, when it is 7:00 A.M. in Philadelphia it is noon in London.

The Sun moves approximately sixty miles every four minutes (more at the equator and less in our latitudes). This average sixty miles forms one degree of longitude, hence the Sun travels one degree of longitude in four minutes of time, or fifteen degrees to the hour. Suppose a certain city to be sixty miles or so west of your birthplace, then when it is noon by your watch at your birthplace the Sun will not reach the other city for four minutes. In former days each city or country place maintained its own time, but as people moved more frequently, they argued about the correctness of their watches so much, that Standard Time was introduced.

When we set up the angles of a horoscope we need true Local Mean Time. Therefore, when the birth time is given in Standard Time, it is necessary to correct it to Local Mean Time.

Standard Time (abbreviated S.T.). On November 18, 1883, Standard Time was inaugurated in the United States (and Canada). However, the geographical limits of the Time Zones were not definitely established until March 19, 1918. For example, Georgia was not changed to Eastern Standard Time until then. Previously, it had been under Central Standard Time. Do not think the dividing line of the Time Zones lies exactly halfway between all zones, otherwise you will come to grief on cities in Ohio and Michigan.*

Time Belts of the United States:

1. **Eastern Standard Time** (E.S.T.) is calculated to the 75th meridian west longitude. This is the meridian close to Philadelphia, Pa.
2. **Central Standard Time** (C.S.T.) is calculated to the 90th meridian west.
3. **Mountain Standard Time** (M.S.T.) is calculated to the 105th meridian west. This passes through Denver.
4. **Pacific Standard Time** (P.S.T.) is calculated to the 120th meridian west.
5. **Alaska** was standardized in 1918 on 150° west, but in actual practice other zones are, and have been, in use— 120°, 135°, 150°, 165°.

---

* If you look at an atlas and find that the place where you were born is exactly on the 75th, 90th, 105th, or 120th meridian, you need make no calculations for Local Mean Time. It will coincide with Standard Time. Again, if you were born previous to November 18, 1883, no correction is needed. In the following exercises the meridians are correct only to the nearest degree.

EXERCISES IN CONVERTING STANDARD TIME TO
LOCAL MEAN TIME

Example 1. If you were born in New York City at 5:20
A.M., Eastern Standard Time (E.S.T.), what
is your Local Mean Time?

A map will show you that New York City is 74 degrees west
of Greenwich, that is, one degree east of the 75th meridian,
hence the Sun has already passed over New York City before
it reaches Philadelphia, or rather the 75th meridian. It will
have taken four minutes to accomplish this distance, hence,
when the Eastern Standard clock at either Philadelphia, or
New York, shows 5:20 A.M., it will be 5:24 A.M. Local Mean
Time in New York City.

Example 2. If you were born at Washington, D. C. at
7:15 P.M., E.S.T. what is your L.M.T.?

A map will show you that Washington, D. C. is 77° West,
that is, 2° west of the 75th meridian—2° yields 8' of time. For
places west of the meridian that sets the time, subtract these
minutes, hence your Local Mean Time is 7:07 P.M.

Example 3. If you were born at Minneapolis, Minn.,
June 2, C.S.T. midnight * (12:00 A.M.),
what is your L.M.T.?

A map will show you that Minneapolis is 93° West, that is,
3° west of the 90th meridian. 3° yields 12' (for west subtract).
Hence your L.M.T. is 12' before midnight of June 2, and you
were born at 11:48 P.M. on June 1.

Example 4. If you were born at Dallas, Texas, at noon
(12:00 P.M.), C.S.T., what is your L.M.T.?

A map will show you that Dallas is 96½° West, that is,
6½° west of the 90th meridian. 6½° yields 26' (for west subtract). Your L.M.T. will be 11:34 A.M.

* Midnight is 12:00 A.M. Noon is 12:00 P.M.

Example 5. If you were born at Los Angeles, Calif., at
noon (12:00 P.M.) P.S.T., what is your
L.M.T.?

A map will show you that Los Angeles is 118° West, that
is, 2° east of the 120th meridian (for east add). 2° yields 8'.
Your L.M.T. will be 0:08 P.M.

We give you below a few examples of the approximate
number of minutes to add to, or subtract from, the Standard
Time of various cities in order to obtain Local Mean Time.

E.S.T. for 75° West			C.S.T. for 90° West		
Albany, N. Y.	Add	5 min.	Austin, Tex.	Sub	31 min.
Augusta, Me.	Add	21 "	Burlington, Ia.	Sub	5 "
Baltimore, Md.	Sub	6 "	Chicago, Ill.	Add	9 "
Bangor, Me.	Add	25 "	Dallas, Tex.	Sub	27 "
Boston, Mass.	Add	16 "	Des Moines, Ia.	Sub	14 "
Buffalo, N. Y.	Sub	16 "	Erie, Pa.	Sub	20 "
Dayton, O.	Sub	37 "	Galveston, Tex.	Sub	19 "
Detroit, Mich.	Sub	32 "	Indianapolis, Ind.	Add	15 "
Hartford, Conn.	Add	9 "	Jackson, Miss.	Sub	1 "
Newport, R. I.	Add	15 "	Kansas City, Mo.	Sub	18 "
New York, N. Y.	Add	4 "	Louisville, Ky.	Add	17 "
Miami, Fla.	Sub	21 "	Memphis, Tenn.	correct	
Philadelphia, Pa.	Sub	1 "	Milwaukee, Wis.	Add	8 "
Pittsburgh, Pa.	Sub	20 "	New Orleans, La.	correct	
Portland, Me.	Add	19 "	Omaha, Nebr.	Sub	24 "
Rochester, N. Y.	Sub	10 "	St. Louis, Mo.	Sub	1 "
Syracuse, N. Y.	Sub	5 "	St. Paul, Minn.	Sub	12 "
Washington, D. C.	Sub	8 "	Topeka, Kans.	Sub	23 "
Montreal, Que.	Add	6 "	Winnipeg, Man.	Sub	29 "

M.S.T. for 105° West			P.S.T. for 120° West		
Denver, Colo.	correct		Sacramento, Calif.	Sub	6 "
Phoenix, Ariz.	Sub	28 "	Los Angeles, Calif.	Add	7 "
Salt Lake City, Utah	Sub	28 "	San Francisco, Calif.	Sub	10 "

FOREIGN STANDARD TIME

Europe is divided into three belts of time:

1. **Greenwich Mean Time (G.M.T.)** is set for zero longitude. At an International Meridian Conference in 1884, it was
agreed by geographers of the leading nations that they would
use the meridian of Greenwich as the zero degree on all maps.

Greenwich Mean Time is used throughout Great Britian, France, Belgium, Holland, Luxemburg, Spain, Portugal, Algeria, and Morocco.

2. **Middle or Central European Time** (M.E.T. or C.E.T.) is standardized on 15° East longitude. It is used in Germany, Sweden, Norway, Austria, Hungary, Poland, Switzerland, Italy, Czechoslovakia, and Yugoslavia. The time is one hour fast of Greenwich. Hence subtract one hour to obtain G.M.T.

3. **Eastern European Time** (E.E.T.) is standardized on 30° East longitude. It is used in Turkey, Greece, Bulgaria, Romania, Estonia, Latvia, Finland, Egypt, Palestine, and the Union of South Africa. The time is two hours fast of Greenwich. Hence subtract two hours to obtain G.M.T.

You may find the following notes on time in foreign countries useful, particularly if you ever become interested in Mundane Astrology.

India went on Standard Time on January 1, 1906. It is standardized on 82½° East longitude, i.e. 5½ hours fast of G.M.T. Note that Calcutta is not on this standard. It is 5 hrs. 53' 21" fast of Greenwich.

Burma is standardized on 97½° East long., i.e. 6½ hours fast of G.M.T.

Indo China and Siam are standardized on 105° East long., i.e. 7 hours fast of G.M.T.

Western Australia, Hong Kong, and the Philippines are standardized on 120" East long., i.e. 8 hours fast of G.M.T.

Japan and Korea are standardized on 135° East long., i.e. 9 hours fast of G.M.T.

Eastern Australia is standardized on 150° East long., i.e. 10 hours fast of G.M.T.

Marshall and Solomon Islands are standardized on 165° East long., i.e. 11 hours fast of G.M.T.

New Zealand, Guam, and Samoa are standardized on 172½° East long. i.e. 11½ hours fast of G.M.T.

Places in the Western Hemisphere:

Argentina and some of the West Indian islands use Atlantic
Time, which is standardized on 60° West Long, i.e. 4 hours
slow of G.M.T.

Newfoundland, Labrador, and Uruguay are standardized on
52½° West long., i.e. 3½ hours slow of G.M.T.

Canada uses Atlantic Time for places East of 60° West longitude, such as Nova Scotia. From 60° West to 90° West,
Canada is standardized on the 75th meridian, i.e. 4 hours
slow of G.M.T.

Puerto Rico, Chile, and Paraguay use Atlantic Time, four hours
slow of G.M.T.

The Panama Canal Zone uses Eastern Standard Time, five
hours slow of G.M.T.

Hawaii is standardized on 157½° West long., i.e. 10½ hours
slow of G.M.T.

The U.S.S.R. is divided into ten zones of time extending from
30° East longitude to 150° East. These zones occur regu-
larly at intervals of 15 degrees, each equivalent to one hour
of time.

From the U. S. Naval Observatory Eastern Standard Time
is sent daily across the country and to all U. S. possessions.

From Greenwich Observatory Greenwich Mean Time is
sent daily to all parts of Great Britain and to all its possessions,
and spheres of influence.

Exercises to Obtain Foreign Local Mean Time:

Exercise 1. If you were born at Paris noon by the clock,
what is your L.M.T.?

A map will show you that Paris is 2° 20′ E, hence you will
add 9′. Your L.M.T. is 0.09 P.M.

Exercise 2. If you were born at Berlin noon by the clock,
what is your L.M.T.?

A map will show you that Berlin is 13° E. 24′. The difference to the 15th meridian is 1° 36′, hence for west of this meridian, you subtract 6′. Your L.M.T. is 11:54 A.M.

Exercise 3. If you were born at Jerusalem at noon by the clock what is your L.M.T.?

A map will show you that Jerusalem is 35° E 14′. This is 5° 14′ East of the 30th meridian, so add 21′. Your L.M.T. is 0:21 P.M.

Exercise 4. The Korean War started at 4 A.M. June 25, 1950, by Korean Standard Time. What was the L.M.T.?

Seoul is 127° East, which is 8° west of the 135th meridian that sets the time, hence subtract 32′ to get L.M.T., which will be 3:28 A.M.

Exercise 5. At the request of the Burmese astrologers, Burma declared itself a republic on January 4, 1948 at 4:20 A.M., Rangoon. What was the L.M.T.?

Rangoon is 96° East and the meridian that sets the time is 97½° East. Thus Rangoon is 1½° west of the time meridian. Subtract 6′ and the L.M.T. will be 4:14 A.M.*

Daylight Saving Time, sometimes called Summer Time. This is the pet aggravation of astrologers. During the summer one has to subtract one hour to obtain correct Standard Time. It started in New York State March 19, 1918 at 2:00 A.M. as an aid to the war effort. Other states joined in this Summer Time during various years. By 1946 twenty states were on Day-

---

* In all of the above examples we take it for granted that the clocks are showing Standard Time, and not Summer Time. If the latter is indicated, all one need do is subtract one hour to get Standard Time, except in New Zealand which uses only one half hour for their Summer Time. This country, being south of the equator has its summer during our winter. Their Summer Time ranges from September 24 to April 28. It is often necessary to question a client about Summer Time. Florida has none, and during some years California and other places had none (except War Time), but they have had it in other years. War Time was a permanent Daylight Saving Time all the year around, so be careful of charts dated during the war years.

light Saving Time and twenty-eight were not. Its duration is now from the last Sunday in April at 2:00 A.M. until the last Sunday in September at 2:00 A.M.

Some states, which originally used Daylight Saving Time, do not use it now. Others which did not use it, now do use it. Washington, D. C., first went on Summer Time May 11, 1947. Astrologers must always ask in what kind of time the birth data is given. Hospitals are supposed to give the time of birth in Standard Time, but one sometimes wonders.

War Time was invented during World War II. This meant that the clocks were one hour ahead during both summer and winter. In the United States War Time began February 9, 1942 and ended September 30, 1945.

In England Daylight Saving Time started in 1916, but was discarded after the war. Raphael in his *Almanac or Prophetic Messenger* calls Summer Time "crazy time." He usually inserts the variations which have affected Great Britain annually during the different years since 1924, when Summer Time became an annual observance.

During World War II some European countries used War Time all the year around, but during the summer had what they called "Double Summer Time."

Greenwich Mean Time (G.M.T.). The position of the planets in some ephemerides is given in Greenwich Mean Time, which is simply the Local Mean Time of the suburb of Greenwich, four miles South East of London. Through this suburb the zero degree of longitude passes. The Royal Observatory is located there. In London time is sometimes stated in Greenwich Civil Time, meaning that no correction has been made from Greenwich for the four mile distance.

Sidereal Time (S.T.). Sidereal Time is time measured by the stars and not by the sun. Sidereal Time is slightly faster than sun or solar time. If a fixed star is exactly overhead on any particular day, and the sun is also overhead, then on the following day, that is, twenty-four hours later, the sun will arrive at the same overhead position four minutes (approximately) later than the fixed star.

The astronomer has what is called a Sidereal clock. If he sets this at zero on a day near the spring equinox, that is, about March 21, then each day his Sidereal clock is about four minutes ahead. In the course of the year this approximate four minutes has amounted to twenty-four hours, or one day.

If your own clock were a yearly clock and you looked at it, say at noon on April 22, it would show twelve o'clock, of course, but the Sidereal clock of the astronomer would indicate about two hours of Sidereal, or star time, since this increases approximately two hours every month.

An ephemeris gives you the exact Sidereal Time for each day in the year. The table below gives you the approximate Sidereal Time for noon on the 22nd day of each month:

Date	Hours
March 22	0
April 22	2
May 22	4
June 22	6
July 22	8
Aug. 22	10
Sept. 22	12
Oct. 22	14
Nov. 22	16
Dec. 22	18
Jan. 22	20
Feb. 22	22
March 22	24 (or 0 hours)

To get the Sidereal Time approximately correct on any date succeeding some date given above, add four minutes for each day. For example, March 31 will be nine days later than March 22. Multiply 9 by 4 giving you 36'. Add this to 0.00 hours, and you have the S.T. on March 31—0:36 P.M.

LESSON SEVEN

How to Cast a Horoscope

♈ ♉ ♊ ♋ ♌ ♍ ♎ ♏ ♐ ♑ ♒ ♓

INTRODUCTION: *Since you are now starting to calculate horo-scopes here are the books you need—your tools for work.*
1. An ephemeris is necessary to give you the planetary positions of the year, month, and day of birth. Ephemerides are published each year, and in most cases back copies can be obtained. There are a number of good ones on the market, but before using them it is important to know whether they are calculated for noon or for midnight.
   a. Raphael's Astronomical Ephemerides are calculated for noon, Greenwich Mean Time.
   b. The Simplified Scientific Ephemerides are calculated for noon, Greenwich Mean Time.
   c. American Astrology Ephemerides are calculated for Midnight, Eastern Standard Time (approximately for the meridian of Philadelphia, Pa.). Each issue gives you a lucid example of how to erect a chart when using the ephemeris. The first of these ephemerides came out in 1940.
   d. The German Ephemerides (Die Deutsche Ephemeride) from 1850–1930 inclusive, are calculated for noon, G.M.T. However, all succeeding issues are calculated for Greenwich, midnight.
2. A Table of Houses is needed. With the help of these tables you are enabled to insert the correct house cusps. The Table of Houses is good for any year. There are several good ones.
3. You need an atlas which will give the latitudes and longitudes of cities.
4. If you desire to know the eclipse preceding your birth, or preceding any important event in your life, The 200 Year Ephem-

eris, 1800–2000 inclusive, and *The Ephemeris of the Moon*,
1800–2000, inclusive, both by Hugh MacCraig, will give you the
dates. The former book also gives the latitudes and longitudes
and longitude in time of over 7000 cities of the world.
5. *World Time Zones*. Maps of these are obtainable.
6. Printed horoscope blanks may be bought.
7. *Ephemeris of Pluto*. The 200 Year Ephemeris, 1800–2000, gives
Pluto positions for the first day of each month, correct to the
nearest degree.
8. Students interested in ascertaining the heliocentric longitude of
the planets will find them in *The 200 Year Ephemeris*, mentioned above, and in *American Astrology Ephemerides*.

We plan to show you first how to cast the simplest of all
possible horoscopes—that of one set for noon, London, January 1, 1951. We shall use *Raphael's Ephemeris* for 1951.

1. On page two of this Ephemeris you will find at the left a
column for the days of the month, then one for the days of
the week. In the third column is the Sidereal Time of the day.
This (in *Raphael's Ephemeris*) is always calculated for noon;
thus the astrological day is from noon of any day to noon of the
following day.

Ephemeris: We reproduce below two lines of the ephemeris noting that the planetary positions are
correct for 0:00 P.M., G.M.T.

D M	D W	Sidereal Time H. M. S.	☉ Long. ° '	☉ Dec. ° '	☽ Long. ° ' "	☽ Lat. ° '	☽ Dec. ° '	MIDNIGHT	
								☽ Long. ° ' "	☽ Dec. ° '
1	M	18 41 19	10♈15 46	23 S 3	13♎50 4	1 S 54	7 S 12	20♎42 23	10 S 21
2	Tu	18 45 16	11 16 55	22 58	27 40 35	2 58	13 25	4♏44 45	16 21

D M	Ψ Long. ° '	♅ Long. ° '	♄ Long. ° '	♃ Long. ° '	♂ Long. ° '	♀ Long. ° '	☿ Long. ° '	Lunar Aspects. ☉ ♇ Ψ ♅ ♄ ♃ ♂ ♀ ☿
1	19♎26	7♋20	2♎16	4♓48	13♒26	22♑ 0	11♑ 7	□ ✱ ☌ □ ⧠ △ □
2	19 26	7 ℞17	2 17	4 59	14 13	23 15	9 ℞45	↙ □

Write down:

	hrs.	min.	sec.
Sidereal Time Jan. 1..........	18	41	19

Since the birth is at noon, London, the above will be the Sidereal Time corresponding to Greenwich Mean Time of noon, which is within seconds of the true Local Mean Time of London.

2. Look at the end of your 1951 ephemeris for the Tables of Houses for London. These lie on unnumbered pages following page 41. The Table is calculated for the latitude of London, approximately 51½° North. Find the columns marked Sidereal Time. We reproduce part of this Table below.

Sidereal Time. H. M. S.	10 ♑	11 ♑	12 ≈	Ascen ♈	2 ♉	3 ♊
18 0 0	0	18	13	0 0	17	11
18 4 22	1	20	14	2 39	19	13
18 8 43	2	21	16	5 19	20	14
18 13 5	3	22	17	7 55	22	15
18 17 26	4	23	19	10 29	23	16
18 21 48	5	24	20	13 2	25	17
18 26 9	6	25	22	15 36	26	18
18 30 30	7	26	23	18 6	28	19
18 34 51	8	27	25	20 34	29	20
18 39 11	9	29	27	22 59	♊	21
18 43 31	10	≈	28	25 22	1	22
18 47 51	11	1	♓	27 42	2	23
18 52 11	12	2	2	29 58	4	24
18 56 31	13	3	3	2♉13	5	25
19 0 50	14	4	5	4 24	6	26
19 5 8	15	6	7	6 30	8	27
19 9 26	16	7	9	8 36	9	28
19 13 44	17	8	10	10 40	10	29
19 18 1	18	9	12	12 39	11	≈
19 22 18	19	10	14	14 35	12	1
19 26 34	20	12	16	16 28	13	2
19 30 50	21	13	18	18 17	14	3
19 35 5	22	14	19	20 3	16	4
19 39 20	23	15	21	21 48	17	5
19 43 34	24	16	23	23 29	18	6
19 47 47	25	18	25	25 9	19	7
19 52 0	26	19	27	26 45	20	8
19 56 12	27	20	28	28 18	21	9
20 0 24	28	21	♈	29 43	22	10
20 4 35	29	23	2	1♊19	23	11
20 8 45	30	24	4	2 45	24	12

Sidereal Time. H. M. S.	10 ≈	11 ≈	12 ♈	Ascen ♊	2 ♊	3 ♋
20 8 45	0	24	4	2 45	24	12
20 12 54	1	25	6	4 9	25	13
20 17 3	2	27	7	5 32	26	13
20 21 11	3	28	9	6 53	27	14
20 25 19	4	29	11	8 12	28	15
20 29 26	5	♓	13	9 27	29	16
20 33 31	6	2	14	10 43	≈	17
20 37 37	7	3	16	11 58	1	18
20 41 41	8	4	18	13 9	2	19
20 45 45	9	6	19	14 18	3	20
20 49 48	10	7	21	15 25	3	21
20 53 51	11	8	23	16 32	4	21
20 57 52	12	9	24	17 39	5	22
21 1 53	13	11	26	18 48	6	23
21 5 53	14	12	28	19 48	7	24
21 9 53	15	13	29	20 51	8	25
21 13 52	16	15	♉	21 52	8	26
21 17 50	17	16	2	22 53	10	27
21 21 47	18	17	4	23 52	11	28
21 25 44	19	19	5	24 51	12	29
21 29 40	20	20	7	25 48	12	♋
21 33 35	21	22	8	26 44	13	1
21 37 29	22	23	10	27 40	14	1
21 41 23	23	24	11	28 34	15	2
21 45 16	24	25	13	29 29	16	3
21 49 9	25	26	14	0♋22	16	4
21 53 1	26	28	15	1 15	17	5
21 56 52	27	29	16	2 7	18	5
22 0 43	28	♈	18	2 59	19	6
22 4 33	29	2	19	3 48	19	7
22 8 23	30	3	20	4 38	20	8

Sidereal Time. H. M. S.	10 ♓	11 ♈	12 ♉	Ascen ♋	2 ♋	3 ♌
22 8 23	0	3	20	4 38	20	8
22 12 12	1	4	21	5 28	21	8
22 16 0	2	6	23	6 17	22	9
22 19 48	3	7	24	7 24	23	10
22 23 35	4	8	25	7 53	23	11
22 27 22	5	9	26	8 42	24	12
22 31 8	6	10	28	9 29	25	13
22 34 54	7	12	29	10 16	26	14
22 38 40	8	13	♊	11 2	26	14
22 42 25	9	14	1	11 47	27	15
22 46 9	10	15	2	12 31	28	16
22 49 53	11	17	3	13 16	29	17
22 53 37	12	18	4	14 1	29	18
22 57 20	13	19	5	14 45	♌	19
23 1 3	14	20	6	15 28	1	19
23 4 46	15	21	7	16 11	2	20
23 8 28	16	23	8	16 54	2	21
23 12 10	17	24	9	17 37	3	22
23 15 52	18	25	10	18 19	4	23
23 19 34	19	26	11	19 1	5	24
23 23 15	20	27	12	19 45	6	24
23 26 56	21	29	13	20 26	6	25
23 30 37	22	♉	14	21 8	7	26
23 34 18	23	1	15	21 50	8	27
23 37 58	24	2	16	22 31	8	28
23 41 39	25	3	17	23 12	9	28
23 45 19	26	4	18	23 53	9	29
23 49 0	27	5	19	24 32	10	♍
23 52 40	28	6	20	25 15	11	2
23 56 20	29	8	21	25 56	12	2
24 0 0	30	9	22	26 36	13	3

SECTION OF TABLE OF HOUSES FOR LONDON

You have to find the nearest Sidereal Time to 18 hrs. 41 min. 19 sec. Note two sets of figures which are close to what you need, but not exactly.

One is ....18 39′ 11″
The other is ....18 43′ 31″

Your needed figures lie about halfway between these two sets of figures. In this lesson we are erecting approximate charts, and we advise you to use the figures succeeding the ones you need. This is because for the time being, we are neglecting all minor corrections, which might have been added to the Sidereal Time of noon, but which never total more than two or three minutes at the most. Since most people do not know their birth time within two or three minutes, there is surely no need to spend a long time making minor corrections until the birth time has been rectified to minutes. These minor corrections are given in Lesson Fourteen.

Taking the *Table of Houses* figure of 18 hrs. 43′ 31″, lay a ruler under this line to keep your place. At the top of the columns are figures 10, 11, 12, Ascen., 2, 3. These figures refer to the cusps of the 10th house, 11th house, 12th house, Ascendant, 2nd house, and 3rd house. Underneath each is a zodiacal sign, and the number of degrees in the sign. The signs must be placed on the cusps of your horoscope blank, e.g. Capricorn on the 10th house, Aquarius on the 11th house, Aquarius on the 12th house, Aries on the Ascendant, Gemini on the 2nd house, and Gemini on the 3rd house. Note, as you go down the columns that, Capricorn has changed to Aquarius for the 11th cusp, and Taurus has changed to Gemini for the 3rd cusp. Next, put the degrees on the cusps (Diagram 41).

In Diagram 41 you have:

10° Capricorn on the 10th cusp
0° Aquarius " " 11th "
28° Aquarius " " 12th "
25° 22′ Aries " " Ascendant
1° Gemini " " 2nd cusp
22° Gemini " " 3rd "

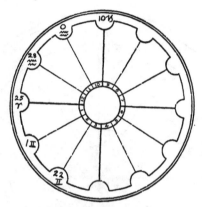

DIAGRAM 41
House Cusps for January 1, 1951
0:00 P.M., London

These signs are in correct order except that Pisces and Taurus are missing. They have to be inserted, and are called **Intercepted Signs.**

The next step is to put opposite signs on the opposite
houses, keeping the same number of degrees. Since Pisces is
intercepted in the 12th house, Virgo will be intercepted in the
7th house, as per Diagram 42.

You have now finished with the *Table of Houses,* which
was necessary only to find the signs and degrees on the cusps.
For the present insert the Ascendant correct only to the nearest
degree. Discard the minutes.

Your next step is to turn back to the ephemeris for January 1, and insert the planets in their correct houses. The Sun is
found in the column next to the Sidereal Time. Under its symbol is the abbrevation *Long.* which is for Longitude. We shall
not at present use any columns marked *Dec.* which is the abbreviation for Declination. The Sun's position is given in degrees, minutes, and seconds. In this map we shall neglect the
minutes and seconds. With the Moon and other planets we
need only the columns marked *Long.*

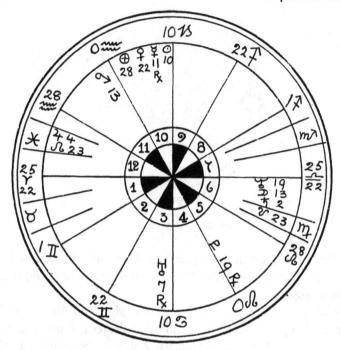

DIAGRAM 42
Horoscope of January 1, 1951
0:00 P.M., London

In the above diagram you have:

Sun ....10° Capricorn
Moon ....13° Libra
Neptune ....19° Libra
Uranus .... 7° Cancer ℞
Saturn .... 2° Libra
Jupiter .... 4° Pisces
Mars ....13° Aquarius
Venus ....22° Capricorn
Mercury ....11° Capricorn ℞

Pluto's position is obtained from page 39 (Raphael)
    Pluto ....19° Leo ℞

Counterclockwise Motion of the Planets. Since the planets move in counterclockwise motion, their motion must be inserted in order of their increasing degrees. Although we have three planets in Libra, they are all less than 25°, which is the degree on the 7th cusp, hence they are all placed in the 6th house, in order of increasing degrees. We also have three planets in Capricorn occupying from 10°–22° of the sign, hence they are all placed in the 10th house, and not in the 9th house. Uranus is less than 10° Cancer, hence it is placed in the 3rd house, and not in the 4th. Your cusp degree acts as a dividing point.

Retrograding Planets. In the ephemeris you will note that the position of Mercury, Uranus, and Pluto is marked with an ℞, which stands for retrograde motion. This symbol must be inserted in the chart.

WHAT IS MEANT BY RETROGRADING PLANETS

We have all traveled in trains that passed other trains. We have noticed that if we are traveling in quite a fast train, and another train passes which is faster than ours, we seem to travel quite slowly. Sometimes when the other train travels at exactly the same rate as ours, we seem to be standing still—yet we are moving. We on the earth experience at times a similar phenomenon in regard to the planets. The planets and the earth never stand still, but travel around the Sun, each at its own rate. Retrograde motion is not a real fact, but only an apparent going backwards. There is also a time when a planet is apparently stationary in relationship to the earth. This is marked S in the ephemeris. When the planet starts to go forward, or direct, again, this fact is recorded in the ephemeris by the letter D. When it is stationary and about to retrograde, this is recorded in the ephemeris by S℞.

Although stationary and retrograde motion is apparent and not real, we are dealing in astrology with how things appear from the earth, and how planets affect persons born upon this earth; hence we have to be careful to record even appearances in our horoscopes. The Sun and Moon can never be stationary, nor retrograde from the point of view of the earth. They are always direct.

Be careful in the correction of retrograde planets. Their longitude is greater **before** noon, and less **after** noon.

How does retrograde motion affect the individual? It is sometimes considered evil, but this is a wrong concept. If a planet retrogrades just before it reaches an evil planet, then the evil would never be reached. If it retrogrades so that it can reach a benefic planet, then a belated benefit might be attained. Generally speaking, when a planet is retrograde some of the power of the planet is lost; hence, the native does not receive the full effect of the planet. Thus if Mercury is retrograde, as it is in the preceding chart, some of the ability of Mercury to move and think freely is restricted. The person may be dominated by others.

In Diagram 42, Mercury rules the Second House of money, and is posited in the Tenth; hence, if the horoscope were that of a person, the native would attain considerable success in business and public life, yet his financial affairs at certain periods might not progress as fast as he might like. Pluto retrograding in the Fifth House would mean changes in romance, also that children would tend to leave home.

We often find that the horoscopes of geniuses and great leaders contain retrograde planets. This may tend to prove that their message to mankind is not readily accepted at first. Also, their ideas may be received, not from actual textbooks, but from their own subconscious—or super-conscious. Retrograde planets sometimes mean that time must be taken for reflection, and not so much for action.

Retrograde and stationary planets in the charts of those who are not geniuses and leaders, may mean either that material success will not be achieved, or that matters under these planets may not come to quick fruition. Also, we might remember that in some cases later in life the planets may become direct in motion; thus, the later period of life may be fortunate.

THE MOON'S NODES ☊ ☋

The Nodes are those degrees on the ecliptic (or pathway of the Sun) where the Moon moves from South to North Latitude, or vice versa. When the Moon moves from South to North, the point on the ecliptic is the ascending, or North, Node, sometimes called the Dragon's Head, or Caput (Latin term for head). Its symbol is ☊. This is similar to the symbol of Leo, but the eyelets are closed. The degree of the North Node is termed benefic.

The South Node, Dragon's Tail, or Cauda (tail), is placed in the sign opposite that of the North Node, and in the same number of degrees. Its symbol is ☋. It inclines to sweep away the things of the house and sign in which it is placed. In the 1951 Ephemeris you will find on page 3 at the top right hand a column marked Node. This gives the position of the North Node on January 1 as 22° Pisces 45'. We shall approximate this to 23° Pisces, and insert the South Node at 23° Virgo.

CRITICAL DEGREES

Certain degrees of signs are said to be very much more important than others, and are termed **Critical**. Before one can accept this ancient statement as correct, much research will be necessary. The critical degrees are as follows:

Cardinal Signs:	Aries, Cancer, Libra, and Capricorn: Degrees 0–1, 12–13, and 25–26
Fixed Signs:	Taurus, Leo, Scorpio, and Aquarius: Degrees 8–9, and 21–22.
Mutable Signs:	Gemini, Virgo, Sagittarius, and Pisces: Degrees 4–5, and 17–18.

In the chart you have just been considering, you find the Moon in 13 degrees Capricorn, hence in a critical degree. The word "critical" does not mean faultfinding or passing judgment, but rather a state of anxiety while waiting for some important matter to change for the better or worse. The critical degrees were formerly used by astrologer-doctors and by those interested in Horary questions.

It must not be thought that critical degrees were chosen in any arbitrary fashion. They were chosen on a system—that of a sevenfold division of the zodiac. If we divide the total 360° by 7, we have 51³/₇°. Neglecting fractions in our total answers, we find that if we keep on adding 51³/₇ degrees of arc to the zero degree of each Cardinal sign, we obtain our critical degrees. Starting with 0° Aries:

0° Aries	plus 51³/₇°	gives	21° Taurus
21° Taurus	" "	"	13° Cancer
13° Cancer	" "	"	4° Virgo
4° Virgo	" "	"	26° Libra
26° Libra	" "	"	17° Sagittarius
17° Sagittarius	" "	"	9° Aquarius

Let us do the same with the other three Cardinal signs:

0° Cancer	21♌, 13♎, 4♐, 26♑, 17♓, 9♉
0° Libra	21♏, 13♑, 4♓, 26♈, 17♊, 9♌
0° Capricorn	21♒, 13♈, 4♊, 26♋, 17♍, 9♏

The above indicates that the old astrologers used the 28 Lunar Mansions, which today are thought to have been used exclusively by the Hindus. Actually, the Hindus had a division based on 27 Lunar Mansions (called Nakshatras). The division into 28 divisions is said to have been invented by the Arabs, who found it very illuminating in their Horary work. Just as we think the entrance of the Sun into the Cardinal zero degrees is important in Mundane Astrology, so the Arab astrologers thought the entrance into a Lunar Mansion was most important, hence they called the entrance degrees *critical.*

Before we give the Arabs full credit for discovering Critical Degrees, let us note that long before the time of Christ ancient Greek doctors prognosticated the course and duration of fevers, etc., by means of Critical Days (founded upon the travel of the Moon through the signs, and lunar mansions).

Note:

$$360° \text{ divided by } 27 \quad \text{gives } 13° \ 20' \text{ per mansion}$$
$$360° \quad " \quad " \quad 28 \quad " \quad 12\%° \quad " \quad "$$

The division into 28 parts, i.e. seven times four, is used at the present day by researchers in Prenatal Astrology. In this the Ascendant, or sometimes the Descendant, of the birth chart is said to show the place of the Moon at conception.

In some textbooks the Critical Degree of the Cardinal signs is written 1°. This means from 0°–1°, not beyond.

INTERCEPTED SIGNS

You will note that in Diagram 42 Pisces is intercepted in the 12th house, Taurus in the 1st, Virgo in the 6th, and Scorpio in the 7th. This will mean that there are more influences playing upon these houses than would be possible if one sign only occupied the whole area, such as happens in the 2nd house where only Gemini has influence. In the 12th house, two degrees of Aquarius have influence (28°–30°), then all 30 degrees of Pisces, plus 25 degrees of Aries. All together we find 57 degrees of arc playing upon the 12th house.*

THE PART OF FORTUNE ⊕

If you are not sure of your birth time, do not attempt to calculate the Part of Fortune, for the calculation is based upon the degree of the Ascendant. The Part of Fortune, as its name

---

* Signs are always 30° in length, but the houses may be much longer or shorter. The matter is somewhat similar to what artists call *foreshortening* in observations of space from the earth.

implies, is supposed to be the most fortunate degree in the horoscope. Today, there is growing tendency among astrologers to say that it is an imaginary degree, and therefore should be discarded.

Rule to Find the Part of Fortune: Add the longitude of the Ascendant to the longitude of the Moon. From your answer subtract the longitude of the Sun.

Let us calculate the Part of Fortune for the chart we have just made:

	Signs	Degrees	Minutes
Ascendant	0	25	22
Add the Moon	6	13	00
	7	08	22

We now have to subtract the Sun's longitude, which is 9 signs 10 degrees. This is larger than our total for the Moon and Ascendant. We, therefore, add the full circle, or 12 signs, to this total before we make our subtraction.

	Signs	Degrees	Minutes
Total of Asc. and Moon ...	7	08	22
Add circle of 12 signs	12		
	19	08	22
Subtract the Sun	9	10	00
Part of Fortune	9	28	22

Nine full signs is zero Capricorn,* hence our Part of Fortune is 28° 22′ Capricorn. We can always check to see if our calculations are correct, because the Part of Fortune is always the same distance from the Ascendant as the Sun is from the

---

* Students nearly always seem puzzled as to why we call Aries the zero sign. It is not a full sign until we reach the end of the sign, i.e. until we finish 30 degrees Aries, and this is actually zero Taurus. So 0° Taurus is one full sign, 0° Gemini is two full signs, and so on. It is just as we say we are in our 21st year as soon as we pass 20 years. We might also remind our students that 60 minutes of arc make one degree, and 30 degrees of arc make one sign.

Moon. In our chart the Part of Fortune is 87 degrees from the ascendant, and the Sun is 87 degrees from the Moon.

HOROSCOPE OF GREATER NEW YORK CITY

Let us next set up a slightly more difficult chart, that of Greater New York City. The five boroughs comprising the city were incorporated on May 11, 1896, and came into corporate existence on January 1, 1898 at 0.01 A.M. We use the latter date for the horoscope of the city, because it was on the latter date that the city began to function as an entity under its charter. New York is 40° 43′ North Latitude and 74° degrees West Longitude.

Since the longitude is one degree east of the 75th meridian, we have to add four minutes to the Standard Time to get Local Mean Time, which in this case will be 0:05 A.M., or 11 hrs. 55 min. before noon.

The Sidereal Time for January 1, 1898 is found in the ephemeris for that year. It is 18 hours, 44 minutes, 38 seconds. From this we subtract the hours before noon.

	Hrs.	Min.	Sec.
Sid T.	18	44	38
Hours before noon	11	55	
Sid. T. of M.C.	6	49	38

Next look at the back of any *Raphael's Ephemeris* for the *Table of Houses* for New York City. Find the nearest Sidereal Time:

6 hrs. 47′ 51″ is followed by 6 hrs. 52′ 11″

We shall take the latter figure, as we are not at the moment using various corrections which never amount to more than two or three minutes. Note the house cusps to the right of the Sidereal Time:

10th house	11th house	12th house	Ascen	2nd house	3rd house
12♋	15♌	15♍	10°♎21′	7♏	8♐

Set these down on the cusps of a horoscope blank, then fill in the opposite cusps. Check your signs to see if any are lacking. In this chart we find no intercepted signs.

Next you have to correct the planets for the time of birth because in *Raphael's Ephemeris* they are correct to noon at London. We have to turn our New York Time into Greenwich Time. This we do by simply adding five hours to the Standard Time. Midnight Standard Time in New York is 5:00 A.M. in Greenwich Time, so one minute after midnight here would mean one minute after five in the morning in London. (For the time being we shall not use this minute.)

Our first problem is to know how far the planets will travel between noon of December 31, 1897 and noon of January 1, 1898. A simple subtraction from the planetary positions in the ephemeris will give us this 24-hour rate of travel. Our next problem is to find the proportional travel they go from noon of December 31 to 5:00 A.M. January 1.

From noon of December 31 to 5:00 A.M. January 1 is 17 hours, which would be $1\frac{7}{24}$th of a day, an awkward fraction. Let us think of the problem in a different way. From 5:00 A.M. January 1 to noon is 7 hours, so we could subtract $\frac{7}{24}$ths of the day from the noon positions of January 1. Even this is an awkward fraction. Since we are only correcting our planets to the degree and not to minutes or seconds, we suggest you take $\frac{6}{24}$ths of the day, which would be $\frac{1}{4}$ of the day.

Let us turn back to our ephemeris and calculate the travel in the 24 hours between December 31 and January 1. This gives us the daily rate of travel, that is, the travel in 24 hours. When we have this, all we need do is divide it by four, and then subtract our answer from the noon positions on January 1, 1898.

2									[RAPHAEL'S	
		JANUARY, 1898.								
D M	D W	Sidereal Time.	☉ Long.	☉ Dec.	☽ Long.	☽ Lat.	☽ Dec.	MIDNIGHT.		
								☽ Long.	☽ Dec.	
		H M. S.	° ′ ″	° ′	° ′ ″	° ′	° ′	° ′ ″	° ′	
1	S	18 44 38	11♑ 9 42	22 S59	0♉12 24	5N16	16N28	6♉13 52	18N30	

D M	♆ Long.	♅ Long.	♄ Long.	♃ Long.	♂ Long.	♀ Long.	☿ Long.	Lunar Aspects.							
								☉	♆	♅	♄	♃	♂	♀	☿
	° ′	° ′	° ′	° ′	° ′	° ′	° ′								
1	20♍37	1♐44	7♐35	9♎28	29♐29	0♑15	22♐18	∠					△	△	

24									[RAPHAEL'S	
		DECEMBER, 1897.								
31	F	18 40 41	10 8 33	23 4	18 0	28 5	12	11 52 24	8 7	14 15

D M	♆ Long.	♅ Long.	♄ Long.	♃ Long.	♂ Long.	♀ Long.	☿ Long.	Lunar Aspects.							
								☉	♆	♅	♄	♃	♂	♀	☿
	° ′	° ′	° ′	° ′	° ′	° ′	° ′								
31	20 38	1 41	7 29	9 24	28 44	29 0	22° 58	✶	⊔	⊔					

Sun's position Jan. 1   11°♑09′
  "   "   Dec. 31   10   08′
                   1   01′ or 61 minutes in 24 hours

Divide this by 4 and you have 15′; hence you take off 15 minutes from the January 1 position of the Sun.

Sun's position Jan. 1   11°♑09′
                          15′
             10   44 or approximately 11°♑.

* Moon's position Jan. 1   0° ♉ 12′
   "   "   Dec. 31   18 ♈00
                      12   12 travel in 24 hours

Divide this by 4 and you have 3° 03′ which has to be subtracted from the noon position on Jan. 1.

Moon's position Jan. 1   0° ♉ 12′
                      3   03
             27 ♈09 or approximately 27° ♈.

You now work in a similar way with all the planets. The planets from Jupiter to Pluto move so slowly that you need not

* Note that in the above subtraction you count 0° Taurus as 30° Aries before you can make the subtraction.

compute them. The position of Pluto has to be found from a
Pluto Ephemeris. It could not, of course, be given in an 1898
ephemeris, since Pluto had not been discovered then. The position of the North Node is found at the top right of page 3 of
the *Raphael's Ephemeris* for 1898. It is 27° ♑ 47′, or 28° ♑.

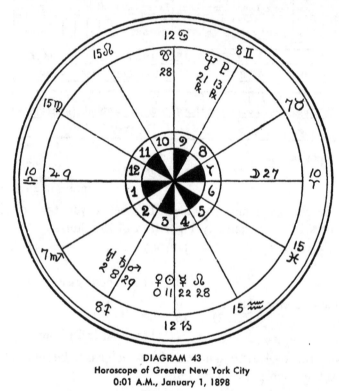

DIAGRAM 43
Horoscope of Greater New York City
0:01 A.M., January 1, 1898

This chart of Greater New York is interesting as Jupiter
ascending in Libra describes the vast appearance of the city.
Three planets in the Third House of local travel indicate the
subways and communications systems. Any mayor since 1898
will be described by the Moon in Aries in trine to Mars—
always energetic.

BIRTHDAY OF ATOMIC CHAIN REACTION

Let us take the moment in time which was given in the newspapers as the Birthday of Atomic Chain Reaction. This was December 2, 1942, Chicago, Ill., at 3:25 P.M., Central War Time.

One hour has to be subtracted from the given War Time to get Standard Time for Chicago. This gives 2:25 P.M. Chicago is 41° 50′ N., and 87° 40′ W. From the longitude we see that Chicago is 2° 20′ from the 90th meridian. Multiplying this difference by 4 gives us 9′ 20″ to add to the Standard Time to get Local Mean Time. We can neglect the seconds and so our time will be 2:34 P.M.

From the *Raphael's Ephemeris* of 1942 we take the Sidereal Time of Dec. 2:

	Hrs.	Min.	Sec.
Sidereal Time Dec. 2.	16	42	47
Add L.M.T.	2	34	00
Sid. T. of M.C.	19	16	47

We next need a *Table of Houses* for Chicago. This is not given at the back of our ephemeris. For the present, we use Tables calculated to the nearest degrees of latitude. From the *Dalton Table of Houses* we find the figures greater or less than we require:

Hrs.	Min.	Sec.
19	13	44
19	18	01

We shall use the latter figure and use the corresponding cusps:

18♑   11♒   14♓   3♉24′   5♊   27♊

Insert these sign positions on the house cusps, noting that Aries and Libra are missing. We place Aries in the Twelfth

House and Libra in the Sixth House respectively, calling them intercepted signs. To correct the planets to the nearest degree, we need Greenwich Mean Time. In Chicago G.M.T. is always six hours more than Standard Time, hence the G.M.T. is 2:25 P.M. plus six hours, or 8:25 P.M.

If we approximate 8:25 P.M. to 8:00 P.M., it is roughly one third of the day. We find the rate of travel of the planets from December 2 at noon to December 3 at noon, then divide this by 3. This factor, added to the noon position of Dec. 2, will give us the approximate position of the planets at 8:00 P.M., G.M.T.

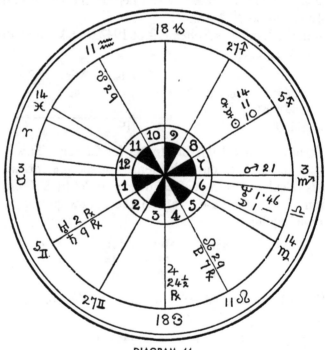

DIAGRAM 44
Horoscope of Atomic Chain Reaction
December 2, 1942, 3:25 P.M., C.W.T.,
Chicago, Illinois

We might note that in the above chart Venus rules the Ascendant, and so represents the United States. Mars occupies the Seventh House which would be the house of the open enemies of the nation. The chart is extremely important and it might in a sense be called the Birthday of the Atomic Age.

RULES FOR CASTING AN APPROXIMATE HOROSCOPE

1. Determine the latitude and longitude of the birthplace to the nearest degree of each.
2. Determine the time of birth, whether Standard Time, Local Mean Time, or Daylight Saving Time. If the time is not given in Local Mean Time, then change it to that. Afterwards, if you are using a *Raphael's Ephemeris*, determine the corresponding Greenwich Mean Time.*

   You need G.M.T. in order to correct your planets.
3. From an ephemeris of the year of birth, write down the Sidereal Time of noon on the day of birth.

   a. For a birth **after** noon, add this Sidereal Time to the number of hours that have elapsed since noon, e.g. if the L.M.T. is 3:15 P.M., add 3:15.

   b. For a birth **before** noon, subtract from this Sidereal Time, the number of hours that are before noon, e.g. if the L.M.T. is 3:15 A.M., subtract 8 hours and 45 minutes.
4. Find the page in your *Table of Houses* for the latitude of the birth place. Using the result from #3, insert the house cusps on your horoscope blank.
5. You need your ephemeris again in order to insert the planets, and when correcting them, you must use the G.M.T. corresponding to the birth hour.

   a. If the G.M.T. is **after** noon, add fractional travel.

   b. If the G.M.T. is **before** noon, subtract the fractional travel.

   Greenwich Mean Time: To obtain G.M.T. find your longitude of birth and multiply by four, since the Sun travels 4 minutes for each degree.

   a. If born at 80° W., multiply 80 by 4, giving 320 min., or 5 hrs. 20 min. **Add** this to your L.M.T.

   b. If born 13° E., multiply 13 by 4, giving 52'. **Subtract** this from your L.M.T.

* You need Local Mean Time for the setting up of the houses.

A simpler method to obtain Greenwich Mean Time, in the U. S. A.
if you have Standard Time:

a. To Eastern Standard Time add 5 hours
b. To Central Standard Time " 6 "
c. To Mountain " " " 7 "
d. To Pacific " " " 8 "

NOTE ON THE APPROXIMATE CORRECTION OF
THE SUN'S POSITION

If you look at the Sun's position on any day in your ephemeris, you will find that it moves between one day and the next,
that is, in 24 hours, about 58 minutes to one degree of longitude. If we take one degree, or 60 minutes, as our average of
travel in 24 hours, then we shall find that the Sun moves:

$$\tfrac{60}{24}, \text{ or } \tfrac{5}{2}, \text{ or } 2\tfrac{1}{2} \text{ minutes per hour.}$$

Hence you will usually find it easier to correct the Sun's position at the rate of 2½ minutes per hour, or 5 minutes of arc for
every two hours.

NOTE ON THE APPROXIMATE CORRECTION OF
THE MOON'S POSITION

If you look at the Moon's position on any day in your
ephemeris, you will find that it moves between one day and
the next, that is, in 24 hours, approximately 12 degrees of
longitude. Since it moves 12 degrees in 24 hours, it will move
in one hour:

$$1\tfrac{2}{24}\text{ths, or } \tfrac{1}{2}^\circ, \text{ or } 30 \text{ minutes per hour.}$$

Hence you can add or subtract the Moon's position at the rate
of 30 minutes per hour, or one degree for every two hours of
G.M.T.

These corrections are accurate enough for practical work
until you learn to correct position by logarithms. The main

objective in these lessons is to let you find out what you are doing, and why. In Lesson 14 you will be introduced to logarithms, but apart from extremely accurate work, you will never be able to be a good astrologer unless you cultivate the habit of thinking at any time of the day just about what sign will be on the ascendant, and in what probable house the Sun and Moon will be. Many young students who start making charts using logarithms find the process so tedious that they will only calculate a few. When you know a simple method you can make many, and so develop your powers of reading from the start.

GETTING ACQUAINTED WITH ASPECTS

When planets are placed at a specific number of signs or degrees away from one another, according to the table that follows, they are said to be in aspect. Aspects are of value when interpreting character, and also when reading events. Some aspects are said to be good, and some bad. The terms might better be called harmonious and inharmonious.

The following aspects are the ones commonly used. They are specific parts of the total 360 degrees of the zodiacal circle.

1/2	of 360°	—180°	called the Opposition	Symbol ☍
1/3	" "	—120°	" " Trine	" △
1/4	" "	— 90°	" " Square	" □
1/5	" "	— 72°	" " Quintile	" Q
1/6	" "	— 60°	" " Sextile	" ✱
1/7	" "	— 51 3/7°	not commonly used (see page 156)	
1/8	" "	— 45°	called the Semi-square.	Symbol ∠
1/9	" "	— 40°	not commonly used	
1/10	" "	— 36°	called the Semi-quintile or Decile	Symbol 36°
1/11	" "	— 32 8/11°	not commonly used	
1/12	" "	— 30°	called the Semi-sextile	Symbol ⊻
3/8	" "	—135°	" " Sesqui-quadrate	" ⚼
2/5	" "	—144°	" " Bi-quintile	" BiQ

$\frac{5}{12}$ of 360° —150° called the Quincunx or
Inconjunct or
Quadra-sextile   Symbol   ⊼
Within 8° orb is   "   " Conjunction   "   ☌

The Opposition: In an opposition there are two factors struggling for mastery. Two good planets cannot bring much difficulty.

The Square: A square causes a continual thwarting of the purpose.

The Semi-Square: This acts something like a square but the conflict is not so intense.

Quincunx: The quincunx tends to sit on the fence when two phases of life are in conflict.

Sesqui-Quadrate: This acts like a square, and is almost as powerful.

Trine: A trine is the most harmonious of aspects, and requires the least effort and work to obtain the desirable things of life.

Sextile: The sextile, like the trine, brings harmony and benefits, but usually some effort is attached. There are two kinds of sextile as you will see from diagrams 45 and 46, on page 169. One links up Masculine signs, which are those of effort. The other links up Feminine signs, which are signs of receptivity.

Semi-Sextile: This aspect is similar in effect to the sextile, but, as a rule it does not bring so much benefit. However, Alan Leo's wife, Bessie, attributed her marriage to a semi-sextile aspect, so one should not neglect it.

Quintile: This aspect is benefic, but seems to act more in the world of thought than in the material world.

Bi-Quintile: This aspect is benefic, but again it seems to act in the world of thought with better results than in the material world.

Semi-Quintile: This aspect is half a quintile, or 36 degrees.

It seems to have quite as strong an effect, or even stronger, than the semi-sextile.

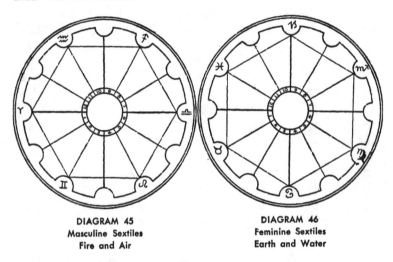

DIAGRAM 45
Masculine Sextiles
Fire and Air

DIAGRAM 46
Feminine Sextiles
Earth and Water

DECANATES

Every sign of the zodiac contains 30°. If we divide any sign into three equal parts, there will be 10° in each. These three sets of 10° are called the three decanates of the sign. The word decanate is derived from a Latin word meaning ten. If we divide Aries into three parts, we have:

1st decanate . . . . 0°–10° Aries
2nd decanate . . . . 10°–20° Aries
3rd decanate . . . . 20°–30° Aries

The whole of the sign Aries is ruled by Mars (or Pluto), but the first decanate of Aries is more powerfully under the domination of Mars (or Pluto) than the following decanates. The second decanate has a flavor of Leo in it (i.e. the second Fire sign), hence it is said to have a subrulership of the Sun. The third decanate has a flavor of Sagittarius in it (i.e. the third Fire sign), hence it is said to have a subrulership of Jupiter.

DECANATES AND THEIR RULERS

Sign	First Decanate	Ruler	Second Decanate	Ruler	Third Decanate	Ruler
♈	♈	♂ ♇	♌	☉	♐	♃
♉	♉	♀	♍	☿	♑	♄
♊	♊	☿	♎	♀	♒	♄ ♅
♋	♋	☽	♏	♂	♓	♃ ♆
♌	♌	☉	♐	♃	♈	♂ ♇
♍	♍	☿	♑	♄	♉	♀
♎	♎	♀	♒	♄ ♅	♊	☿
♏	♏	♂ ♇	♓	♃ ♆	♋	☽
♐	♐	♃	♈	♂ ♇	♌	☉
♑	♑	♄	♉	♀	♍	☿
♒	♒	♄ ♅	♊	☿	♎	♀
♓	♓	♃ ♆	♋	☽	♏	♂

There is another method of enumerating decanates based on the sequence of the planetary hours. This we are not giving you at present.

LESSON EIGHT

Basic System of Reading the Horoscope

♈ ♉ ♊ ♋ ♌ ♍ ♎ ♏ ♐ ♑ ♒ ♓

INTRODUCTION: As soon as you have mastered the simple method of erecting an approximate horoscope, you should construct many horoscopes with other data, and then analyze them systematically. So many students, when they have erected the chart in which they are personally interested, run around asking everyone they know how to interpret it. Learn to rely upon yourself. If you follow the basic method laid down in Lesson Eight, you will be able to analyze your own or any horoscope. In this lesson are eighteen factors that must be considered before you worry about aspects. You are now coming to the art of astrology, which is comparable to that of weaving, in which dominant colors and figures make the design.

Draw your charts neatly, so that the figures can be recognized at a glance. Write all signs and figures so that they can be read without having to twist the chart. When you do this you lose your power of concentration. Place your planets close to the cusps to which they belong. If you do this, you need not insert the sign after them, unless you wish to do so.

We plan to go through the horoscope of the late President Calvin Coolidge, first, as a brief exercise in the erection of a chart, and second, in order to give you a systematic plan of the factors that have to be considered when reading either his horoscope, or that of any other person. You will find that all you have learned in the previous seven lessons has to be put into action. Nothing has been unnecessary.

Calvin Coolidge was born in Vermont (latitude 44° N., longitude
73° W.) July 4, 1872, 9:00 A.M. No Standard Time was in operation at that date, hence 9:00 A.M. was Local Mean Time, and
3 hours before noon.
1. The Ephemeris for 1872 gives the Sidereal Time on July 4, noon
as:

	Hours	Minutes	Seconds
Sid. T. of birthday	6	51	13
Subtract 3 hours	3		
Sid T. of birthtime	3	51	13

2. Look in the Table of Houses for Latitude 44° N. This shows:

10	11	12	Asc.	2	3
0♊	5♋	7♌	5♍21	28♍	26♎

We shall find that Scorpio is intercepted in the Third House,
and Taurus in the Ninth House.
3. Turn back to the ephemeris in order to get the planetary positions. Since these are calculated for Greenwich Mean Time, we
have to transpose the Local Mean Time into G.M.T. as follows:

Birthplace............73° W. long.
Multiply by...............4 = 292′
Divide by........292′=4 hrs. 52 min.
                  60

Since Vermont is west of Greenwich, we add our answer to 9:00
A.M. Our G.M.T. is 1.52 P.M.

This is almost 2:00 P.M. which is 1/12th part of the whole
day of 24 hours, so that if we take the travel of the planets
from noon on July 4 to noon on July 5, and divide their difference by 12, then add this difference to the noon positions of
July 4, we shall obtain their approximate positions as of 2:00
P.M. G.M.T. July 4.

POSITION OF PLANETS FROM 1872 EPHEMERIS

D M	D W	Sidereal Time	☉ Long.	☽ Long.	♅ Long.	♄ Long.	♃ Long.	♂ Long.	♀ Long.	☿ Long.	D M	Nept Long.
		H. M. S.	° ′ ″	° ′	° ′	° ′	° ′	° ′	° ′	° ′		° ′
1	M	6 39 23	9♋52 12	22♉41	0♌11	18♒35	3♌57	28♊ 6	5♋47	17♋41	1	26♈ 9
2	Tu	6 43 19	10 49 25	4♊54	0 14	18♑31	4 9	28 46	7 0	19 44	4	26 12
3	W	6 47 16	11 46 38	16 58	0 18	18 27	4 22	29 27	8 14	22 46	7	26 14
4	Th	6 51 13	12 43 52	28 54	0 21	18 22	4 35	0♋ 7	9 28	23 46	10	26 16
5	F	6 55 9	13 41 5	10♋47	0 25	18 18	4 48	0 48	10 42	25 .45	13	26 17

1. Sun's Position

```
                                    °     ′
Sun at noon, July 5............13 ♋ 41
Subtract position on July 4......12    44
                            12/ 0   57 = rate of travel in 24 hrs.
                                       (approximately)
Divide by 12 to get travel in 2 hrs.    05
Add this to July 4 position......12    44
Result is position at 2:00 P.M....12 ♋ 49
```
We shall set this down in the chart as ☉ 12° ♋ 49′.

2. Moon's Position

```
                                    °     ′
Moon at noon, July 5........*10 ♋ 47
Subtract position on July 4......28 ♊ 54
                            12/11   53 = rate of travel in 24 hrs.
Divide by 12 to get travel in 2 hrs. 0   59
Add this to July 4 position......28    54
Result is position at 2:00 P.M....29 ♊ 53
```
We shall set this down in the chart as ☽ 29° ♊ 53′ (approx.).

3. Uranus, Neptune, Saturn and Jupiter

As their rate of travel is so slow, we can use the noon position on July 4.

4. Mars' Position

```
                                    °     ′
Mars at noon, July 5............0 ♋ 48
Subtract position on July 4......0    07
                            12/ 0   41 = rate of travel in 24 hrs.
Divide by 12 to get travel in 2 hrs.   03
Add this to July 4 position.......0    07
Result is position at 2:00 P.M.....0 ♋ 10
```
We shall set this down in the chart as ♂ 0° ♋ 10′.

* When subtracting we find it necessary to add 30°, thus 10°♋ become 40°♊, and a subtraction is possible.

5. Venus' Position

	°	′	
Venus at noon, July 5..........	10 ♋	42	
Subtract position on July 4.......	9	28	
	12/ 1	14	= rate of travel in 24 hrs.
Divide by 12 to get travel in 2 hrs.	0	06	
Add this to July 4 position.......	9	28	
Result is position at 2:00 P.M.....	9 ♋	34	

We shall set this down in the chart as ♀ 9° ♋ 34′.

6. Mercury's position

	°	′	
Mercury at noon, July 5........	25 ♋	45	
Subtract position on July 4......	23	46	
	12/ 1	59	= rate of travel in 24 hrs.
Divide by 12 to get travel in 2 hrs.	0	10	
Add this to July 4 position......	23	46	
Result is position at 2:00 P.M....	23	56	

We shall set this down in the chart as ☿ 23° ♋ 56′.

7. The Moon's Nodes

Their travel is quite slow, hence is given in the ephemeris, as also is that of Neptune, only every three days. In one day the Node decreases only 3′. We shall not divide this by 12, but insert the position as of noon on July 4, i.e. 10° Gemini 53′. The South Node will be 10° Sagittarius 53′.

8. The Part of Fortune

Our rule for obtaining this was to add the longitude of the Ascendant to the longitude of the Moon and subtract therefrom the longitude of the Sun.

	Signs	Degrees	Minutes
Ascendant	5	5	21
Moon	2	29	53
	7	35	14
Sun	3	12	49
	4	22	25

We shall set this down in the chart as ⊕ 22° ♌ 25′.

So far in our charts we have not been concerned with parallels.

WHAT IS A PARALLEL

In order to understand the parallel, we have to understand how we define the position of a planet. We do it very much like we do a town on a map—that is to say, how far it is east or west of Greenwich and also how far it is north or south of the equator. So we give:

1. The planet's position along the Sun's path: i.e., through the signs. This is its celestial longitude, being measured in the heavens and not on the earth as on an ordinary geographical map.
2. The planet's position north or south of the equator. This is its declination and is comparable to the latitude lines on a map of the earth.

When we say two planets are conjunct, we do not mean that they really have touched one another, for they are all swinging along on their own orbits which never meet. We mean that they are each the same angle or number of degrees in the zodiacal signs.

When, however, two planets are the same angle north or south of the equator we do not say they are conjunct, but we say they are parallel. We have therefore, when making the index of the Aspects, to see if there are any parallels. Just write down from the ephemeris the **declinations** of all the planets on July 4, 1872. They are as follows:

	°		′					
☉	22	N.	51		♃	19	N.	40
☽	24	N.	56		♂	24	N.	05
♆	8	N.	31		♀	23	N.	35
♅	20	N.	37		☿	23	N.	12
♄	21	S.	58		☋	4	N.	—

All you have to do with these is to find those that are within two degrees of one another and call them parallel. If both are north, then the parallel is like a conjunction in effect. If one is north with another south, they are like an opposition in effect.

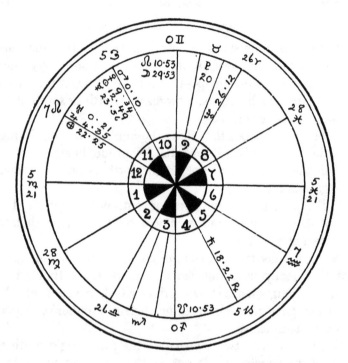

DIAGRAM 47
Horoscope of Calvin Coolidge
July 4, 1872

DECLINATIONS		☉	☽	☿	♀	♂	♃	♄	♅	♆	♇	⊕	ASC	MC
22 N 51	☉			σ	σ	σ		♂ᵒ					✱	
24 N 56	☽				σ				⊻	✱			✱	⊻
23 N 12	☿							♂ᵒ		□	✱	⊻		
23 N 35	♀					σ		♂ᵒ		Q		∠	✱	
24 N 05	♂						⊻	♂ᵒ	⊻	✱			✱	⊻
19 N 40	♃							σ		□		⊻	✱	
21 S 58	♄								□	△	▽	⊡	⊡	
20 N 37	♅									□				✱
8 N 31	♆										⊻	△		
3 N —	♇											□		
	⊕													
	ASC													□
	MC													

The parallels are:

Sun	parallel	Moon
"	"	Uranus
"	"	Saturn
"	"	Mars
"	"	Venus
"	"	Mercury
Moon	"	Mars
"	"	Venus
"	"	Mercury
Uranus	"	Saturn
"	"	Jupiter
Saturn	"	Jupiter
"	"	Venus
"	"	Mercury
Mars	"	Venus
"	"	Mercury
Venus	"	Mercury

This is a very interesting array of parallels, for the Sun throws its life and radiance on no less than six planets. Notice that Saturn is in South Declination, while all other planets in parallel to the Sun are in North Declination, hence this parallel will work out somewhat in the nature of an opposition. Those that are all North will act somewhat as conjunctions.

We are now ready to insert all the aspects in the Index of Aspects. You will learn in Lesson Nine how to interpret these aspects, and also the position of the planets in the signs and houses (see Diagram 47).*

* When calculating the orbs of the planets, it is sufficient to allow a six-degree orb at first, that is, three degrees each side of the exact degree. Later, you may find that except with the minor aspects you can allow wider orbs of influence. In the case of weak aspects, such as, the Semi-sextile, Semi-square, Bi-Quintile, and Quincunx, two degrees either side of the exact degree is sufficient. You will notice, however that in the *Table of Aspects* for the Coolidge chart, we have considered Saturn to be in opposition to all the group in Cancer. This group, stellium, or satellitium, as it may be called, extends from 0°–24° Cancer, hence, since they are pulled together as a conjunction, they can all be considered as in opposition to Saturn.

Steps in Reading the Horoscope:

1. **The Sign of the Sun:** Read what has been told in previous lessons concerning the Sun in Cancer. It is important in this President's chart to note that his Sun is the same Sun sign and degree as that of the United States, which came into being with the Declaration of Independence, July 4, 1776.

2. **The House of the Sun:** This is the Eleventh House, which rules not only friends and the objective of life, but which, in a President's chart, also rules the House of Representatives, and probably the Senate too, places of organized conference on governmental business.

3. **The Ascendant:** The Ascendant is Virgo which will help our Cancerian to bring greater precision into his work than is usual with a Cancerian. Both Cancer and Virgo being somewhat shy signs, we should judge it was difficult for Coolidge in early life to meet people (except friends) with facility.

4. **The Moon:** This is in Gemini in the Tenth House; hence on business matters he would be able to talk well. This position of the Moon aids in overcoming the natural shyness of Cancer.

5. **The Descendant:** This is Pisces ruled by Jupiter and Neptune, the former well placed in regard to the Ascendant and Midheaven; therefore, we judge his wife was harmonious to him, and an asset in his public work. Neptune, the other ruler, is square to Saturn in Capricorn (wide orb). In the chart of a man in public work, the Seventh House represents the public as well as the partner; hence the square of Saturn to Neptune may well represent some of the political enemies of Coolidge, particularly because the political Ninth House enters into the square.

6. Make a table of the planets in Cardinal, Fixed, and Mutable signs:

Cardinal: 6 Mercury, Venus, Mars, Neptune, Saturn, and Sun.
Fixed: 3 Jupiter, Uranus, and Pluto
Mutable: 1 Moon.

7. Make a table of the planets in their elements:

Fire: 3 Uranus, Jupiter, and Neptune.
Earth: 2 Saturn and Pluto.
Air: 1 Moon
Water: 4 Sun, Venus, Mercury, and Mars.

The synthesis of #6 and #7 is Cardinal Water, giving feeling, intensity of emotion, and an inner dramatic power. It will be restrained because Saturn occupies the Fifth House, and the Virgo Ascendant is not dramatic.

8. Note which planets are in Angular, Succedent, and Cadent Houses.

Angular: 2 Moon and Mars.
Succedent: 6 Sun, Venus, Mercury, Uranus, Jupiter, and Saturn.
Cadent: 2 Neptune and Pluto.

The six planets in Succedent Houses increase the will power.

9. Note planets in opposition: Saturn really opposes all the planets in Cancer, and acts as a balance to this group. It will, however, bring great sorrow at times.

10. Note the intercepted signs: These are, Scorpio in the Third House, and Taurus in the Ninth House. These intercepted signs will increase the variety of experiences to be met in Third and Ninth House affairs.

11. Note the planets above and below the horizon:

Above: 9
Below: 1

This preponderance of planets above the horizon made Coolidge an extrovert. It is well that the ponderous heavy planet was below acting as a balance to the Cancerian stellium; otherwise, he would have been liable to "fly off the handle" many times. Saturn counseled him to hold his peace.

12. Note the planets east and west of the Meridian:

East: 7
West: 3

With seven planets rising, Coolidge would have relied largely upon his own powers and efforts to forge ahead. The three setting planets would not have been too helpful to him. Neptune and Pluto in his Ninth House would have brought many strange people to him during the tenure of his various office.

13. Note the Planetary Dignities:

Saturn in its own sign
Moon accidentally dignified in the Tenth House

14. Note planets in their debilities:

Mars in its fall
Uranus in its detriment

15. Retrograding Planets:

Saturn is retrograding, and was partly
responsible for the death of one of his sons

16. Note any planets in Mutual Reception:

The Moon in Gemini, Mercury's sign
Mercury in Cancer, the Moon's sign

17. Find the Final Dispositor of the chart. The section immediately following this will tell you how to find this.

18. Note the eclipse preceding the day of birth. It helps you to see which house will be accentuated at birth. The eclipse preceding Coolidge's birthday was in 16° Gemini, in his Tenth House; hence the whole focus of the chart is towards public life.

TO FIND THE FINAL DISPOSITOR OR DISPOSITORS

The final dispositor, or dispositors, of a horoscope can become the most important clue to the understanding of the objective in life. Some horoscopes have no final dispositor, and in this case, unless there is mutual reception, the central focussing power seems to be lost. Mutual reception gears two forces into one line of action.

We proceed with Calvin Coolidge's chart (or any other) as follows:

The Ascendant is Virgo	ruled by Mercury
Mercury is in Cancer	ruled by the Moon
The Moon is in Gemini	ruled by Mercury
Mercury is in Cancer	ruled by the Moon

We note that Mercury and the Moon are in each other's sign, hence they are in Mutual Reception. This reception enabled Coolidge to appeal to the public.

Next let us take Neptune which is elevated:

Neptune is in Aries	ruled by Mars
Mars is in Cancer	ruled by the Moon

Once again we come back to the Moon-Mercury reception. Suppose we try Uranus in Leo:

Uranus is in Leo	ruled by the Sun
The Sun is in Cancer	ruled by the Moon

We have come back a third time to the Moon-Mercury reception.

Saturn is in its own sign Capricorn, hence it is a final dispositor of itself. Mercury and the Moon take care of all the other planets; thus, Calvin Coolidge was able to deal with his Congress with facility, and to maintain his leadership as long as he chose to run.

In Franklin D. Roosevelt's chart (Diagram 48) the most important reception lies between Mercury and Uranus. This takes care of most of the planets. The Moon is in its own sign, and is the dispositor of itself.

In Harry S Truman's chart (Diagram 49) there is a link between Mercury and Uranus, through Gemini and Virgo. This gives the ability to speak ad lib, as occasion may necessitate.

In Thomas A. Edison's chart (frontispiece) there is reception between Saturn and Neptune, enabling ideas to be brought into the realm of practicality.

In Evangeline Adams's chart (Diagram 50) there is no reception, unless we consider Jupiter as the ruler of Pisces, in which case there is reception between Jupiter and Uranus, enabling her to make a living through her astrological work.

Here are a few extra charts, in order that you may apply your systematic analysis to them. We should, however, like to call attention again to the Edison horoscope, which was drawn many years ago by Charles H. Forbell. The artist's quick vision seized immediately upon the main factors apparent in the horoscope, and set them forth in pictorial fashion.

Edison had Scorpio rising, the sign par excellence for research work and the understanding of matters not known to the average person.

Nine planets below the horizon conferred an introspective mind. The Moon in Capricorn represented ambition, industry and organizing power.

The Sun in Aquarius represented the wide distribution of his work. Neptune with the Sun gave him vision as well as intuition. Knowledge came from he knew not where. His Mercury in Aquarius caused all people to accept his work.

Saturn in Pisces gave the ability to materialize the results of what was sensed through intuition. Uranus, the planet of invention, was in Aries, the sign of new theories.

Jupiter, ruling the ideational mind, was in Gemini, the sign of the practical mind. The whole chart is a curious combination of genius, vision, and new ideas, brought into the realm of reality.

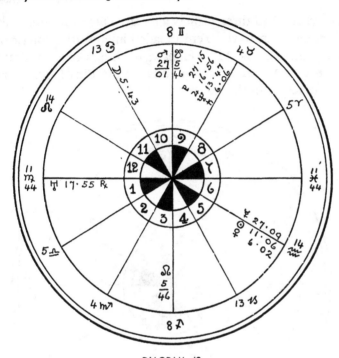

DIAGRAM 48
Horoscope of Franklin Delano Roosevelt
January 30, 1882

Franklin D. Roosevelt had no less than five planets in Earth signs. These happened to be all heavy planets; hence he was able to make such changes in the nation.

His Moon was highly elevated and in its own sign; hence, on the whole, the people loved and admired him, as did his own mother. The Sun, however, rules the Twelfth House; hence many important people did not admire him. Since the Sun is in the Fifth House, among these nonadmirers would be many of the great financiers. The Sun is square to various planets in the Ninth House, so these men would dislike some of the new legislation he put into force.

Roosevelt had three planets angular. These gave him a flair
for action. Mars in the Tenth made him a wartime president.
Two planets in the Fifth House gave him a sense of drama.
Mercury in Aquarius, with its ruler in the First House, made
him interested in the future.

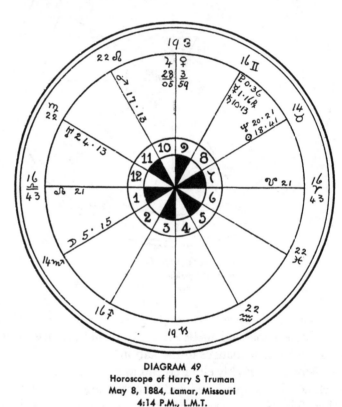

DIAGRAM 49
Horoscope of Harry S Truman
May 8, 1884, Lamar, Missouri
4:14 P.M., L.M.T.

Harry S Truman has one planet in a Fire sign while the
others are evenly distributed among Earth, Air, and Water
signs. Since his ascendant is an Air sign, we give precedence to
the Air signs, indicating his ability to meet people freely and
easily. The elevated Jupiter brought him to the Presidency.

The Sun in his Eighth House shows that he would reach major elevation through the death of some important friend, for the Sun rules his house of friends.

The Moon rising and in trine to Venus in Cancer, apparently is the cause of his popularity with the people. His foreign policy is under Mercury in Gemini conjoined with Pluto, indicating far-reaching changes. His Saturn, also in Gemini, tends to bring a stabilizing note after numerous changes. Mars in the Tenth House makes him, like Mr. Roosevelt, a wartime president.

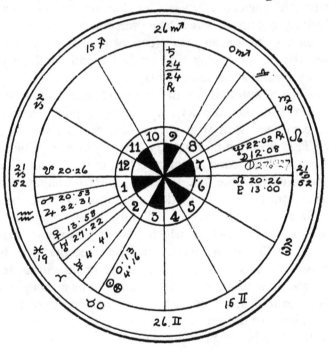

DIAGRAM 50
Horoscope of Queen Elizabeth II of England
April 21, 1926, 2:43 A.M., Summer Time

' Official hour of birth given as 2:43 A.M. (Summer Time)

The horoscope of Queen Elizabeth II is an extremely difficult one for any beginning student of astrology to analyze.
This is because the most obvious note is struck by a three-
legged Fixed Cross, consisting of Saturn, Mars, Jupiter, Neptune and the Moon—a factor that could bring apparently un-
surmountable obstacles if there were not compensating values
in the chart to offset it. However, we must always penetrate
deeply into a chart before we give precedence to mere aspects.
We should try to discover the powers that enable the soul to
triumph over obstacles. Has Elizabeth any impregnable towers
of strength? She certainly has. Her chart resolves into two in-
terlocking receptions, which take precedence over squares and
can convert the squares into agents of power as beneficial as
trines, the benefits being won by fusing and combining apparently incompatible ingredients.

The first reception is that of Mars and Saturn, indicating the
ability to overcome obstacles by means of quick decisive action, combined with wise government and a knowledge of
facts. This reception takes care of Mercury in Aries, England's
ruling sign. The second reception is that of Jupiter and Uranus
(interlocked with the first, because Jupiter is conjoined with
Mars). Here we have the wisdom and intuition that bring success. This reception takes care of Venus, the Sun, Neptune, the
Moon, and Pluto, all of which planets contribute specific
qualities to the second reception. These receptions increase
Elizabeth's ability to size up the nature of new ideas, to in-
corporate these ideas, if necessary, into her own thought, and
then to express and present them to the peoples of her far-
flung spheres of influence.

In this way her reign will stand out as one that meets the
future without fear. Who is more courageous than a person
with Mars conjunct Jupiter? Who can deal with international
difficulties with more wisdom, speed, and effectiveness? Who
can expend her energies so freely in the cause of her peoples

overseas? She should travel constantly and visit these domains, for wherever she goes, she can gain in prestige. Who is so basically sympathetic as a person with Venus in Pisces? With that planet's trine to Pluto she will find new ways to help people in trouble. With Uranus in Pisces she will be able to discover new ways to raise the finances of her Commonwealth, and, since Uranus is trine Saturn, she will bind the separate parts together in a stable financial commonweal. The Sun in Taurus gives her a fundamental awareness of material values. She is no theorist, but practical. With the Sun sextile Pluto she will find new ways of dealing wisely and·justly with conflicting groups.

No less than five planets are angular in the Queen's horoscope; hence, she cannot be idle. The Seventh House indicates her sailor husband Philip. It also represents, in a ruler's chart, her powerful allies and her powerful foes. When we see Neptune in the seventh, we see the fight against Communism, but as the Sun disposes of Neptune, and Venus in turn disposes of the Sun, we need not be discouraged over the final outcome. Elizabeth gained her throne when the progressed Midheaven sextiled Mars, the ruler of her Tenth House. In two years the progressed Midheaven will sextile her radical Jupiter, so that she gains in wisdom and in popularity.

The Queen will not find life easy. She will not wear her heart on her sleeve, but she will stand as a tower of strength during danger, which is what should be required of any ruler. She will attract wise councillors and friends, and her military, naval, and air commanders will be outstanding and successful.

The elevated Saturn fortunately is not in her Tenth House, and since it will retrograde all her lifetime, going away from the Midheaven, it will not mean, as some astrologers have said, that she will lose her throne and empire. It means, rather, that the crisis of empire took place nearer her birth year. Elizabeth was born at a time when the growth direction of the empire indicated new lines of expression, and these looked so like the forces of total disintegration that in 1926 an Imperial Conference was called. This Conference helped to point out the useless dead branches, and to concentrate upon the living tree. It paved the way for the new growth to have full expression in the Statute of Westminster, which passed the House of Commons on November 24, 1931. Without this statute, Great Britain might never have weathered World War II.

Saturn elevated in Elizabeth's chart and in trine to Uranus indicates that the monarch understands, and will work with, the new concepts of the relationship of the mother country to the dominions, which is one of perfect freedom—such that we now have the curious anomaly of a country like India, a free and sovereign republic, numbered in the Commonwealth of Nations (with the word *British* omitted). Elizabeth understands that she does not rule the dominions, but that they stay in her sphere of influence just as long as they wish to do so, and no longer. The important thing is that they shall admire, respect, and honor her as the symbol of the unity of the Commonwealth. There is no doubt from the Queen's horoscope but that she can hold their respect. Actually, she will do more. She will command their love and affection.

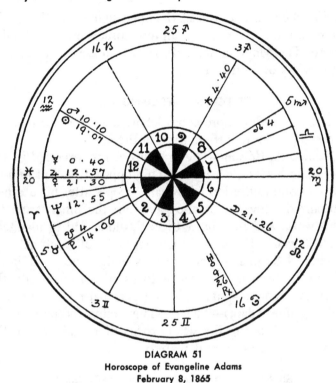

DIAGRAM 51
Horoscope of Evangeline Adams
February 8, 1865

Evangeline Adams has three Water planets surrounding her Ascendant. These planets include the two benefics, Jupiter and Venus. Jupiter rules her Midheaven; hence she would become well-known through her own personal efforts. Jupiter also rules her Ninth House; hence, she would be successful in legal cases, though the presence of Saturn in the Ninth would not prevent lawsuits. Neptune rising, and being one ruler of her Ascendant, gave her an intuitive sense which helped in astrological reading. She did not have a full Fixed square of planets since the sign Scorpio contains no planet. We call such a configuration as this, a three-legged square. Considerable difficulty can enter the life when malefics transit the open sign, so on the whole, it is sometimes better to have all four corners of a square filled at birth. The Moon in her Sixth House, in Leo, gave her both love of work and pride in it.

THE ECLIPSE PRECEDING BIRTH

In the preceding horoscopes let us note the effect of the eclipses just prior to birth in three of them.

Thomas A. Edison—The previous eclipse occurred in 26° Libra in his Twelfth House. This, apparently, shut him off from communication with many people after his deafness occurred. However, it also gave him the inner vision for his work, and the ability to work alone and to meditate. The Twelfth House is the natural home of Neptune.

Harry S Truman—The previous eclipse occurred in 6° Taurus, throwing the whole focus of his chart into the Seventh House—public life and personal relationships.

Evangeline Adams—The previous eclipse occurred in 7° Scorpio, throwing the whole focus of her chart into the Eighth House of occult matters.

SIGNS OF LONG AND SHORT ASCENSION

The simplest way to understand signs of long and short ascension is to look at the *Table of Houses* at the back of *Raphael's Ephemeris*. Let us look first at the table for New York City. Study the column where Aries is given as the Ascendant. Note that the corresponding Midheaven runs from 0°–16° Capricorn. This means that while 16 degrees of Capricorn pass over the Midheaven, the whole 30 degrees of Aries travel quickly over the Ascendant. Aries is a sign of short ascension; that is, it ascends, or passes over the Ascendant in a very short time in our northern latitudes.

Now look at Libra as an Ascendant. During the time when Libra occupies the Ascendant, all of Cancer has to move over the Midheaven and then five degrees of Leo. Libra is, therefore, a sign of long ascension. It takes a long time to move.

Now study the *Table of Houses* for London and Liverpool, which are much farther north than New York City, and you will find that the time for Aries to ascend is even shorter than in New York City, while the time for Libra to ascend is longer.

The signs of short ascension are:

> Capricorn, Aquarius, Pisces,
> Aries, Taurus, and Gemini

The signs of long ascension are:

> Cancer, Leo, Virgo,
> Libra, Scorpio, and Sagittarius

At or near the equator, we find the signs ascend evenly, but not so in places north or south of the equator. If you think the matter over seriously, you will realize that in northern latitudes fewer people can be born under Ascendants of short ascension, than under Ascendants of long ascension. In other words, there are fewer people born with Ascendants from Capricorn to Gemini inclusive, than there are people with Ascendants from Cancer to Sagittarius inclusive.

LESSON NINE

Signs and Planets Affecting the   ·   Twelve Houses

♈   ♉   ♊   ♋   ♌   ♍   ♎   ♏   ♐   ♑   ♒   ♓

INTRODUCTION: *Lesson Nine is extremely important. The sign on the cusp of a house gives the basic clue to the consciousness impinging upon the affairs of the house, and it also gives a clue to the type of events denoted by the house. You need to know the meaning of each house, and of each sign, very thoroughly before you can weave both together. In order to test yourself, make a rough horoscope wheel, and try to work out for yourself what each sign can mean on each cusp.*

The second part of this lesson is a brief study of what each planet can effect when in a specific house.

Apply the knowledge gained in this lesson to your own chart, and to that of other people's charts. You will discover many added meanings. You may also think you discover statements that do not suit particular horoscopes. Do not be discouraged. The contradiction may be due to the aspects which the planet in the house, or the ruler of the cusp, happens to make. For example, suppose Jupiter rules the cusp of your Second House, or should happen to be posited in your Second House. Jupiter may be making good aspects and so bring you money, or Jupiter may be afflicted by various other planets; hence, though it is possible you may have what some people would call considerable money, your earnings, or income, may be smaller than your necessary expenditures. Tabulate your aspects before you draw absolute conclusions.

When you have set up your own, or any other chart, the next step is to discover how to read it. You will learn to do this only gradually, and you may think it a long difficult process. But in time you will remember quite easily what the houses, signs, and planets mean; hence, you will merely have to glance at a symbol and understand it. Just as the pianist learns to read music at sight, so you will learn to interpret the manifold details of a chart almost instantaneously.

You have found that the twelve signs are always in sequence around the chart. You have to interpret each particular sign that happens to be on the cusp of a chart. Note first if it is the natural sign of that house, or some other. Next, determine whether it is a sign that is harmonious to the nature of that house. For example, the Seventh House deals with other people; therefore, a highly individualized sign, such as Leo, Aries, or Capricorn, can create difficulty when on the Seventh cusp, for none of these signs enjoy co-operation, except from other people. Again, with regard to the Fifth House, which deals with children, or romance, the signs Capricorn or Virgo, may be quite out of place, since neither sign is temperamentally inclined to love either children or romantic situations unless, of course, their ruler is well aspected by Venus.

MATTERS AFFECTED BY THE HOUSES

House 1

The body, the head and face. Physical appearance. Temperament. Health (as well as the Sixth House). Natural tendencies. Childhood years. Beginnings of all enterprises.

House 2

Money, possessions, property, investments, household furniture, etc. Since liberty is largely a matter of money, House Two is the house of liberty. Is the house of matters concerning Taurus, the throat, etc.

House 3

· Relatives, acquaintances, environment. Communication, short journeys, speech, letters, writings, telephones, telegraphs, street cars, automobiles, railways, etc. Shows the adaptability of the mind for learning.

House 4

The home, property, lands, mines. Private life. The mother (sometimes the father), inheritance, inherited tendencies. All that is secluded, the base of character. Closing years of life. Endings of all matters. Fame after death.

House 5

Love, romance, pleasures, games, theatres. Speculations, games of chance, enterprise. Type of affection given and met. House of what the native creates, whether children, inventions, books, etc. Education of children. Publications

House 6

Sickness, employment, servants. Conditions you meet in employing others or in being employed. House of uncles and aunts related to parent in Fourth House. House of service you have to give others, whether in the home, social life or in employment.

House 7

Partner in business or marriage. Dealings with the public and other people. Legal difficulties, contracts. Open enemies. House of what we lack most in ourselves. House of the ideal.

House 8

Deaths, wills, legacies, sex. Money of the partner, dowries. In conjunction with House Six shows the type of illnesses.

House of what is secret. House of detective work. House of the occult, of regeneration and new life, or of decay and death.

House 9

Long journeys (over 24 hours), ocean voyages. The ideational mind, science, religion, law, philosophy, publications, foreign countries, commerce, the church as a spiritual factor. House of one's in-laws, being the third from the Seventh House. They call out one's philosophy. Note too that cosmically this house is always in opposition to the third, that of one's own relations.

House 10

Profession, honor, public life, professional status. The church as an organization. Government. The father (sometimes the mother),* the employer.

House 11

Hopes and wishes. Capacity for friendship. Effects of friendship. Spiritual joys (the Fifth House represents physical and mental joys). House of what one desires most in life. Humanitarian work, clubs, societies. Money obtained from the profession, since it is the second from the Tenth House.

House 12

Secret enemies. Charity, sympathy. The cause of the troubles of life. Self-undoing. The debt one owes to humanity. Things that are hidden from the world. House of institutions, places of detention, jail, hospitals, limitation and suffering.

* The Fourth and the Tenth Houses are those of the parents. Sometimes when the mother's influence is strongest and when she has the main care in the upbringing of the child, the Tenth House is that of the mother, but normally when the status in life comes through the father, the Tenth House is that of the father. Often, when a father dies young, the Tenth House is that of the mother. When a mother dies young, the Fourth House is that of the father.

ARIES ON THE CUSPS OF THE TWELVE HOUSES

House

♈ on 1 Physical activity; restless; headstrong; electric; direct rather than diplomatic.

♈ on 2 Activity, new ideas and directness in money making; desires quick turnover.

♈ on 3 Good brain capacity; mentally, energetic; impulsive; many journeys; often separates from brethren.

♈ on 4 Energy in the home; mind is stimulated by the home; strife in home or in environment; many new homes.

♈ on 5 Energy for pleasures; mental realization through love; love at first sight; rash in speculation.

♈ on 6 Energy in work; new kinds of work; accidents and fevers; risky work; works well with metals.

♈ on 7 Energy used by partners or for partners; quarrels with partners; hasty marriage.

♈ on 8 Sexual energy; accidents or fevers cause death; strife in respect to legacies.

♈ on 9 Love of travel; strife through travel; atheistic.

♈ on 10 Mechanical pursuits; engineering; critical position; scandal; risky profession; enemies in profession.

♈ on 11 Assertive among friends, or has assertive friends; original, forceful, or quarrelsome friends.

♈ on 12 Actions cause enmity; self-undoing through violence and haste.

TAURUS ON THE CUSPS OF THE TWELVE HOUSES

House

♉ on 1 Strong physique; magnetic but slow; self-centered; practical; keen desires; stolid physically.

♉ on 2 Determination to make money; jealous of possessions; hoards money and possessions.

♉ on 3 Determined; set in mind and opinions; does not travel much.

♉ on 4 Stable home; good table; conservative type of home.

♉ on 5 Strong feelings and sensations; not inclined to speculate; happy with children; fond of pleasure.

♉ on 6 Reliable in work; dogmatic towards servants; throat troubles.

♉ on 7 Pleasant marriage partner if allowed own way; marriage partner does not exert himself much.

♉ on 8 Gain through partners; marriage partner has many possessions; does not part readily with them.

♉ on 9 Reserved in religious views; does not travel much.

♉ on 10 Stable position; somewhat lethargic in public life.

♉ on 11 Dogmatic, stubborn friends; does not change friends much; romance through friends; possessive toward friends.

♉ on 12 Self-undoing through possessions and emotions.

GEMINI ON THE CUSPS OF THE TWELVE HOUSES

House

♊ on 1 Dexterity; gift of imitation; body suitable for mental pursuits; nervous; high-strung.

♊ on 2 Two ways of earning money; earns through mind; finances often involve relatives.

♊ on 3 Refined; logical; fond of detail; conventional.

♊ on 4 Good memory; two homes; relatives in home; sends and receives many letters from home.

♊ on 5 Dual love affairs; love letters; mind tries to get above sensation; love with relative or friend.

♊ on 6 Two kinds of work or many changes; hobbies; intellectual work preferred; critical.

♊ on 7   Probability of two marriages; may marry a relative or friend; changeable towards mate.

♊ on 8   Mind occult; turns on death and sex; problems regarding partner's money; mind never settled; morbid tendency.

♊ on 9   Conflict of faith and reason; optimism v. despondency; fond of travel; travels with relatives.

♊ on 10 May have two professions; professionally associated with others.

♊ on 11 Clever, literary friends; dual attachments.

♊ on 12 Sorrow through brethren or friends; secretive mind interested in institutions.

CANCER ON THE CUSPS OF THE TWELVE HOUSES
House

♋ on 1   Sensitive body; tenacious; receptive; liable to extremes; dependent; retreats from the unpleasant.

♋ on 2   Economical; tenacious; saves for old age or children. Interest in real estate or commodities related to home life.

♋ on 3   Sensitive; indolent; fanciful; tenacious of opinions; loves antiques.

♋ on 4   Class conscious; love of home; attachment to parents, yet often changes the home.

♋ on 5   Impressionable; receptive to feelings of others; fond of children.

♋ on 6   Fond of food; growth through service; likes change of work.

♋ on 7   Desire for popularity; mate demonstrative in affection.

♋ on 8   Interested in psychic matters; emotionally interested in problems of death.

♋ on 9   Mystical; religious; prophetical; tenacious of religious views.

♋ on 10   Ability to meet public when shyness is overcome; work with drama, foods, liquids; office may be at home.

♋ on 11   Attachments to inferiors or children; socially active; dramatic friends; friends are often in family.

♋ on 12   Sorrow through home or emotions; very kindly to those in trouble.

LEO ON THE CUSPS OF THE TWELVE HOUSES

House

♌ on 1   Strong vitality; independent; enthusiastic; usually well liked.

♌ on 2   Hopeful concerning money; prefers to work for himself rather than in partnership or under someone else.

♌ on 3   Ambitious; enterprising; fearless; zealous; kindly disposed towards relatives.

♌ on 4   Often favorite at home; likes to entertain regally.

♌ on 5   Many loves; one real one; happy with children; rarely many children of his own; fond of gambling and speculation.

♌ on 6   Not really happy unless working for himself; faithful in service, however.

♌ on 7   Partner often fine and noble; expects entire devotion; wholehearted.

♌ on 8   Sometimes money through legacy from a loved one; wants full control of partner's money, yet generous to partner.

♌ on 9   Great love of truth; idealistic philosophy but built on ideas of a benevolent despot.

♌ on 10   Well-liked in his profession; his leadership easily accepted.

♌ on 11   Noble, generous friends; ardent; idealistic; happy among friends.

♌ on 12   Sorrow through love or children or speculation; not able to express his love so well in this house.

VIRGO ON THE CUSPS OF THE TWELVE HOUSES

House

♍ on 1   Sensitive body; highly nervous; practical; discriminating; restless; difficult to understand; picayunish.

♍ on 2   Money through organizations, civil service or commerce; businesslike, exact and shrewd.

♍ on 3   Laborious; analytical; scientific; critical; fond of writing; sometimes writes or speaks on questions of diet.

♍ on 4   Neat and orderly in the home; critical of effects; desires company; business or work sometimes in the home.

♍ on 5   Discrimination in love; analyzes the emotions; prudish; exacting in love.

♍ on 6   Hygienic; accurate and painstaking in work; good at detail work; interested in diet.

♍ on 7   Somewhat critical partner who wants every detail correct; often works for partner.

♍ on 8   Practical with partner's money; needs much convincing before he is interested in the psychic or occult.

♍ on 9   Many changes of ideas concerning religion; takes practical outlook on religion and philosophy.

♍ on 10   Often has two professions during life; a good teacher.

♍ on 11   Works for friends or among friends; interested in humanitarian work.

♍ on 12   Sorrow through employment or illnesses; tries to understand nature of diseases; interested in institutional work and problems.

LIBRA ON THE CUSPS OF THE TWELVE HOUSES

House

♎ on 1 Gentle; well-proportioned body; daydreams; mentally indecisive, if not balanced; adaptable; fawning manner.

♎ on 2 Money bound up in partnership.

♎ on 3 Love of justice; makes good comparisons; happy among brethren.

♎ on 4 Artistic home; harmonious or opposite.

♎ on 5 Refined feelings; love of opposite sex; dualistic love affairs.

♎ on 6 Patient in sickness; good nurse or servant; may marry or ally with someone socially inferior.

♎ on 7 Marriage partner poised; pleasant partner; does not exert himself too much; artistic; balanced.

♎ on 8 Gain through partner; legacies probable; death peaceful; liability to kidney trouble.

♎ on 9 Harmonious; reserved in religious views; idealistic; harmony when traveling but not overfond of travel.

♎ on 10 Stable position in life; artistic pursuits; social success; liked by the public.

♎ on 11 Artistic friends; platonic unions; marriage to friend.

♎ on 12 Philosophical in trouble; troubles through partnership; secret marriage.

SCORPIO ON THE CUSPS OF THE TWELVE HOUSES

House

♏ on 1 Acute; proud; reserved; self-controlled; hard to penetrate; ability to stand strain.

♏ on 2 Financial strain; secretive regarding finance.

♏ on 3 Decisive mind; research; satire; mystical; occult; secretive; suspicious; difficulties among brethren.

♏ on 4   Secretive regarding home affairs; stress in home life.

♏ on 5   Secret loves; self-control or none; regeneration through love; not lucky in speculation.

♏ on 6   Constructive; reserved; secret work.

♏ on 7   Marriage partner has to work hard; secretive regarding marriage; regeneration through marriage.

♏ on 8   Secretive regarding partner's finances; strain through partner's finances; occult.

♏ on 9   Occult; enemy of ceremony; difficulties on journeys; litigation causes trouble.

♏ on 10   Succeeds in government office; secret work; research work.

♏ on 11   Secret attachments; fatalistic; tragedies among friends.

♏ on 12   Secret enemies; work among occult societies; fond of mystery novels.

SAGITTARIUS ON THE CUSPS OF THE TWELVE HOUSES
House

♐ on 1   Restless; irrepressible; well-proportioned body; excitable; verbose; slow to sense attitude of others.

♐ on 2   Luck in money or none; liberal; demands freedom; gambles; selfish.

♐ on 3   Foresight; legal mind; imaginative; religious; prophetic; impulsive; rebellious.

♐ on 4   Reacts to fine surroundings; changes in home; mystical; idealistic; pride of family.

♐ on 5   Idealistic in love; intense; fond of pleasure and speculation; sometimes great benefit through children.

♐ on 6   Pride in work; prudent; loves religious work or speculates; air of superiority to work.

♐ on 7   Humane partner; sociable; popular; just, or a gambler and pleasure-seeker; often two marriages.

♐ on 8   Researcher; occult; inventive; subtle; benefit through partner.

♐ on 9   Devout; religious; idealistic; just; legal mind; travels; conventional.

♐ on 10 Studies etiquette; socially important; a leader; accurate; ambitious; a climber.

♐ on 11 Loyal friends; gain through friends; philanthropic; leader in organizations; gay friends.

♐ on 12 Zeal in philanthropy; work not appreciated.

CAPRICORN ON THE CUSPS OF THE TWELVE HOUSES

House

♑ on 1   Bony structure evident; childhood years difficult; grows stronger the older he becomes; in poor types fawning manner; pride; ambition; coldness; reserve.

♑ on 2   Ambitious for money; desire to save; money through organizations; sometimes money through father.

♑ on 3   Persistency; reflective; suspicious; cautious; ambition attained through brethren or acquaintances.

♑ on 4   Poverty in home but also pride; restriction in home of parents.

♑ on 5   Cold exterior in love but highly sexed; trustworthy or capricious; absorbs feelings of others; ambition sometimes attained through a loved one or through children.

♑ on 6   Organizes work; efficiency expert; often works in and through large organizations or in governmental employ.

♑ on 7   Delays marriage, or gives difficult, domineering marriage partner; marriage partner ambitious.

♑ on 8   Death as a rule by old age; careful regarding partner's money; hard to get money from partner.

♑ on 9 Orthodox in religion; not overfond of travel; good legal mind.

♑ on 10 Seeks responsibility; very ambitious; a good executive; likes governmental positions.

♑ on 11 Ambitious friends; friends may hold office in government or be executives; inconsistent friends.

♑ on 12 Sorrow through ambitions thwarted; ambition may be to work in institutions.

AQUARIUS ON THE CUSPS OF THE TWELVE HOUSES
House

♒ on 1 Very positive; sometimes blunt; uncertain, sudden impulses; mental fantasies.

♒ on 2 Money through organizations or government.

♒ on 3 Intuitive; co-ordinating; capricious; good judges of others' minds.

♒ on 4 Desire to mix with elders during childhood; much change in the home or many restrictions.

♒ on 5 Many loves; one special lover who is often a friend first; interested in the welfare of children; not much luck in speculation.

♒ on 6 Wants to work in own way; expects co-operation from others; somewhat nervous and restless in employment; ever seeking ideal conditions; worries much concerning illnesses.

♒ on 7 Many difficulties in partnership; wife or husband often a better friend than marriage partner.

♒ on 8 Difficulties and unexpected circumstances concerning partner's money; often much sorrow over death of friends; interest in occult study.

♒ on 9 Desire for travel; friends made during travel; own ideas concerning religion.

♒ on 10 Interested in societies and groups; friendly to those in his profession.

≈ on 11   Varied friends; may be in groups or societies; eccentric friends but attached mentally rather than emotionally. ·

≈ on 12   Desire to organize and systematize institutions of all kinds; much dislike of restraint; often is benefactor or friend to those in trouble.

PISCES ON THE CUSPS OF THE TWELVE HOUSES

House

✕ on 1   Plastic body; kindly, but not very practical; sometimes absent-minded or moody; apparently happy in company, then slips away to be by himself.

✕ on 2   Difficulties and sorrow through money affairs; often two ways of making money.

✕ on 3   Receptive; mediumistic; fond of music; sorrow through relatives.

✕ on 4   Sorrow or limitation in the home; a good host when in the humor for friends.

✕ on 5   Impressionability in love; dual attachments; sorrow through love and children.

✕ on 6   Not overstrong physically; irritated over trifles; very many ideas in work or employment, but needs courage and strength to carry them out.

✕ on 7   Partner often a person of high ideals, but not very practical; sorrow in marriage.

✕ on 8   Very psychic; trouble and sorrow through partner's money.

✕ on 9   Very mystical in religion; much inspiration and vision; desire for sea travel.

✕ on 10   Can make an executive with much vision, but not always practical.

✕ on 11   Mediumistic friends; sorrow through friends; hopes and wishes not often realized.

✕ on 12   Much loneliness and disappointment in life.

LESSON TEN

The Moon and Planets in the Signs

♈ ♉ ♊ ♋ ♌ ♍ ♎ ♏ ♐ ♑ ♒ ♓

INTRODUCTION: You discovered in Lesson Three that the Sun has a different effect in each sign of the zodiac. We now have to consider the effect of the Moon and of the eight planets in every sign. To do this, we have to examine the basic activity of each, and then decide whether it can express its full action in the signs.

From the data in the ephemeris for your birthday, note in what signs the planets are placed. These factors have meant much in your life, so reflect upon their meaning; then do the same with the horoscopes of persons you know quite well.

Use the current ephemeris each day, and note the daily position of the planets, particularly the positions of the Sun and of the Moon. We call these daily positions of the planets, **Transits**. See what houses of your chart they are affecting. Note whether the Sun or Moon in their daily motion are harmonious, or not, to any planets in your chart. Note what happens on the days when they form a good aspect to your natal planets, and what occurs on the days when they form an inharmonious aspect. Thus you learn.

The Moon takes roughly twenty-eight days to travel through the twelve signs; that is, it takes two and a third days to move

through each sign. In one year it travels approximately thirteen times around the zodiac. The Moon reflects the light of the Sun, and in its monthly travel, it throws radiance, light and vitality on the particular house and sign where it is. The new Moon and full Moon mark the important factors of the month. If the lunation and full Moon degrees coincide with the degree positions of any planets in your horoscope, the month becomes important to you.

New Moon is the conjunction of the Sun and Moon, and is called the lunation. The lunation period comprises the twenty-eight days following the new Moon.

Full Moon is the opposition of the Sun and Moon. Its influence extends for fourteen days, but its influence is subordinate to that of the new Moon.

The First Quarter is the first square the Moon can make to the Sun after new Moon. It has minor influence for one week.

The Last Quarter is the square that the Moon makes to the Sun after full Moon. It has minor influence for seven days.

Growth in vegetation manifests in waves, and the growth of the affairs of your life seems to do the same. From the new to the full Moon, there is a manifestation of growth and activity. What is promised at the new Moon may come to fruition at the full Moon. After the full Moon growth seems to proceed at a more leisurely rate.
If the Moon in your own chart is decreasing in light, you are introspective; if it is increasing, you act quickly.

THE MOON IN THE TWELVE SIGNS

Moon in Aries: This causes growth in the matters under Aries—new beginnings, new ventures, and new enterprises.

The brain will be stimulated, hope and optimism being aroused. Watch the beginning of the Moon's entrance into Aries each month, and take advantage of its rays if you want to start anything new, or if you want to obtain new ideas on any subject in which you are interested. Do not quarrel or be too headstrong on these days.

Moon in Taurus: Taurus is substance, so if you wish to collect your forces and consolidate your ideas, take advantage  each month of the Moon in Taurus. Taurus gives devotion, common sense, and perseverance; hence all these things can develop when the Moon passes through this sign. Do not be too grasping on these days nor let your feelings run away with your judgment.

Moon in Gemini: Gemini has to do with mental efforts, with short journeys, relatives, correspondence, so you should  watch each month for the Moon in Gemini to get new stimulation in your business. It will be a time when your mind seems brighter. You can know best how to deal with relatives, or decide on short journeys. The days when the Moon is in Gemini are busy.

Moon in Cancer: Cancer has to do with the emotions, home, parents and old age. Take care when the Moon is in Cancer to  try to keep emotionally balanced. Do not get too dramatic or make too many changes in the home. Try not to be too possessive of everybody and everything. It will, however, be good to consider plans for the future and for old age; how to deal with parents and old people, for the rays of the Moon at this time will give you illumination.

Moon in Leo: Leo governs the heart, romance, and children, speculation and authority, so that all these things grow during  the days when the Moon is in Leo. Knowledge and understanding of how to deal with all these things will come when the Moon is in Leo if you will try to tune in on Leo's rays. Be careful, however, not to increase in vaingloriousness, conceit and pride.

Moon in Virgo: Virgo has to do with work and with health. You can analyze and think out what to do for the best in these matters if you will watch each month for the Moon in Virgo. You can understand the relationship with your employer or employee better, as well as your health, food and need for exercise. Concentrate on these things during the two and a half days each month when the Moon is in this sign.

Moon in Libra: Libra has to do with other people, partnership, law and the fine arts. You will be happier in society during the period when the Moon is in Libra. You can appear more attractive to your partner. You will understand legal problems better. You will want to make life more beautiful. Be careful under these rays not to sit on the fence and argue both ways, but come to some definite conclusion. Do not postpone doing what you intend to do when you know it is right to do so.

Moon in Scorpio: Scorpio is emotional, intuitive and introspective. It has to do with death, legacies, the partner's money, detective work, and the occult. It is not a good time to set a new enterprise into motion, but rather to make the plans for a new start, to think things out to their foundations, to know the why and wherefore. There is often ability to carry on research work and occult studies. The Moon in this sign gives not only great courage but also tremendous endurance. The memory under this position is almost abnormal, reaching to very early childhood days. Often, however, the memory tends to dwell on the unhappy things, on slights and fancied wrong, so it is always well for a person

who has the Moon in Scorpio in the natal chart to resolve to dwell on the cheerful side of life. It is a position of great introspectiveness.

Moon in Sagittarius: Sagittarius is interested in travel, sport, change and movement. The Sagittarian is always enthusiastic

over his ideas and knowledge. Therefore the Moon in this sign gives him ability to make his ideas known to the world. A strong liking for large animals and outdoor life is manifested. Diplomacy may be shown, but Sagittarius is not a sign that can keep a secret, like Scorpio; thus Sagittarian diplomacy seems to express itself in a love of all that is polished, civilized, and refined, rather than in the handling of delicate and intricate problems. The Moon in Sagittarius tends to lack caution, and may talk too freely. When the Moon transits the sign, it is good time to dwell on the ideal side of life.

Moon in Capricorn: Capricorn is the sign of ambition, honor and public advancement. The Moon here gives a great

desire for such things. It confers steadfastness and reliability. Conscience is awakened and there is a strong moral purpose and rectitude. Capricorn being a Saturnine sign, however, tends to reserve and distance, so that the Moon in this sign is unable to express the tender, emotional and devotional side. Thus, there often grows up under the Moon in Capricorn a tendency to melancholy and a feeling of not being appreciated. When the Moon is in this sign, try not to feel too economical, discontented, or too full of pride and self-complacency.

Moon in Aquarius: Since Aquarius is the sign of distribution, when the Moon is here, there can be a great desire to

meet and see all kinds of people and conditions in life. In unevolved types there is at
times a certain disconnectness of ideas and
a continual jumping from one subject to the
other. In evolved types, the co-ordinating
factors are under control, hence they can see
in and through all conditions of life with im-
partiality, and they have clear notions as to

how and where people can work best. The Moon in Aquarius
people can obtain mountains of facts, and they can use each
one to the best advantage in any work on hand. There is great
zealousness in this configuration to tear down the old social
order and build up a new. When the Moon is in this sign, do
not let the average person think you want to improve him.
Most people resent enforced improvement.

Moon in Pisces: Pisces represents the desire for freedom
from the limitations of matter. The Moon is Pisces desires to
live in a dream world and in his feelings,
rather than in the practical world. The
Moon here fosters this tendency and often
causes strange dreams and psychic powers.
Since the Moon is collective in instinct, the
Moon in Pisces tends to make the native
gather money and possessions of which he
will later wish to rid himself. Pisces holds on

to them until they become ties and limitations, holding him
in bondage and distress. Because of this, Pisces is called the
sign of self-undoing and limitation. As a rule the freedom of
Pisces has to be obtained through sorrow and loss. It is not a
freedom in activity, as is that of Aries, but a freedom of spiritual consciousness, much more difficult to attain.

We do not have pictures of the Sun and the planets in the
twelve signs, but your imagination will suggest to you equally
vivid illustrations for them.

MERCURY IN THE TWELVE SIGNS

Sign

☿ in ♈ Keen analytical mind, adaptable, full of new ideas and invention; good traveler, correspondent; able to argue effectively; observant; spontaneous in action, a leader.

☿ in ♉ Somewhat stubborn and set in ideas; learns slowly but thoroughly; artitistic as a rule; shrewd sense of money values.

☿ in ♊ Fond of travel and change; good position for salesman; wants to know the why and wherefore of everything; quick, adaptable; witty, tactful, keen, shrewd.

☿ in ♋ Some conflict between reason and emotion; retentive memory; fond of company in the home; stays young looking to advanced age; emotions and opinions change.

☿ in ♌ Kindhearted; open and generous in nature; a good executive; likes pomp and style; much dignity; fond of children.

☿ in ♍ Systematic study of detail; careful of health; somewhat nervous in manner.

☿ in ♎ Desire to work with others; co-operative in spirit; a strong sense of comparative values; a strong sense of legal values; likes to appear before the public.

☿ in ♏ A penetrative intellect; concentrates easily; works in secret; subtle in mind and acute; a good detective; can write on little known subjects.

☿ in ♐ Fond of travel; can write and talk of what he has seen and thought; often atheistic in youth since he wants everything to be reasonable; very impulsive.

☿ in ♑ Ambitious, practical; a good organizer; great sense of detail; expects everything to be done thoroughly and systematically; economical, critical.

☿ in ♒　Usually fond of gathering large groups of friends; interested in politics or public welfare work.

☿ in ♓　A good interpreter of all that is mysterious and strange; much interest in institutional work; mind often inclined to feel oppressed with the sorrows of the whole world.

VENUS IN THE TWELVE SIGNS

Sign

♀ in ♈　Original, artistic mind; many new loves; Venus tends to soften and restrain the Arian impetuosity, except as regards love affairs where it often produces hasty marriage.

♀ in ♉　Steadfast in love; very strong feelings; desires beautiful surroundings; often makes money through artistic products; marriage may be for money.

♀ in ♊　Poetical, artistic, happy among associates; changeable in love; often makes money through artistic products.

♀ in ♋　Exceptionally emotional; attachment means everything; a somewhat clinging love nature; loves children; fond of home and parents; desires beauty in the home.

♀ in ♌　Faithful in love; fond of pleasures; especially theatres; magnificent in style and colorful in expression; usually lucky in speculation unless afflicted.

♀ in ♍　Prefers line to color; inclined to put off marriage because he sees imperfections in everyone; harmonious in work; benefits through servants or inferiors.

♀ in ♎　Peaceful and contented among others; fond of art and music; usually happy in marriage; a good position for social life.

♀ in ♏　The position of Venus here tends to soften the reserve of Scorpio and to present to people in a

happy manner much of the hidden research work
of Scorpio; there can be financial benefit from the
partner or from legacies; in low types, coarse, self-
indulgent, passionate.

♀ in ♐ Love usually idealistic in nature; there is gentleness
but strength in presenting views on religion; love
is sometimes met on a journey or in the study of
new things; love changes as the ideal changes.

♀ in ♑ Intensifies the ambition and desire for fine surroundings; there is sometimes timidity in love and
reserve in expressing the feelings. Marriage for social gain; late marriage.

♀ in ♒ Faithful to friends; becomes mentally absorbed in
friends and in helping others; fond of mental pursuits; a keen sense of comparison; hopes and wishes
usually realized.

♀ in ♓ Highly emotional; often suffers through love; desires to help those in distress; poetical and musical;
psychic; emotionally absorbed in loved ones.

MARS IN THE TWELVE SIGNS

Sign

♂ in ♈ Increases the physical and mental activities; courage, rashness, impetuosity, enthusiasm, adventure.

♂ in ♉ Persistency of effort and action; activity in making
money; interested in matters concerning real estate;
in farming or in artistic work.

♂ in ♊ Mentality alert and energetic; witty, sarcastic; strife
with relations or acquaintances, but quite ready to
make friends again; fond of machinery or mechanical work.

♂ in ♋ Many emotional exhibitions; active in the home;
strife in the home; inclined to imaginative work;
much travel and recklessness.

♂ in ♌ Quick, dynamic action; a born leader; endless activity to make a good position for himself; quarrels with those he loves; sometimes accident to loved ones; love of gambling.

♂ in ♍ A very energetic mental worker; often sarcastic; quarrels with servants or dependents; sometimes love of dangerous work.

♂ in ♎ An enthusiastic and active partner; often strife in partnership or in marriage; severed connections.

♂ in ♏ The energy of Mars is "fixed" in this sign, hence action is based on deliberate plans; strife concerning partner's money or legacies.

♂ in ♐ Very active traveler; presents ideas on religion or philosophy with tremendous zeal; sometimes creates bitter strife through this; impulsive.

♂ in ♑ Active in making a name and position for himself; much hostility aroused through these efforts; strife with one of parents.

♂ in ♒ Fond of working for friends, clubs and groups of people; desires to put new life into them; causes hostility at times through these efforts.

♂ in ♓ The activities are limited in this sign which is not physically energetic, hence there may be sullenness and brooding; a good sign for secret service men or detectives; bitter enemies if afflicted.

JUPITER IN THE TWELVE SIGNS

Sign

♃ in ♈ Benefits mentally and physically through travel; new dynamic conceptions in philosophy; kind but positive methods of action.

♃ in ♉ Ability to make money; philosophic; likes the best of everything; appearances count for much.

♃ in ♊   Happy disposition; fond of change and travel; kindly disposed towards relatives and acquaintances; a good writer on law or philosophy; sound judgment.

♃ in ♋   Deep emotional nature; idealistic concepts concerning mother and home; good judgment concerning finance, but economical.

♃ in ♌   Fond of pleasures, theatres, children, speculation; self-esteem; capable leader and executive.

♃ in ♍   Benevolent to dependents but requires very painstaking service; a good investigator.

♃ in ♎   Humane and generous partner; idealist concerning marriage; often a collector of fine arts; well liked by public; lucky in legal matters.

♃ in ♏   Shrewd, penetrative judgment; subtle in methods; fond of law; resourceful in finding out every fact and factor; philosophic concerning death.

♃ in ♐   Benefits in foreign lands; fond of travel and outdoor life; humane, optimistic and just; success in law and speculation; fond of gambling.

♃ in ♑   Interest in large organizations; make good appearance before the public; authoritative; interest in governmental matters; conservative views; materialistic.

♃ in ♒   Benefits and help from friends; has many friends of superior social position; interested in governmental and social reform.

♃ in ♓   Interested in all psychic matters; kindness expressed to all in trouble and sickness; likes to give secretly, or is not able to give as much as he would like.

SATURN IN THE TWELVE SIGNS

Sign

♄ in ♈   Limits the enterprise and flamboyance of Aries, but makes it more stable; gives ability to concentrate the mind and to organize the ventures.

♄ in ♉   Care and economy in money matters; rarely moves from home town; very great will power and persistence.

♄ in ♊   Plodding type of mind; often unhappy among relatives and friends; dislikes travel; often melancholy.

♄ in ♋   Limitations are usually in the home circle; inability to express the emotions to the full; loneliness in old age.

♄ in ♌   Sorrow through love or children; sometimes deprived of affection; gives pride that carries through affliction.

♄ in ♍   Not popular in employment; often has to work without much recognition; cannot tolerate inaccuracy; often has to work for an older person or the father.

♄ in ♎   Sorrow through marriage or partnership; often gives a jealous partner or one who limits the native.

♄ in ♏   Philosophic understanding of life but usually through sorrow and death of loved ones; loss of legacies and financial trouble.

♄ in ♐   Thoughtful outlook on life; feeling of responsibility in religion; orthodox in religion; not fond of travel and not lucky in travel.

♄ in ♑   Extreme ambition but gets little joy out of it; as a rule makes enemies and causes jealousy in the attainment of ambition; a great organizer.

♄ in ♒   A feeling of isolation when among friends; sorrow through inability to obtain hopes and wishes; interested in govermental work.

♄ in ♓   Periods of isolation and sorrow; fear of illness and also of psychic matters; trouble through enemies; sometimes early loss of parents.

URANUS IN THE TWELVE SIGNS

Sign

♅ in ♈   Inventive, ingenious, difficult to understand; action is quick and spasmodic; unexpected adventures.

♅ in ♉   Many unexpected upsets in finance; rarely remains long in one position; feelings often upset.

♅ in ♊   Not understood by brethren or acquaintances; continually on the move; may become a writer or teacher of the occult; likes modern literature and music.

♅ in ♋   The unexpected occurs in the home; one of the parents may be inventive or merely difficult; highly imaginative; many changes in old age.

♅ in ♌   Likes new and original pleasures; love at first sight; hunches concerning speculation; an inventive or original child if well aspected, otherwise trouble through children.

♅ in ♍   Dislikes routine work; the unexpected occurs in employment; often a great worker for astrology and the occult.

♅ in ♎   The unexpected in marriage and partnership; highly artistic and mentally original; legal troubles.

♅ in ♏   Surprises in finance, especially the partner's; very sensitive; somewhat difficult to know; much intuition; can throw light on psychic and occult matters.

♅ in ♐   Interested in all kinds of travel, particularly flying; quick, intuitive mind; advanced views in religion; sometimes publishes books on inventions or theories.

♅ in ♑   The unexpected in the profession; sometimes profession is connected with new inventions or with the occult; strange ambitions; intuitions concerning the profession.

♅ in ♒ Unusual experiences among friends; highly original friends; new ideas in social reform, and business.

♅ in ♓ Strange dreams and premonitions; original ideas concerning fate and destiny; gets into institutions unexpectedly and gets out just as unexpectedly.

NEPTUNE IN THE TWELVE SIGNS

Neptune was only discovered in 1846, hence none of the ephemerides previous to that date give the position of Neptune. These positions are contained in books devoted to this purpose.

Sign

♆ in ♈
(1861–1874) A new impetus in psychic, religious, and philosophical thought; somewhat destroys the facility for rapid action by causing distrust in one's own powers; the mind becomes introspective.

♆ in ♉
(1874–1887) Feelings somewhat oversensitive; a tendency to rely on *hunches* in regard to earning money. New concepts concerning money; new concepts in art. Public presentation of occult studies.

♆ in ♊
(1887–1901) Mental sensitivity; the ability to put the mysteries and occult knowledge into writing. Restlessness, desire for change; not understood by acquaintances. New theories concerning trade, commerce, travel, and communications.

♆ in ♋
(1901–1915) Sensitive emotions; strange conditions in the home. Nurtures mystical thought.

Ψ in ♌
(1915–1929)   Strange conditions in love, or in connection
                with children; exceptionally fond of specula-
                tion; does not accept authority very easily; new
                conditions in government.

Ψ in ♍
(1929–1943)   New concepts concerning health, diet; new
                conditions of employment. The form side of
                new religious thought is established; new
                phases of art; strange conditions in public
                service.

Ψ in ♎
(1943–1956)   New concepts concerning marriage; strange at-
                tractions. The subtle and mysterious is appre-
                ciated in art; confusion in legal matters; strange
                alliances individually and nationally.

Ψ in ♏
(1956–1970)   Highly secretive; problems concerning life, and
                life after death; much occult study. Great prog-
                ress in chemistry, oils, liquids, and new ma-
                terials.

Ψ in ♐
(1970–1984)   Desire for distant travel; new types of religious
(1806–1820)   propaganda; revolutionary ideas concerning phi-
                losophy; confusion and deceit in law; distrust
                among nations.

Ψ in ♑
(1984–1996)   Revolutionary ideas concerning government;
(1820–1834)   new concepts in politics. Hunches help in ob-
                taining the ambitions.

Ψ in ♒
(1834–1847)   New ideas and concepts in social life; strange
                conditions among friends; widespread interest
                in psychic truths.

♆ in ♓

(1847–1861) Psychically sensitive; strange dreams, often prophetic; love of poetry and music; new concepts concerning social necessities, such as, people in unfortunate conditions, or in institutions.

PLUTO

The discovery of Pluto was announced March 13, 1930. Until we know more about its meaning and work, it would be foolish to dogmatize upon its effects in the twelve signs.

Pluto in Capricorn	1762–1777	15 years
" " Aquarius	1777–1799	22 "
" " Pisces	1799–1823	24 "
" " Aries	1823–1852	29 "
" " Taurus	1852–1884	32 "
" " Gemini	1884–1914	30 "
" " Cancer	1914–1939	25 "
" " Leo	1939–1957	18 "
" " Virgo	1957–1972	15 "
" " Libra	1972–1984	12 "

As it changes signs, Pluto retrogrades, or goes direct, during such long periods that we have merely given the date when it was established in the sign, and not necessarily when it first entered the sign.

Pluto travels the circle of the zodiac in about 248 years, but, as you see from the above table, it has a very uneven rate of travel through the signs.

In the horoscope of the Declaration of Independence, Pluto was at approximately 28 degrees Capricorn. Its action in Capricorn was to change definitely the type of government of the country.

In whatever sign Pluto is placed, it causes changes to occur, so that new methods can be established to meet all modern requirements.

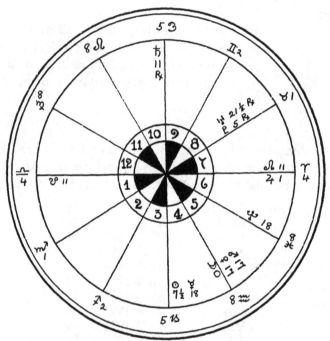

DIAGRAM 52
Horoscope of Woodrow Wilson
December 28, 1856

Woodrow Wilson had Libra ascending, a sign governing law. Libra is concerned with law as between two individuals, whereas Sagittarius is more concerned with jurisprudence. Why then was Wilson Professor of Jurisprudence at Princeton for twelve years? The answer seems to lie in the fact that he had Jupiter in his Sixth House of employment.

Note Saturn in the Midheaven. In the Tenth House, Saturn can incline towards governmental work, or work in large institutions. Wilson found more interest in the study of government than he did in law. Saturn is in its fall in Cancer, a sign which has to do with the public. Wilson was unable to be entirely successful when dealing with the masses. Saturn in the

Tenth House is said by some astrologers to promise a downfall. It need not do so unless it is afflicted, and in this chart it is afflicted by sign and by aspects.

Fame after death is denoted by the Fourth House; fame in life by the Tenth House. Wilson had three planets in the Fourth House.

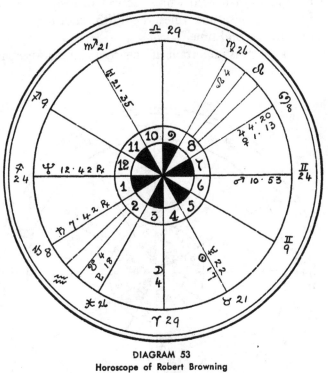

DIAGRAM 53
Horoscope of Robert Browning
May 7, 1812

Browning had Sagittarius rising which tends to ideality of thought and zeal in presenting new ideas.

The sign of poetry is Pisces, which is on the cusp of the Third House, the house of writing. The ruler Neptune is in the Twelfth House, the house of poetry (and the sign Pisces).

Gemini, the sign of writing, is on the cusp of his Sixth House, the house of work. Its ruler, Mercury, is in the Fifth House in Taurus. Taurus inclines towards beauty and stability. Mercury in the Fifth House shows that some of his inspiration was derived from his romance with Elizabeth Barrett Browning. Mercury rules the cusp of the Seventh House, hence he married the woman with whom he was in love. Venus is in the Seventh House and rules the Fifth, showing the same thing for the second time.

When a factor is important in a chart, it is sometimes shown more than once.

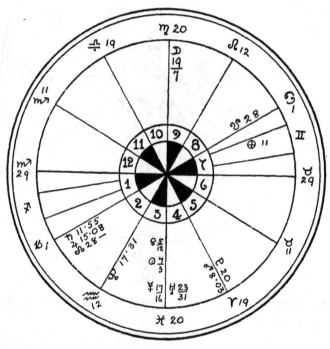

DIAGRAM 54
Horoscope of Camille Flammarion
February 26, 1842

Here we have the horoscope of the well-known French astronomer. The Ascendant is Scorpio which confers the desire to penetrate the mysteries. Its ruler Mars is in Aries showing love of the new. Flammarion wrote and lectured much on the possibility of life on Mars. The powerful ascendant counteracts the influence of the satellitium (group of planets) in Pisces, which might otherwise have exhausted itself in daydreaming. Pisces, however, desires to penetrate the unknown. Mercury acts as the interpreter of his findings. Uranus gives originality and insight. Venus, also in Pisces, meant that his mind worked with his emotions, hence he could popularize astronomy. The Moon in Virgo gave attention to details.

Neptune in the Third House accounts for his writings on spiritualism. He wrote *Dreams of an Astronomer*, also *Death and Its Mystery*.

The Planets in the Twelve Houses

♈ ♉ ♊ ♋ ♌ ♍ ♎ ♏ ♐ ♑ ♒ ♓

INTRODUCTION: *People often ask why the astrologer asks for the place of birth. House cusps and their sign degrees depend upon the location of your birthplace. This lesson makes you realize how much the latitude of your birth has affected your life. The consideration of geographical factors enables you to discover in which house each planet will be posited. At the end of Lesson Eleven you are given a few hints upon the effects the rulers of the house cusps have when placed in various houses.*

A planet can be in any house; therefore, it is necessary to note in which house it is posited. Planets express their best qualities when in houses whose nature is like their own, but they may cause difficulty when in houses that are inharmonious to them. Saturn in the Fifth may cause sorrow in connection with romance or children. The house is one of joy and pleasure, while Saturn's nature is not. In the Seventh House Saturn may not be too bad. Here it might describe a serious, or older partner, and not sorrow. Saturn in the Ninth House is fairly well placed, because it can confer a deep philosophical trend. It is not so good, however, for long journeys. Saturn in the Eleventh House can bring stable friends. As regards Saturn on the Ascendant, we might recall that both Goethe and Alan Leo had this position. Goethe lived to be eighty-three; Leo died at fifty-seven.

THE SUN IN ANY OF THE TWELVE HOUSES

House

☉ in 1   Joy, radiance, good health, strong constitution; a happy childhood; general success.

☉ in 2   Ease in making money; generosity; parent may be financially successful.

☉ in 3   Joy among relations; happy when traveling; fond of letter writing.

☉ in 4   Happiness in the home; kindly parents; health in old age; favorable for real estate.

☉ in 5   Joy through love and children; lucky in speculation; fond of pleasure.

☉ in 6   Faithful in work; not over strong; cheerfulness can overcome sickness.

☉ in 7   Happiness in marriage; lucky in lawsuits; pleasant to other people.

☉ in 8   Legacies likely; money through partnership or marriage.

☉ in 9   Noble ambitions; success in law or long journeys; orthodox religion.

☉ in 10   Success in the profession; happy when before the public.

☉ in 11   Good and noble friends; happiness in friendship; hopes and wishes realized.

☉ in 12   Some lack of self-confidence; desire for solitude; will work well for the poor or afflicted; interested in all kinds of institutions.

THE MOON IN ANY OF THE TWELVE HOUSES

House

☽ in 1   Emotional, sensitive, timid, acquisitive, changeable; when timidity is overcome, contacts the public with success.

☽ in 2   Many changes in finance; acquisitive; money
          through liquids or contacts with the people; some-
          what changeable concerning money; gain through
          mother or wife.

☽ in 3   Emotional mind; dramatic; retrospective; timid,
          but clings to own thought; likes to travel; help from
          brother or associates.

☽ in 4   Love of home, family, caste, antiques; gain through
          mother; comfort in old age.

☽ in 5   Emotions strong in love; desire for children; highly
          dramatic; fluctuating luck in speculation; success
          as teacher.

☽ in 6   Change of occupation; somewhat inclined to bring
          on illness through imagination; success through in-
          feriors.

☽ in 7   Indecision in marriage; partner sensitive or moody;
          changes in feeling during marriage; popular with
          the public.

☽ in 8   Psychic tendencies; interested in all problems con-
          cerning death; public attention at death or sickness;
          money through partner or women. *Sexual - Inheritance*

☽ in 9   Much imagination; many journeys; orthodox in re-
          ligion as a rule; inclined to dream.

☽ in 10 Many changes in profession; loves to contact the
          public; help from women; success through Moon
          occupations.

☽ in 11 Many friends; always hoping and wishing for
          friends; lucky through friendship, or club life.

☽ in 12 Too sensitive and retiring; psychic and restless; in-
          terested in all kinds of institutions.

MERCURY IN ANY OF THE TWELVE HOUSES

House

☿ in 1   Mental opportunities; adaptability; restlessness;

nervousness; may stammer under affliction; eloquent under good aspects.

☿ in 2   Mind acts on memory; reserve regarding money, or none; patient and obedient, or the reverse; tricky regarding finance; likes quick sales.

☿ in 3   Reason, accuracy; thoughtful relatives, or irresponsible ones; conversational or literary powers; if afflicted, deceitful, exaggerates.

☿ in 4   Mind retentive; economical; love of antiques; family pride; wants new emotions; afflicted, trouble in home, many changes of home; interested in real estate.

☿ in 5   Speculative, autocratic; leaders in thought; literary creation; mind evolves through love; usually no children.

☿ in 6   Practical, reserved, systematic observation; irritable; too many irons in the fire; fond of mental work.

☿ in 7   Well-balanced thought, or not; talented mate; cooperation; early marriage; refined; dishonest to partner, if afflicted.

☿ in 8   Penetrative insight; mind turns on death or the mysterious; early sex experiences; sly, sarcastic.

☿ in 9   Earnest; religious, or a doubter; propagandist; rash or dissolute, if afflicted.

☿ in 10 Wants facts; quick rather than thorough; changes in occupation, or many occupations at one time; usually cheerful and successful.

☿ in 11 Mind active; original; comprehensive; wants cultured friends; new ideas; intuitive; idealistic; treachery to or from friends, if afflicted.

☿ in 12 Secretive-in thought, or towards brethren; interest in the psychic; if afflicted trouble through brethren, or through writings. Can analyze people's problems clearly.

VENUS IN ANY OF THE TWELVE HOUSES

House

♀ in 1 Kindness, beauty, harmony, intuition, balance, compromise, vanity, good luck; happy disposition.

♀ in 2 Prosperity; contentment; intuition in getting money; money through partner or art; lucky.

♀ in 3 Harmonious with brethren; profit in travel; luxurious travel or for art; sees other person's point of view; compromises; mentally refined; or lazy; dilettante.

♀ in 4 Fond of parents; parents well off; good endings to enterprises; fond of eating; marriage usually late, but happy.

♀ in 5 Happy love affairs; success in speculation; artistic creativeness; gain through children.

♀ in 6 Gives happy and contented service; has good will of servants; sometimes works for a woman; love of artistic work.

♀ in 7 Happy in marriage; ability to harmonize; partner does work; popular with the public; success in law.

♀ in 8 Legacy or gain through partner; gain by insurance; peaceful death; sometimes the death of a loved one.

♀ in 9 Harmony with in-laws; good for long journeys; but not much inclination for them; keen intuitions, religious harmony, or lazy indifference.

♀ in 10 Social success; gain through women or art; well liked; lucky; one of the parents helpful in profession.

♀ in 11 Happy associations; benefits from friends; romance among friends; artistic friends.

♀ in 12 Joy in occult things; many secret love affairs; undoing through love or through women; resigned in trouble.

MARS IN ANY OF THE TWELVE HOUSES

House

♂ in 1 Self-assertiveness, combativeness, boisterousness, positiveness, martial bearing, courage, physical strength, pride.

♂ in 2 Money through enterprise: extravagant; strife regarding money; has to work hard for money.

♂ in 3 Many journeys for new ideas; trouble on journeys; trouble with brethren; impulsive mind; anger; does not consolidate plans.

♂ in 4 Works in home; strife in home; changes in home; danger of fire, lack of order; strife at end of life.

♂ in 5 Ardent in love; restless; reckless in speculation; gambling; trouble with and through children; quarrelsome in games.

♂ in 6 Energetic worker both in mind and body; friction in work; high fevers when ill; accidents.

♂ in 7 Energies stimulated by marriage; early or hasty marriage; strife with partner, legal difficulties.

♂ in 8 Strife over partner's money; strife regarding legacies; accidents or fevers may cause severe illnesses.

♂ in 9 Enthusiastic mind; independent; religious zeal; skepticism; strife with in-laws; strife in foreign lands; much travel.

♂ in 10 Mechanical ability or pursuits; risky positions; strife with public; scandal; trouble with father.

♂ in 11 Friends with mechanical ability; military friends; sometimes risky friends; strife with friends or loved ones.

♂ in 12 Works and fights for all in trouble, if well aspected; if not, violent enemies; false accusations; confinement in public institutions; works to escape from them.

I

JUPITER IN ANY OF THE TWELVE HOUSES

House

♃ in 1   Benevolence; loves travel and open air; breezy; opportunities through rich people; kindly, happy; if afflicted, impatient, rash, noisy.

♃ in 2   Sympathetic, benevolent, spendthrift, showy; good judgment, or none, regarding finance.

♃ in 3   Witty; helps relatives; likes change; lofty ideals, practical. or superficial; credulous; happy-go-lucky; good judgment, unless afflicted.

♃ in 4   Devoted to home; likes fine surroundings; benefit through real estate; greedy, if afflicted; benefits in old age.

♃ in 5   Love of grandeur; speculation; expects gain through love; sensuous; values approbation.

♃ in 6   Interested in philanthropy; chooses servants well; expects reward from work; ability to organize groups of workers.

♃ in 7   Conscientious in marriage; marries generous person, or for money; good judgment, or none, regarding marriage.

♃ in 8   Resourceful; occult; good judgment regarding partner's money; none, if afflicted; is subtle.

♃ in 9   Faith, toleration, devotion, aspiration; love of sport; interested in publications; sectarianism, travels expensively.

♃ in 10 Leader, authoritative, conventional, trustworthy, self-reliant; proud, ambitious.

♃ in 11 Has generous, helpful friends; social reformer; or restless, lazy, sponger among his friends.

♃ in 12 Kind to poor and needy; hospitable; gives secretly; doubting; self-indulgent; mediumistic; resourceful in own trouble; luck when in difficulty.

SATURN IN ANY OF THE TWELVE HOUSES

House

♄ in 1   Reserved, serious, conscientious, patient, aristocratic; desire for power; limitations during childhood; wants to go forward but is timid in early life.

♄ in 2   Anxiety concerning money; earns it through hard work; his lesson is the conquest of fear and conquest of desire to economize unjustly; invests safely; afflicted, causes poverty.

♄ in 3   Patience, tact; matter-of-fact; difficulties among relatives, especially in early life; sometimes lack of early education.

♄ in 4   Anxiety concerning old age; discontent; oversensitive; forebodings; unhappy in home; sometimes early death of a parent or difficulty with parent; old people in the home.

♄ in 5   Sorrow through love or children; speculates wisely; never rash; may lose through timidity and delay.

♄ in 6   Unpopular in employment; very exacting, but reliable; success in municipal or government employ.

♄ in 7   Difficulties and disappointments in partnership and marriage; one or the other partner has a feeling of arrogance; superiority; sometimes disparity in age or temperament.

♄ in 8   No financial gain through marriage; disappointments in legacies and money; resentful; death by old age.

♄ in 9   Orthodox; distrustful of new ideas; earnest; desires to know everything thoroughly.

♄ in 10   Accepts responsibility and desires it; demands respect; much arrogance and ambition; melancholy; jealous; trouble through father; if afflicted, may lose position.

♄ in 11 Reserved among friends; must be respected; feels responsibility towards friends; hopes and wishes rarely realized; trouble through children, since this is opposite Leo's house.

♄ in 12 Morbidly sensitive; inclined to isolate himself; fearful of fate; needs to cultivate hope.

URANUS IN ANY OF THE TWELVE HOUSES

House

♅ in 1 Original ideas; inversion of ideas; breadth of vision and insight; explosive, perverse, abrupt; difficult to know or understand; tactless, dictatorial.

♅ in 2 Original methods of gaining money; upsets in finance.

♅ in 3 Genius; inventiveness; abusive in speech, if afflicted; sudden journeys; brilliant writer; unconventional, a crank.

♅ in 4 Many changes in home life; does not understand one of the parents; mother original.

♅ in 5 Many strange love affairs; love at first sight; unaccountable upsets through children; fond of speculation and gambling.

♅ in 6 Inventive; likes to work his own way; nervous; many changes in work; peculiar illnesses.

♅ in 7 Sudden marriage or sudden divorce; an original partner.

♅ in 8 Upsets concerning partner's money; interest in the occult, and life after death.

♅ in 9 Illumination; strange journeys; inventive, resourceful; not orthodox in religion; the unexpected in legal affairs.

♅ in 10 Not understood by public; inventive; original work brings native before the public; father may be inventive.

⛢ in 11   Strange and original friends; desire to help humanity in original ways.

⛢ in 12   Desire to break through convention and restraint;
works in original ways; if afflicted, sudden reversal
of fortunes; breaks out of restraint.

NEPTUNE IN ANY OF THE TWELVE HOUSES

House

♆ in 1   Refinement; gentleness; vagueness; unreliable;
fussy; imaginative; discontented; a dreamer; changes
plans and ideas with moods; may be musical.

♆ in 2   Philanthropic in ideals; careless regarding money
matters; often extremes in fortune and misfortune;
danger of trickery in money; may earn through
music or the sea.

♆ in 3   Mediumistic; not understood by relatives; needs to
cultivate courage and action; hallucinations; fond
of travel; strange adventures.

♆ in 4   Dreams of ideal home; strange conditions in the
home; many changes; bad for real estate or mining;
music in home.

♆ in 5   Idealism in love; loss through deception or the unexpected; trouble with, or loss of, children; inclined
to gamble.

♆ in 6   Illness often brought on by morbid fancies; strange
conditions in employment; deception by servants;
sickness is difficult to diagnose.

♆ in 7   Idealistic concepts of marriage; love to work with
mystics and artists; must be content without material gain in any alliance; afflicted, trouble or deceit
in partnership.

♆ in 8   Psychic; thinks much regarding after-life; disappointment through money.

♆ in 9   Love of long journeys and sea travel; mystical in religion; strange dreams; fond of music.

♆ in 10   Often presents new vision to the world; ordinary people think him queer; under affliction, scandal and downfall; good position for musician.

♆ in 11   Unusual friends; meets friends in strange ways; may be deceived through friends; musical friends.

♆ in 12   Love of the mysterious; secret orders; strange troubles in life; morbid; needs to exert himself for others, and not day dream.

PLUTO IN THE TWELVE HOUSES

House

♇ in 1   Changes in personality during early life.

♇ in 2   Changes in financial standing.

♇ in 3   Changes brought about by relatives, or letters.

♇ in 4   Changes in the home.

♇ in 5   Changes in romance.

♇ in 6   Changes in health conditions, or work.

♇ in 7   Changes in partnership.

♇ in 8   Changes regarding wills or legacies.

♇ in 9   Changes in religious outlook.

♇ in 10   Changes in the profession.

♇ in 11   Changes among friends, hopes, and wishes.

♇ in 12   Changes during restrictive periods.

Note that the changes brought about by Pluto arrive subtly, and not the obvious or expected way. When the change is perceived, one wonders why it has not been noticed before.

POSITION OF THE HOUSE RULER

The Ruler of the First House:

In the 1st: Generally fortunate. Able to achieve.

In the 2nd: Money through own desires and efforts.

In the 3rd: Interest in relatives and short journeys.

In the 4th: Interest in real estate and parentage.
In the 5th: Love of children, drama, or speculation.
In the 6th: Questions regarding health are important.
In the 7th: Desire for marriage. May be own enemy.
In the 8th: Legacy, or money from others.
In the 9th: Interest in travel, law, or philosophy.
In the 10th: Public success through own efforts.
In the 11th: Many friends. Strong hopes, and wishes.
In the 12th: Creates own restrictions.

The Ruler of the Second House:

In the 1st: Spends on the self.
In the 2nd: Main objective is wealth.
In the 3rd: Gain by writing, short journeys.
In the 4th: Money spent on home or family.
In the 5th: Money spent on children or speculation.
In the 6th: Gain through inferiors, pets, or health.
In the 7th: Marriage, or law brings money.
In the 8th: Legacy from partnership.
In the 9th: Travels in prosperity.
In the 10th: Spends on social life and profession.
In the 11th: Spends, or makes, through friends.
In the 12th: Gain through public institutions.

The Ruler of the Third House:

In the 1st: Many short journeys or removals.
In the 2nd: Gain through relatives or journeys.
In the 3rd: Interest in relatives, letters.
In the 4th: Travel through parent or property.
In the 5th: Romance on short journeys.
In the 6th: Short journeys due to health or work.
In the 7th: May work for, or marry, a relative.
In the 8th: Money through travel.
In the 9th: Love of long journeys.

In the 10th: Traveling salesman. Journeys for profession.
In the 11th: Journeys with, or due to friends.
In the 12th: Difficulties on journeys.

The Ruler of the Fourth House:

In the 1st: Personal help from a parent.
In the 2nd: Financial help from the home.
In the 3rd: Property interests with a relative.
In the 4th: Property in the family.
In the 5th: Gives property to children.
In the 6th: May work in, or from, home.
In the 7th: Property from partnership.
In the 8th: May inherit property.
In the 9th: Home may be abroad.
In the 10th: May use home as business place.
In the 11th: May give property to friends.
In the 12th: End of life is restrictive.

The Ruler of the Fifth House:

In the 1st: Love of children, and speculation.
In the 2nd: Money from children, or theatre.
In the 3rd: Love of drama and theatre.
In the 4th: Investments in property.
In the 5th: Fortunate in children or drama.
In the 6th: A child may be sickly.
In the 7th: Tends to romantic marriage.
In the 8th: Money spent on children.
In the 9th: Children love travel.
In the 10th: One child may be famous.
In the 11th: Romantic friendships.
In the 12th: Ill luck through gambling.

The Ruler of the Sixth House:

In the 1st: Causes own sickness.

In the 2nd: Money spent on servants or sickness.
In the 3rd: Likes service on short journeys.
In the 4th: Servants in the home.
In the 5th: Sickness through pleasure.
In the 6th: Servants helpful.
In the 7th: Hired help may become a partner.
In the 8th: Serious illnesses. Loss through inferiors.
In the 9th: Legal problems through inferiors.
In the 10th: Health ideas may become the profession.
In the 11th: Health of friends causes concern.
In the 12th: Servants may become enemies.

The Ruler of the Seventh House:

In the 1st: Early marriage. Obvious enemies.
In the 2nd: Gain through marriage.
In the 3rd: Marriage to relative or neighbor.
In the 4th: Marriage to person from home town.
In the 5th: Romantic marriage.
In the 6th: Marriage to an inferior.
In the 7th: Lucky in law, or marriage.
In the 8th: Money from partner.
In the 9th: Foreign partner. Inclines to lawsuits.
In the 10th: May marry employer, or superior.
In the 11th: May marry a friend.
In the 12th: Secret troubles through partnership.

The Ruler of the Eighth House:

In the 1st: During childhood many relatives die.
In the 2nd: Chances of legacies.
In the 3rd: Dangerous short journeys.
In the 4th: May die in own home.
In the 5th: Death through pleasures.
In the 6th: Death of servants.
In the 7th: Death of known enemy.

In the 8th: Gain through the dead.
In the 9th: Dangerous long journeys.
In the 10th: Public notice at death.
In the 11th: Death of friends.
In the 12th: Death of private enemies.

The Ruler of the Ninth House:

In the 1st: Foreign contacts.
In the 2nd: Money from law, or long journeys.
In the 3rd: Much travel or removal.
In the 4th: A parent may be foreign.
In the 5th: Teaches religion to own children.
In the 6th: Health problems arise on journeys.
In the 7th: Inclines to lawsuits.
In the 8th: Lawsuits expensive.
In the 9th: Interest in foreign languages.
In the 10th: Profession may be religion, law, or science.
In the 11th: Friends made on long-distance journeys.
In the 12th: Enmity experienced during travel.

The Ruler of the Tenth House:

In the 1st: A parent helps in business or profession.
In the 2nd: A parent helps the finances.
In the 3rd: Social contacts on short journeys.
In the 4th: A parent in the home.
In the 5th: Gain or prestige through children.
In the 6th: Business affected through sickness or em-
                 ployees.
In the 7th: Gain by partnership or marriage.
In the 8th: Gain through social status of parent.
In the 9th: Profession may be connected with law or reli-
                 gion, or may entail foreign contacts.
In the 10th: A parent helps profession or business.
In the 11th: Social standing helped by friend.
In the 12th: Profession connected with institutions.

The Ruler of the Eleventh House:

In the 1st: Realization of hopes depends on self.
In the 2nd: Finances increased through friendships.
In the 3rd: Friends on short journeys and by letters.
In the 4th: Friends in the home.
In the 5th: Gain by children, or speculation.
In the 6th: Servants are on friendly basis.
In the 7th: Friendship helps marriage.
In the 8th: Death of friends.
In the 9th: Friends made during long-distance travel.
In the 10th: Important friends.
In the 11th: Friends help the objective of life.
In the 12th: Friends may become secret enemies.

The Ruler of the Twelfth House:

In the 1st: Secret enemies cause difficulties.
In the 2nd: Enemies cause financial loss.
In the 3rd: Troubles through relatives, or letters.
In the 4th: Danger of theft in the home.
In the 5th: Sickness to children, or difficult children.
In the 6th: Enemies among inferiors.
In the 7th: Strife with partner.
In the 8th: Death of enemies.
In the 9th: Troubles over religion, or law.
In the 10th: Secret enemies in the profession.
In the 11th: Enemies among groups of friends.
In the 12th: Enemies harm themselves.

LESSON TWELVE

The Meaning and Value of Aspects

♈ ♉ ♊ ♋ ♌ ♍ ♎ ♏ ♐ ♑ ♒ ♓

INTRODUCTION: In astrology, it is not the distance of one planet from another that affects us; it is the angle between them. Centuries of observation have proved that certain astrological angles cause a harmonious action, whereas others cause conflict and disharmony. These angular distances are called aspects.

It puzzles some students at first to understand why a good aspect can sometimes lead to difficulty and trouble. Here we have to go back to the basic nature of the planets. An aspect is merely a linking together of two planetary forces. For example, if Mars is undisciplined, it is not likely to be disciplined by the nebulous Neptune, even under a good aspect. It could, however, be disciplined by a good aspect of Saturn. Saturn trine Mars might lead to the appreciation of discipline. Saturn square Mars might be a discipline which would be enforced in spite of all resistance. Mars trine Neptune might lead by the easy path to drink, dope, accident, or gambling.

The terms good and bad as applied to aspects make the student think that good or bad events must result. The terms merely mean aspects that enable, or aspects that block or prevent. Evil can be prevented or blocked by a square. Saturn opposing Uranus helped to end World War I.

In this lesson we have not included Pluto aspects, since these still require research. Note all the Pluto aspects in the charts you study, and start your own research notebook.

During the process of learning the meaning of the planets in the various signs, you noted that harmony was established when certain planets swung through signs with which they had affinity, whereas inharmony began when planets swung into signs with which they had no affinity. Friction can be useful or troublesome, according to the soul development of the native.

There is another factor by means of which we determine harmony, or inharmony, within the horoscope—aspects. Aspects fall into two major groups—good and bad, harmonious and inharmonious; aspects of inclination and those of compulsion, those of ease and those of friction. Do not be afraid of so-called "bad" aspects. Some of the noblest and finest people have had the greatest array of inharmonious aspects. Because they have had to overcome the forces that hindered them, they have become strong. Too many trines in a chart merely represent what has been handed to the native on a silver platter. Trines do not call forth effort. Sextiles call forth considerable effort, but the action succeeds without too much friction. Friction is the result of inharmonious action, but without friction we should live in a world without heat or light, and we should slide along polished surfaces without a brake. Trines keep the status quo, and make little progress.

Evil does not have to enter with inharmonious aspects if the basic character is strong; hence, before the student attempts to study aspects in an actual chart, he must go through the horoscope, as we have previously shown him, and size up the character. Until this has been done, aspects throw the student on wrong tracks.

Planets in their dignity or exaltation, can withstand all the adverse aspects possible without being thrown off balance for long. Planets in their fall or detriment, may not show any inspiring conduct even under good aspects.

A person with a weak Ascendant, or a weak Mercury, may have difficulty in handling slightly bad aspects, while a person with a strong Ascendant, and a strong Sun and Moon, will conquer every obstacle. The beginner goes wrong on this subject of aspects because he seems to think they are all-important. They merely represent the helps, or hindrances, of life. The weak soul needs help all the time, while the strong soul exults in having overcome something worthy of his strength.

Aspects are important in bringing about specific events. Events lie within the birth chart as potentialities. The good or ill brought about through events is modified by the development of character that has taken place during the intervening years. The timing of events is revealed through Progressions and Transits.

Events, and the greater part of what we call destiny, result from character. People who have not developed patience, conscience, strength and grit, bring into manifestation events which are the result of their own inharmony. Selfishness is the keynote of practically all the sins. For example, laziness is simply a dislike of putting the activities of the body and brain into use, because it pleases the self not to do so. Theft is indulgence of the desire to appropriate to ourselves what belongs to others. Envy, jealousy, and meanness result from wanting to possess people or things that belong to others.

The student will realize from the above that the interpretation of aspects must be based upon a real knowledge as to whether the native puts self first, or whether he has risen to a stage of consciousness wherein he co-operates and can work in harmony with, other people.

Bad aspects in charts of these latter people can only be interpreted as the evil things that other people do to them, or the difficulties encountered in the fulfillment of their ideas and enterprises. Very few things are under destiny. We cannot choose our birth, nor our childhood experiences. We all have to die some time, and so does everyone else. The time when loved ones die is under destiny. It is not something we can avert. However, most of our actions are those of our choice, under given circumstances. We should strive to meet all events in a mood that is constructive, and not destructive.

Under the aspects of Mars we can meet people and events with fortitude and courage. Under Saturn's aspects, we can meet events with moroseness and melancholy, or with patience and philosophy. Under Neptune, we can meet events in chaos of spirit and in confusion, or with an understanding such as will reveal the whole mystery of life.

We cannot understand an aspect from a mere statement that one planet is trine or square to another. We must know the sign and house of each planet. The effect of Venus square Moon is very different when the square is from the Fifth to the Eighth Houses, than it is when the square involves the Second and Fifth Houses. Again, Venus in Libra square Mars in Capricorn is very different in effect from Venus in Scorpio square Mars in Leo.

If two planets are each strongly placed by sign and house, but are in conflict with one another, then the inharmonious aspect will call forth the strength and power of each planet, and the aspect will cause the native to accomplish something that no one under good aspects would take the trouble to do. If, however, one planet is strong by sign and house, and the other is debilitated, then the latter will represent the thing, person, matter, or defect in character that causes difficulty.

The birth chart represents the moment in time when the child is born. This moment has been acted upon by all kinds of vibrations. It has been subjected to change and modifications. The character has been maturing, yet just as a maple does not grow into an oak, so the birth chart will keep the individual within his own pattern. Within that pattern, he can make improvements. When Theodore Roosevelt was young it was thought that he was subject to tuberculosis, but by care and thought he made his body strong and efficient. The stars impel, but they do not compel.

Aspects between planets show tendencies, abilities, and disabilities, rather than attainment. We often see greater attainment in the chart of a person who has less ability, than in one with more, because we find greater persistance, greater zeal, or greater enthusiasm.

The harmonious aspects are: the trine, sextile, semisextile, quintile, and bi-quintile.
The inharmonious aspects are: the opposition, square, semi-square, quadra-sextile, and sesqui-quadrate.
The conjunction is harmonious, or otherwise, according to the agreement, or disagreement, in the nature of the planets conjoined.

CONDITIONS AND CIRCUMSTANCES CAUSED BY SUN ASPECTS

The Sun is the significator of the person in authority; hence, aspects to the Sun manifest in positions of authority, success, and honor. In a woman's chart, the Sun can represent marriage, or success to the marriage partner. In both male and female charts, it can refer to the father, or to the employer; hence ill aspects to the Sun can represent difficulties with, or to, the father or employer.

Sometimes a well-aspected Sun merely indicates cheerfulness, happiness, social contacts, and good health. The ill-aspected Sun indicates the reverse. Under good aspects from the Sun and Venus, romance or success may come into the life. One may have pleasant times with children, or receive a gift. One might visit the jeweler and make a purchase. Under bad aspects one is more likely to visit the pawnbroker or moneylender, and pleasant times and success seem to recede.

When the Sun makes good aspects to the planets of mind, Mercury and Jupiter, a constructive attitude is fostered. Things that have formerly presented difficulties become easy to accomplish. The mind takes new strides.

The Sun with the Ascendant and its ruler, are the main

factors in estimating the general health and vitality of a man. The Moon with the Ascendant and its ruler, are the main factors in estimating the health of a woman.

ASPECTS OF THE SUN

☉ to ☽   **Harmonious**—Harmony between parents. Harmony with parents. Contented in mind. Confident. Well liked by employer and by men and women in general. Personality is genial and helpful in employment. Optimistic; usually happy in marriage; works without friction.

Inharmonious—Some inharmony or lack of understanding between parents, or with parents. Disparity in marriage. Disagreements with employer. Inclined to change the profession. Often conflict between some actual work and some hobby, which is more interesting.

☉ to ☿   **Harmonious**—Intensifies the importance of the Sun sign, if conjoined. Has mental understanding of the Sun sign, and of its purpose in life.

Inharmonious—The aspect can never be more than 28 degrees from the Sun, hence can never be evil. It may not, however, be in the same sign as the Sun, in which case it calls forth extra fields of interest.

☉ to ♀   **Harmonious**—Active demonstration of affection and love nature. Gives kindness, affection, and benefits from the father, husband, or employer. Love of fine arts and beautiful surroundings, or love of pleasure.

Inharmonious—The aspect can only be 48 degrees from the Sun; hence the semi-square is the only ill aspect. Inclines to jealousy and separation from the loved one.

⊙ to ♂   **Harmonious**—Desire for freedom, adventure, action, and hard kinds of work. To think is to act. The type of courage will depend on the sign and house position of both planets.

Inharmonious—Confers great energy, but creates disagreements and separation. Lacks poise. Rarely reaps the benefit of his activities.

⊙ to ♃   **Harmonious**—Contentment, benevolence, kindness. Gives benefits from superiors and from men of wealth and standing. Religious but orthodox. Tact and diplomacy. Success in legal matters.

Inharmonious—Discontent with parents, employer, or with religion. Many differences of opinion and judgment with those in authority. Little luck in law. Ability to branch out into new methods of earning money, new philosophies, and new endeavors.

⊙ to ♄   **Harmonious**—Patience, responsibility, depth of character, industrious. Wins the favor of older people, and those in settled walks of life. The father is usually successful and helpful.

Inharmonious—Lack of sympathy with the father, or with older people. Must work hard to make a success. Lacking in tact or self-expression. Inferiority complex. In a woman's chart, restriction through father or husband. Marriage may be delayed.

⊙ to ♅   **Harmonious**—Independence of thought and outlook. Highly magnetic, forceful, original, and inventive. Ability to lead and enthuse others. Unexpected good luck. Brilliance of thought. Powerful friends. Strong-willed.

Inharmonious—Capable of leadership and authority, but often loses through unexpected circumstances, or precipitate action. The unexpected comes through the father or employer with men. With women through the father or husband.

⊙ to ♥ **Harmonious**—Ability to see a completed work in all its details before starting it. Love of the sea, also of large animals. Profession may be connected with the sea or with liquids, religion, or psychic matters. **Inharmonious**—May contact deceit through people who promise too much. Misfortune through things of Neptune. Father or husband not a good provider, but may try to be. Feeling of insecurity.

CONDITIONS AND CIRCUMSTANCES CAUSED BY MOON ASPECTS

Aspects from the Moon to other planets can be understood only when you have a thorough understanding of the qualities of the Moon. The house and sign in which it is placed is important since aspects to the Moon may call into action the sign of Cancer and the Fourth House.

Since the Moon represents the personality, aspects from other planets can modify the personality. Moon aspects may reveal likes and dislikes, desires and interests, changes in the family, etc. Under good aspects to Neptune and Venus there may be a tendency towards daydreaming. Under aspects of Mars and Jupiter activity is called forth, and there can be an expansion of interests. Under aspects from Saturn patience and responsibility can be developed, or inhibitions, frustration, and sadness, may be caused.

ASPECTS OF THE MOON

☽ to ☿ **Harmonious**—Mind and emotion work together. Ability for writing and communicating mental efforts to other people. Ability to teach. Directness of mind. Stays young in ideas. Clear logical mind. **Inharmonious**—Conflict between mind and emo- ·

tion. Difficulties with women, the public, or one's reputation. Mind not conventional; hence the public does not understand one's ideas and actions.

☽ to ♀   **Harmonious**—Tends towards love of the mother or child. Popularity. Benefits from public work, or through women. Inclines to geniality, self-confidence, love of music, art, and sociability. Life may be too easy, and native may become selfish, self-indulgent, or frivolous.

Inharmonious—Difficulty in being recognized or appreciated by the public. Women and the public rarely confer benefits. Conflict or separation from a loved one. Some early inhibition may destroy confidence in the self.

☽ to ♂   **Harmonious**—Somewhat brusque in manner. Physically strong and active. Courage is a natural gift. May espouse an unpopular cause, and win. Straightforward. Direct expression.

Inharmonious—Dislike of control. Strife with mother or in the home. Liable to extremes of thought and action. Sarcastic and sharp spoken. May act rashly and think too late. May mean well, but is perverse.

☽ to ♃   **Harmonious**—Inclines to cheerfulness, contentment, and good health. Meets people of higher social status. Fond of horses and large animals. Likes open air life and sports, or may become interested in Ninth House affairs, e.g. law, religion, travel, publications, etc. May be merely diffusive and easygoing.

Inharmonious—May not agree with parents or people in family circle concerning religion. May lose social status at some time, perhaps only temporarily through journeys, or own ideas. Little luck in law,

or in foreign lands. Some lack of judgment. May
have much pride. Inability to humble the self for
gain.

☽ to ♄   **Harmonious**—Increases practicality. Careful and
prudent. Rarely express feelings. Contented, and
inclined to stay in a rut. Holds to traditions. May
fear the new. Attracted to old people, stable people,
leaders in industry, and government.

Inharmonious—Desires to move out of ruts and
traditional courses. The personality outgrows family
routine. Some fear felt in moving out of the old,
but finally will do so. Unpopular with women and
the public. Shy, reserved, and discontented in early
life, but later may be more patient and reliable
than people with good aspects to Saturn.

☽ to ♅   **Harmonious**—Tends to act spasmodically and without foresight. Acts from intuition rather than from
reason. May be inventive or merely destructive.
Very independent. Dislikes routine and restraint.
Love of what is unusual. Unexpected events in the
life. Original, dramatic, and dynamic methods of
presenting self or work to the public.

Inharmonious—Unexpected difficulties with family
or home. Disruptive to family life. Acts spasmodically and apparently without reason. Breaks up old
conventions and traditions. Life may become haz-
ardous and unconventional. Always has a new plan.
The aspect is often found in charts of reformers, inventors, occultists, astrologers, etc.

☽ to ♆   **Harmonious**—Neptune lures and allures with all
kinds of visions, good and bad. It depends upon the
innate strength and worth of the character whether
the native will walk into a fool's paradise, or into a
real one. Neptune can make a confirmed gambler,

or a saint. It inclines to mysticism in religion. May be musical or poetical.

Inharmonious—Under bad aspects, as well as under good ones, there is a dislike of facing reality, hence laziness, morbidity, etc. are often given high-sounding names. May be deception from the home circle, or some lack of interest. Danger of scandal or discredit. Queer accusations may be made against the native. In early life, fear of death, but later a desire to study spiritualism, and occult things. Easily upset by music or poetry wherein the rhythm is not to his liking.

CONDITIONS AND CIRCUMSTANCES CAUSED BY MERCURY ASPECTS

The planet of mind, Mercury, confers the ability to communicate ideas; hence, thought, speech, letter-writing, the alphabet, telephones, telegraphs, travel by land, sea and air, all may be brought into prominence through aspects of Mercury. Mercury was the god of commerce and industry. He gave facility in making and in selling. The planet rules brethren, relatives, and acquaintances. Under good aspects pleasant associations are enjoyed; under adverse aspects it is difficult to please. When young people want to start a new study, it is easier for them to do so when Mercury forms a good aspect with a planet whose nature signifies the type of study; thus, artistic development would come under Mercury to Venus, engineering from Mercury to Mars, or law under Mercury to Jupiter.

Short journeys may be started under aspects of Mercury, so can new ventures in business and trade. Under favorable aspects matters progress without so much effort; under adverse aspects thought and nervous energy have to be expended if .success is to result.

☿ to ♀   **Harmonious**—Facility for expressing thought gracefully and agreeably. Cheerful among relatives and acquaintances. Affectionate interest in friends. Witty, laughs readily. Entertaining.

            Inharmonious—Difficulties among relatives and acquaintances. Desire to tease or to say the wrong thing. Friction with women, and children. Somewhat irritable or critical.

☿ to ♂   **Harmonious**—Sharp keen intellect. Courageous in speech and action. Good position for military strategists, trial lawyers, and engineers. Works hard for relatives and friends. Tends to popularity. Trustworthy.

            Inharmonious—Irritable, may indulge in displays of temper. Nervous system easily upset. Inability to harmonize with mother and friends. As brilliant mentally as with the good aspect, but the native is generally disliked until he reforms. Sarcastic.

☿ to ♃   **Harmonious**—Tends to optimism, good nature. Thoughtful. Generally prosperous. Not overambitious. Not too fond of hard work. Orthodox in religion. Well liked. Wants to be thought a public benefactor, and often is so.

            Inharmonious—Unorthodox in religion. Reason (Mercury) is in conflict with faith (Jupiter). The geniality of Jupiter tends to be lost in this combination, which tends to sharpness of expression, possibly in conceit. Judgment may be expressed without much reason. Tendency to quarrel about ideas. Ready debater.

☿ to ♄   **Harmonious**—Ability to organize large schemes down to the smallest details. Somewhat hard in nature. Little sympathy with careless people. Reserved and somewhat solitary. No interest in small talk.

Inharmonious—Conflicts with relatives and acquaintances. Rarely popular among friends. Inclined to be melancholy, full of inhibitions, and fears. Critical of old ideas.

☿ to ♅ Harmonious—Great insight and originality. Keen intuitions. Loves change, variety, and strong drama. Independence of thought. Inventive. Advanced views on many subjects. No sympathy with dull people.

Inharmonious—Displays nervous tension. Dislikes routine. Conflicts with relatives and acquaintances. The will power (Uranus) is in conflict with common sense (Mercury). Never still. Works hard, if interested. Defies all kinds of restraint.

☿ to ♆ Harmonious—The mind is open to suggestion, hence it depends upon the quality of the ego whether it responds to beauty or to dissoluteness. Usually kind and gentle. May write on artistic matters. Can interpret intricate problems. Interest in the sea or soil.

Inharmonious—Other people may decieve the native, or he may decieve others. Restless, dissatisfied, knowing not why. Subject to slander or loss of popularity through inexplicable reasons. Losses through products under Neptune.

CONDITIONS AND CIRCUMSTANCES CAUSED BY VENUS ASPECTS

Venus is the principle of attraction and coagulation. It welds people and things together; hence all attachments come under Venus. Under good aspects these come into happy manifestation. Being a feminine planet, it rules women in general. The native's liking for women, or dislike, is disclosed by aspects to Venus. Art goods and beauty of environment are indicated or denied by the aspects to Venus. Inharmonious aspects to Venus may show lack of appreciation of art. Good aspects between Venus and Mars may give desire for possession. Inharmonious ones may bring loss of valuable objects. When placed in signs or houses inharmonious to itself, Venus can become very unlike itself, and become selfish, lazy, and gluttonous.

ASPECTS OF VENUS

♀ to ♂   **Harmonious**—Strengthens the affectional nature. Highly romantic. Fond of children. Courage in love. Will work for the loved one. Can make artistic metal products.

            Inharmonious—Inclines to faultfinding with loved one. Quarrels, separations, or tragedies. In a man's chart gives pride and arrogance. In a woman's quick temper. In both there is little peace or harmony.

♀ to ♃   **Harmonious**—Brings many romances, much praise and many benefits. Fond of flattery. In highly developed characters there is graciousness, and ability to express lofty sentiments. Generally fortunate. Liked in foreign countries.

            Inharmonious—Excess of feeling through love, religion, and politics, yet may change opinions and beliefs. Popularity may not be sought,* but detractors may be numerous. Troubles through law and authority.

♀ to ♄   **Harmonious**—Difficult and hard experiences through love, but native's own love nature wears well. Joy consists in being patient, and dutiful. Will work hard and be helpful. Love of an older person, or one previously married.

            Inharmonious—May become a tyrant to the loved one, or suffer from the tyranny of loved ones. Few benefits through women or children. Sorrow through love. Separation from loved one. Inclines to jealousy, and coldness.

♀ to ♅   **Harmonious**—Sudden benefits or popularity. Many loves at first sight. Eccentric in manner. May have great charm. Is entertaining and dramatic. Loves designing artistic things.

Inharmonious—Just as sensitive and emotional as the good aspects, but may have a stronger urge to do something definite. Anxiety or misapprehension in love matters. Inability to keep financial affairs straight. Dislike of conventions. Lack of interior peace.

♀ to ♆   **Harmonious**—Inclines to dreams and visions rather than to practicality. Sympathetic, emotional. Tends to love of the sea, mysticism, poetry, and music. Fond of large animals. Tends to luck in gambling.

Inharmonious—Confusion or deceit in romance. Loss of loved ones. Tendency to lose valued articles. People exaggerate native's slightest actions. Often wrongly suspected.

CONDITIONS AND CIRCUMSTANCES CAUSED BY MARS ASPECTS

Mars is the principle of dynamic activity. It causes new things and new conditions to manifest themselves. These will be of the nature of the sign and house of Mars, modified by the nature of the planet that is acted upon. Under good aspects to Venus romance can come in; under inharmonious aspects romance can be broken. Under good aspects to Mercury literary activity can be stimulated or selling campaigns organized, also relatives can be helpful or recieve help. If in the Second House, Mars can cause rash spending when under good aspects. Under bad ones it can cause loss. Afflicting the Midheaven, Mars can cause calumny. Under good aspects it can cause progress. Mars can bring benefit from military men, surgeons, workers in metals, and mathematicians. When afflicted in Water signs Mars disturbs the emotional nature; in earth signs it may cause loss to property. In Air signs it can cause rash ideas and ventures; in Fire signs it can cause relentless zeal.

ASPECTS OF MARS

♂ to ♃   **Harmonious**—Leads the activities into new and worthwhile channels. Fond of open-air exercise, travel, and sports. Often this aspect is found in those with religious zeal. Gives a desire to reconstruct the world. Inclines to be an engineering architect.

Inharmonious—Highly excitable, desire for strong drama. May cause precipitate legal action. Inclines to act first, and think later.

♂ to ♄   **Harmonious**—The activities are disciplined by prudence, foresight and hard work. Much is accomplished without fuss.

Inharmonious—There may be periods when action is inhibited; also periods when inhibition may break out into rash acts.

♂ to ♅   **Harmonious**—The energy of Mars is stimulated in all kinds of original ways. Courage to carry out activities that are dangerous. The will power is strong. The native may undertake great risks. Usually successful.

Inharmonious—Tends to irritability and high tension. Goes own way regardless of what people think. Tends to sudden losses in money and position. Abrupt. May be foolhardy. The aspect is disruptive, and native does not build steadily.

♂ to ♆   **Harmonious**—Ability to carry out what is visualized. Straightforward and practical, but intuitive. May

work in occupations connected with the sea, or oil.
Creatively artistic.

Inharmonious—Intensifies the imagination. Can be
creatively artistic as much as with the good aspect.
Gives ability to surmount obstacles in own way, e.g.
Helen Keller. The obstacles may be too strong for
a weak soul to master.

CONDITIONS AND CIRCUMSTANCES CAUSED
BY JUPITER ASPECTS

Jupiter rules the principle of expansion. It confers interest
in abstract thought, religion, jurisprudence, and foreign travel.
It governs people of wealth and social standing, also scholastic
standing. Under good aspects the judgment is reliable; under
unfavorable aspects there can be some warping of the judgment.

Jupiter bestows a protective influence. Help may come in
various ways signified by the sign and house position of the
planet. Contrary to popular opinion Jupiter does not always
confer wealth. Under good aspects the native may feel he has
much. Under contrary aspects he may think he needs more,
or he may spend more than he should. However, under these
aspects he may desire to branch out and expand. Rich men may
have Jupiter afflicted, indicating that they may have been discontented with what they had, and so continually have sought
more.

ASPECTS OF JUPITER

♃ to ♄   **Harmonious**—Gives persistency in carrying ideas
through. Ability to carry responsibility without ap-
pearing overburdened. Note, it is Saturn rather than
Jupiter in this aspect that indicates the hard work.
Jupiter prefers others to work, hence Saturn is necessary before the Jupiterian will work hard.

Inharmonious—Good fortune may be obtained only by a maximum of hard work. Is just as efficient as with the good aspect, but perhaps not so popular. Saturn dampens some of the joviality of Jupiter. May have a father who is unlucky.

♃ to ♅   Harmonious—Ability to form lasting friendships with people who have unusual ability. Thoughtful, inventive, and resourceful. Tends to good advertising campaigns. Interested in propaganda—on radio, etc. Can find new solutions for old problems.

Inharmonious—Views may be too original to be immediately acceptable. May be conflict with church or political party. Should not go to law. Makes quick, swift judgments of his own.

♃ to ♆   Harmonious—Idealistic. Inclined to help all people in trouble. Tends somewhat to daydreaming, and love of ease. May run blindly into get-rich-quick schemes. Interest in international affairs, importing and exporting, shipping.

Inharmonious—Deceit from others or to others. Difficulties in law or religion. Troubles on long voyages. Love of the mysterious. Dislike of authority. Desires freedom, even license.

CONDITIONS AND CIRCUMSTANCES CAUSED BY SATURN ASPECTS

Saturn rules the principle of contraction and of crystallization; hence it rules conservative types of people and thought. Under inharmonious aspects it can cause delays, sorrow, and poverty. Under harmonious rays it confers stability of character, honesty of purpose, and rectitude. It gives the ability to accumulate facts and experience; hence Saturn aspects are important when building up a business. Most business executives have a strongly placed Saturn. Saturn provides the determination to succeed. It inclines towards governmental work, and an interest in church organizations.

Under affliction it may cause fear and worry, despondency, suspicion and jealousy. In whatever astrological house it is placed, it indicates the native's necessity for duty. The aspects show whether the duty is accepted with pleasure or with rebellious feelings.

ASPECTS OF SATURN

♄ to ♅   **Harmonious**—One's will harmonizes with the will of those in authority. Orginality is combined with practicality. Gives patience in bringing ideas into concrete expression. Executive ability. Courageous. Unexpected good luck.

         Inharmonious—Inharmony between one's own will and those in authority. Lack of patience with routine. Strife with parent, employer, or government. A hard struggle to promote one's ideas. Unexpected hard luck. Social status may suffer or be thrown aside.

♄ to ♆   **Harmonious**—The vision of Neptune can be put into practical form, however difficult. Good position for composers, writers, etc. Interest in the sea, chain-store promotion, oil, perfume, etc.

         Inharmonious—Much disappointment before success manifests, e.g. Henry Ford. Lack of support for ideas, also suspicion. Father may be involved in fanciful schemes, or dies early.

CONDITIONS AND CIRCUMSTANCES CAUSED BY URANUS ASPECTS

Uranus rules the principle of emancipation and freedom; hence it rules all that is inventive, since invention implies a departure from old methods. The position of Uranus in the horoscope indicates where one departs from the norm. Its aspects represent the things that lead to changes. It is very difficult for the astrologer to estimate its action, for great inventions are products of highly developed minds. With lesser types of beings, Uranian aspects merely represent discontent and a general desire to remain out of step with convention.

Under the influence of Uranus the native may be seized by a blind impulse to act in such a way that later in the light of reason he may wonder at his action. It is separative in effect, and lacking in kindness. However, when aspected by Venus or Jupiter it may not seem so. It is the planet of astrology. In whatever astrological house it is placed, it tends to bring light to the affairs of that house. The matters of that house cannot be hidden.

ASPECTS OF URANUS

♅ to ♆   **Harmonious**—People with this aspect may be born to carry their age to higher levels. Ordinary people partake of the ideas and work done by these higher souls. In 1881 Uranus was in Virgo trine Neptune in Taurus. The trine aspect did not occur again until 1942, when Uranus in Gemini made a trine to Neptune in Libra. The former group of people brought great inventions and ideas to the world, and many of the 1942 group will do the same for future ages. **Inharmonious**—Indicates periods in history when children are born who will contact great difficulties, not necessarily of their own making, but of national or international import, e.g. in 1910, Neptune was in Cancer in opposition to Uranus in Capricorn. These children faced in early life some of the problems created by World War I—loss of home, or parents, etc., also in some countries great changes of government. In high souls under this aspect there is a release of cosmic forces resulting in new projects; in lesser souls, there has been manifested a total disregard for authority (Capricorn), and much emotional instability (Cancer).

CONDITIONS AND CIRCUMSTANCES CAUSED BY NEPTUNE ASPECTS

Neptune represents the principle of distillation and fermentation; hence it is difficult to estimate the effects of good or bad aspects to it. The decayed leaves can form leaf mold which can feed the new plants. The distillation of rose leaves can produce attar of roses. Sometimes an ill aspect to or from Neptune can represent the circumstances that make the native turn his consciousness from purely material affairs to those affecting his own soul. Aspects from Neptune may cause mere visionaries, or they may cause visions that ennoble humanity. Ill aspects cause lack of support, deceit, treachery, slander, intrigue, or death. In a chart that has no real strength, they may indicate easy paths to bad habits.

Good aspects to Neptune may represent a complete assurance of divine grace, and the attainment of spiritual knowledge. Sometimes they represent the ability to seize opportunity at the right moment—to see in advance. However, even the good aspects can lead to the quicksands. With a born gambler they can tempt him to gamble all he has, and more; the Neptunian is a born gambler. He can gamble, not merely with money, but with good name and fame. Neptune is a very subtle tempter. Beware of mirages when it makes aspects. These aspects test the depths of the soul. They can manifest in fourth dimensional consciousness wherein inner power is attained. The low type soul is attacked through his desires and wishes.

The effect of Neptune-Pluto aspects is still a matter for research. The last conjunction of the two planets occurred at the end of the nineteenth century at about seven or eight degrees Gemini—July 22, 1891, October 31, 1891, and April 25, 1892. Before this, they had not conjoined for about 492 years. These 1891–1892 conjunctions impinged almost exactly upon the Uranus of the United States horoscope of July 4, 1776, and they may have heralded a coming necessity for vast changes in foreign policy due to future inventions which would break down time and space.

Heavy planets do not always act quickly. They are like the giant liners that require the little tugboats to push, pull, and shove for hours before they show appreciable motion. The effects of what was set in motion in 1891–1892 will be felt for nearly five hundred years. As we said previously, Pluto has something to do with the atomic age. Perhaps it was because the conjunction impinged upon the inventive Uranus of the United States that this country was the first to make and to use the atomic bomb. Atomic energy will become a factor in industry in due course; hence, the next few hundred years will be so changed that present-day impossibilities will become realities.

Applying aspects are those in which a faster-moving planet moves towards the exact aspect of a heavier body.

Separating aspects are those in which a faster-moving body has passed the exact aspect of a heavier body.

Health and Occupation

♈ ♉ ♊ ♋ ♌ ♍ ♎ ♏ ♐ ♑ ♒ ♓

INTRODUCTION: *Until the sixteenth and seventeenth centuries practically all doctors studied astrology in their medical courses. Some of their findings have come down to us, and a few are in Lesson Thirteen. More modern astrologers have added thoughts on health factors under the rule of the newer planets. Students of astrology who wish to practice medicine are advised to take a recognized medical course.*

What occupation to follow makes an interesting astrological study. However, before a student advises a person too specifically about the profession, he should study numerous charts of people who have succeeded in this occupation.

Generally speaking, the Sixth House is the basic factor in regard to health. One should study the planets in this house, if any, and then the ruler of the cusp. The Ascendant must also be considered, because it acquaints you with the physical body. Since the Second House is the natural house of Taurus, it may disclose factors relating to the neck and throat. Since the Third House is the natural house of Gemini, it may disclose factors regarding the lungs and arms; and so on, throughout all the houses.

THE SUN IN REGARD TO HEALTH

The Sun is the life. It governs the heart, the spinal cord, the right eye in the male, and the left eye in the female. The Sun through its sign and house position declares where the main vigor lies. Bad aspects to the Sun do not always deplete the health. Even under affliction, the Sun may not reveal the seat of disturbance, but only the fact that vigor is being depleted. The planet aspecting the Sun may indicate what helps or saps strength. Good aspects, particularly from Venus and Jupiter, may indicate self-indulgence, overactivity, and too much pleasure, so that these aspects can cause sickness as much as can ill aspects.

THE MOON IN REGARD TO HEALTH

The Moon governs the stomach, alimentary canal, breasts, fluids of the body, tear ducts, mucous membranes, the left eye of males, and the right eye of females.

The Moon governs the movement of the tides in the physical world, and the ability of the body to grow, and to perform its instinctive functions. Since the Moon is the ruler of the night, it governs sleep; thus any too violent aspect from Mars, the Sun, or Uranus, is likely to cause insomnia. The Moon is the most important factor in the health of women, as its phases control the periods of conception, pregnancy, and child-birth.

The house and sign of the Moon are of importance in estimating the functional ability of the body. Planets in good aspect render help. Planets in bad aspect disturb the rhythm of the body, and tend to upset the sympathetic nervous system. Trouble may manifest in the eyesight, stomach, mucous membranes, etc. Since the Moon rules the fluids of the body, inharmony may manifest in abcesses, boils, etc.

MERCURY IN REGARD TO HEALTH

Mercury governs the nervous system, hence good aspects can give cool reliable nerves. Inharmonious aspects can cause irri-

tability, and tension. Mercury governs the five sense percep-
tions: taste, touch, sight, hearing, and smell. Note that Mercury does not necessarily rule the organ causing perception.
For example, Mars rules the nose and tongue, but Mercury
rules the nerves that must react to cause smell and taste. Our
tongue may not have received any injury, yet everything may
taste like ashes, due to inactivity of the nerve, perhaps through
a cold.

Mercury rules the bronchial tubes, the thyroid glands, and
the function of respiration, thus if afflicted, this planet may
cause asthma, difficulty in breathing, or lung trouble.

It will depend to a large extent upon Mercury's sign and
house where the strength or weakness of the nervous system
lies. The aspecting planet will help, or hinder, through its own
nature, as well as through its sign and house.

VENUS IN REGARD TO HEALTH

Venus rules the venous blood. Good aspects to Venus carry
away the impurities of the blood. Afflictions may cause impurities, which will manifest as lassitude, ennui, swelling, cysts,
varicose veins.

Venus also rules the neck and throat. With good aspects
there will be beauty in these parts, and the ability to talk and
sing well. Afflictions, however, may give rise to sore throat,
mumps, quinsy.

Venus rules the kidneys. Good aspects can bring perfect action of the kidneys, while bad aspects can cause kidney and
bladder trouble.

Since the venous blood pours into the right auricle of the
heart, thence to the right ventricle, and from there to the
lungs, we see that too many impurities in the blood stream
put a great strain upon the heart and lungs. In other words we
have to consider not only Venus, but also the Sun and Mercury.

MARS IN REGARD TO HEALTH

Mars governs the face, head, brain, nose, and tongue. Even the presence of Mars in the First House may cause cuts, bruises, and burns upon these parts of the body. Mars also governs the reproductive organs; hence good aspects increase the number of children, while ill aspects decrease the likelihood of children.

Mars governs the muscular system. Under good aspects to Mars from Mercury, the muscles can be trained in specific ways, denoted by sign and aspect. In musicians, the muscles of the arms, shoulders, and hands are trained to do specific work. Under bad aspects from Saturn the muscles can become stiff and set. When in Water signs Mars tends towards violent temper, and hysteria. When in Earth signs Mars tends towards bodily hurts.

Mars rules the temperature of the human body. People may run very high temperatures when under bad aspects of Mars. Fevers, however, may act as cleansing fires that throw out disease.

Mars rules the red corpuscles of the body, also the iron in the blood. When the planet is near the Ascendant, it tends to impart a ruddy countenance. Evil aspects from Saturn in particular tend to sap Martian vitality, deplete the energies, and possibly to cause anemia.

JUPITER IN REGARD TO HEALTH

Jupiter rules the arterial blood, the liver, thighs, hip bones, and feet.

Since the condition of the arterial blood depends upon the heart action, Jupiter has to be considered in its relationship to the Sun. Good aspects from the Sun or Mars are not always too beneficial to Jupiter, for these tend to over activity. Good aspects from Venus incline to self-indulgence, and too much fat. Jupiter rules cellular growth.

The Jupiterian is fond of open air life, and of sunshine. Actually, he needs these things in order that the blood may be purified, and the liver kept in order.

Under affliction, Jupiter can cause painful swellings in the feet, also fallen arches.

SATURN IN REGARD TO HEALTH

Saturn rules the bony structure of the body, the skeleton, skin, tendons, cartilages, and teeth. Under affliction to Saturn by Mars or Uranus, trouble may manifest in these parts.

Saturn placed in the Ascendant, or ruling the Ascendant, may give delicate health in childhood, but the native usually grows out of this, and lives to quite an advanced age. As noted previously, both Alan Leo and Goethe had Saturn on their Ascendants, and the latter lived to be eighty-three.

Saturn's function is to accumulate; hence it is usually involved in illnesses that begin slowly, last a long time, and are the result of cold, depression, or fear. Saturn tends to impede the circulation, harden the arteries, give uric acid deposits, and rheumatism. At times Saturn can be involved in anemia and tuberculosis, especially when these are the result of poverty, privation, malnutrition, or excessive reducing diets.

URANUS IN REGARD TO HEALTH

Uranus, like Mercury, has some rule over the nervous system. It is usually concerned in sudden illnesses, cramps, and spasms. Uranus may bring sudden falls, or falls from great heights, and yet the native may be uninjured. The planet tends to bring accidents due to electricity, lightning, or explosions.

Under good aspects we find Uranus can bring sudden and almost miraculous recovery from illnesses.

NEPTUNE IN REGARD TO HEALTH

Neptune may be involved in sicknesses that refuse to be diagnosed, also in cases of poison, alcohol, and narcotics. It inclines to melancholy and depression, sometimes to delusions.

Neptune aspects are found in cases of trance, religious ecstasy, and dreams. The planet may cause death by drowning or asphyxiation. In such cases, however, the whole horoscope would have to point to such endings. If a thing is important in a horoscope, it is always indicated in more ways than one.

PLUTO IN REGARD TO HEALTH

Very little has been tabulated on the effects of Pluto on health. It rules the enzymes of the stomach, and probably it rules metabolism.

METALS AND SUBSTANCES RULED BY THE PLANETS AND THEIR SIGNS

Planets	Signs	Substances
Sun	Leo	Gold, precious stones.
Moon	Cancer	Silver, the sea, liquids.
Mercury	Gemini-Virgo	Quicksilver, mirrors.
Venus	Taurus-Libra	Copper, brass, art goods, clothes, silk, velvet.
Mars	Aries-Scorpio	Iron, steel, diamonds, sparkling substances.
Jupiter	Sagittarius-Pisces	Tin.
Saturn	Capricorn-Aquarius	Lead, stone, bone, coal.
Uranus	Aquarius	Electricity, magnetic substances.
Neptune	Pisces	Oil, gas, petroleum products, perfumes, alcohol, phosphorescent substances.
Pluto	Aries-Scorpio	Atomic products.

The knowledge of the substances ruled by the planets sometimes gives us the clue to the trade, or profession. Typesetters are often found under Capricorn and Aquarius, goldsmiths under Leo, engineers under Aries or Scorpio—if not under the Sun sign, then perhaps under the sign on the Midheaven.

We understand the character of people more clearly when we relate their planets to substances. In the chart of Calvin

Coolidge, we noted that his Saturn opposed all his Cancer planets. Saturn acted like lead upon the keel of a ship, steadying the emotionalism of Cancer.

OCCUPATION AS SEEN IN THE HOROSCOPE

When studying occupation, the astrologer must study the total chart. The Eleventh House discloses the objective, and the hopes and wishes. The Sun may disclose something too of the purpose; the Moon may show natural inclination. Mercury declares the mental ability, also capacity for taking instruction. Mars signifies the energy and strength. Venus shows the artistic faculties. The Ascendant discloses the impression that the physical body can make upon the world.

Next look carefully at the cusp of the Sixth House, for this is the house of service, or work for others (in this case the Tenth House will represent the employer). The position, by sign and house, of the ruler of the sign, will modify the nature of the work. For example, if Virgo is on the sixth cusp, and the ruler Mercury is in an Earth sign, the native will prefer a more practical type of work than if Mercury happened to be in an Air sign. If Mercury is in a Fire sign, it will give greater zeal and enthusiasm for work. If it is in an angular house, the native will go out and seek business. If it is in a succedent house, there may be a tendency to stay in the same work for very long periods of years. The Sixth House shows the adaptability for work, the general way in which contacts between inferiors and superiors are conducted.

The Tenth House may declare the actual profession, particularly if the native should work for himself (in which case the Sixth House represents his employees). The ruler of the Tenth House has to be considered in the sign and house in which it is posited. The position of this ruler often indicates the field of activity.

The Second House needs consideration because it yields the

key to the money earned by the native. It also represents the money available for training and for education. It is the house of the money made by the native's own efforts (being the second from the first). The Eleventh House represents money made through the profession (being the second from the tenth).

OCCUPATIONS OF THE SUN AND LEO

Since the Sun is the center and pivot of the solar system, when it is in its own sign Leo, it inclines the native to desire occupations in which it will be the pivot. The native of Leo likes to direct, govern, and organize the work of others. He prefers to be his own employer.

There is an enormous fund of energy in the Leo man, and when he works, he works very hard. Since Leo is also the sign governing pleasures, Leo may work hard at his amusements. He has the capacity to organize games, theaters, and all places of entertainment. Such matters can become his career. Being fond of children, he is often interested in educating them. All children love a Leo teacher, but because little independence of thought is possible in the teaching profession, Leo is rarely among the rank and file of teachers. He is fond of animals and well able to train them, hence many Leo people enter the circus. Leo has a good sense of showmanship, and is usually very convincing when he talks.

Because of his innate faith, Leo may enter the ministry, and succeed very well. Also, because he believes in himself, he can become a good salesman.

Leo rarely succeeds, however, when irritated by the control of others. He is too independent. When in authority he has such confidence in himself that his orders are rarely disobeyed, or questioned.

Since gold is the metal of the Sun, the Leo man is interested in jewelry, the money exchanges, and the speculative markets.

Leo people may succeed as:

actors, artists
movie workers and
  directors
educators
foremen and men in
  authority
financiers
gamblers
goldsmiths

governmental lead-
  ers
horse dealers and
  trainers
jewelers
jockeys
judges
money-lenders
publishers
promoters

pawn-shop dealers
religious leaders
salesmen
showmen
speculators
stock brokers
theatrical managers
  and producers
trainers and coaches
  for games

OCCUPATIONS OF THE MOON AND CANCER

A Moon-type person is fond of travel and amusement, though he likes to have a home to which he may return. He loves to meet people and the public, after he has overcome his natural timidity. He is not overenergetic, but is imaginative and plastic, loving variety of experience, and strong dramatic situations. He is innately psychic, and has a strong sense of what the public wants, hence he is successful when marketing commodities that have wide and quick sales. He has not the patience for long slow selling. Since the Moon is a Water planet, the Cancerian is adaptable, and able to change his methods quickly in order to meet growing needs.

Cancer sometimes uses the home as the base for his energies, and for his work. His work may entail contacts with the homes of his clients, for example, interior decorators, salesmen from house to house, insurance agents, etc. His employment may be connected with women's or children's goods. The sign may include seamen, fishermen, grocers, general tradesmen, dressmakers, cooks, and domestic servants. Cancer has a strong leaning towards banking.

In this occupation the tenacity of the sign enters, encouraging thrift and saving.

Cancer people may succeed as:

actors	dressmakers	pilots
artists	fishermen	real-estate brokers
antique dealers	fortune tellers	salesmen
advertising	food experts	store keepers
banking	houseworkers	sailors
builders' merchants	hotel-keepers	silversmiths
children's nurses	laundry workers	tea and coffee mer-
cooks	mediums	chants
dealers in food and	midwives and nurses	tradesmen
liquids	naval men	news analysts
domestic servants	navigators	

OCCUPATIONS OF MERCURY AND ITS SIGNS

The Mercury person is nimble of hand. His sense of touch is highly developed, hence he is usually good at any work wherein this factor is necessary. Like lunar-type persons, Mercury types enjoy travel and movement. Any occupation that ties them down is trying. In ancient mythology Mercury was the god of the roads, of communications, and of all movement of merchandise. The planet rules travel by road, rail, or airplane. It rules communication of ideas, information conveyed through speech, letter, telegraph, telephone, books, newspapers, magazines and other printed material. It rules trade, the circulation of money, and commerce generally.

Mercury was also the scribe and bookkeeper of the gods. Today we say the planet rules accounting and all secretarial work. Gemini being an Air sign, confers the ability to express harmony in music. Virgo types are, as a rule, more stable than Gemini types. The Earth element inclines to make them practical and inclined towards manual work, if necessary. Virgoans may take up farming, gardening, or woodwork, as a means of livelihood, or as hobbies.

Gemini people may succeed as:

airmen	electricians	railway employees
auctioneers	inventors	reporters
brokers	letter-carriers	secretaries
bankers	messengers,	speakers
bookkeepers	mathematicians	salesmen
booksellers	musicians	teachers
clerks	orators	telegraph operators
composers	postal employees	telephone operators
drivers of vehicles	radio announcers	writers

Virgo people may succeed as:

analytical chemists	historians	physical culturists
bookbinders	literary critics	routine workers
clerks	makers of instru-	secretaries
carpenters	ments	sanitary engineers
dieticians	mathematicians	stationers
doctors	medical men	teachers
druggists	messengers	telegraph operators
editors	nurses	telephone operators
farmers	precision workers	weavers
gardeners	professors	writers

OCCUPATIONS OF VENUS AND ITS SIGNS

Venus rules the principle of attraction, coagulation, adaptation, and beauty. It is not conducive to energy, but it is persistent. The Venusian does not succeed, as a rule, in occupations where it is necessary to go out and seek a market, but he is wonderfully good in occupations where the public will seek him. In fact, the public always seeks Venus. Libra and Taurus rule dress goods, silks, velvets, feathers, ornaments, beauty parlors, art goods, foods, and candy. Since Venus seeks peace and harmony, it rules the principle of justice, particularly that between individuals. Many lawyers, therefore, come under Libra.

Taurus people may succeed as:

agricultural workers
accountants
beekeepers
botanists
cashiers
collectors
cooks, chefs
candy makers
domestic servants
farmers

food manufacturers
financial agents
interior decorators
lawyers
mathematicians
musicians
municipal accountants
manufacturers of women's wear

masseurs
manual workers
nurses
perfumers
paper manufacturers
restaurant keepers
stock breeders
stock brokers
singers

Libra people may succeed as:

artists
adjusters
brokers and those who negotiate affairs for others
comparison shoppers
clothing designers

clothing manufacturers
decorators
dress-goods salesmen
dancers
embroiderers
jewelry workers

lawyers
managers of places of entertainment
milliners
beauty operators
secretaries
wine merchants
writers

OCCUPATIONS OF MARS AND ITS SIGNS

Mars rules the principle of dynamic energy. It gives the ability to cope with hard materials, and rules workers in iron, and metals, engineers, and mechanics. It governs all sharp instruments, hence surgeons, dentists, barbers, clothing cutters, etc., come under its sway. Mars tends to confer resourcefulness and inventiveness, hence it governs those who put new ideas into already existing businesses. It gives aggressiveness and courage, hence its natives can work in extremely dangerous trades. Military men, workers in firearms, and munitions, all come under Mars. It also rules advance salesmen, and such as pioneer a business. In the sign Aries the native likes to go forward with his own activities; in the sign Scorpio the energy is more hidden, hence Scorpio can often be the mainstay of a business, even if he has not the leading title.

Aries people may succeed as:

actors	firemen	nature-cure doctors
architects	footballers	novelists
agents of all kinds	guides	soldiers
company promoters	herbalists	surgeons
carvers	iron workers	salesmen
designers	journalists	steel workers
electricians	metal workers	surveyors
engineers	military men	travelers
explorers	munition makers	workers in foundries

Scorpio people may succeed as:

analysts	iron workers	salesmen
butchers	iron dealers	surgeons
dentists	military men	smiths
doctors	magnetic healers	sanitary inspectors
druggists	metal workers	sanitary engineers
embalmers	naval men	secret service men
engineers	occult workers	submarine workers
executives	police	tanners
hypnotists	researchers	workers in leather

OCCUPATIONS OF JUPITER AND SAGITTARIUS

Jupiter rules the principle of expansion. The people under this planet are interested in sport, travel, religion, jurisprudence, philosophy, hospitals, and public institutions. Under the planet we find ambassadors, writers on jurisprudence, salesmen to foreign countries, astronomers, professors, clergymen, workers in governmental positions, and workers in public institutions.

Sagittarian people may succeed as:

advance agents	ambassadors	clergymen
advertising experts	bookmakers	civil engineers

doctors	inspectors	publishers
ecclesiastical digni-	inspirational writers	professors
taries	judges	professional athletes
explorers	lawyers	stockbrokers
foreign traders	military officers	salesmen
horse dealers	money lenders	trustees
importers	politicians	writers on law

(For Pisces occupations see "Occupations of Neptune and Pisces," page 279.)

OCCUPATIONS OF SATURN AND CAPRICORN

Saturn rules the principle of contraction, and all that is concrete, organized, and scientific. It favors ambition, hence it rules executives of large corporations, men of stability, men in governmental office, and those in power. It governs men who may stay in an office, but who from that office, distribute their products over wide areas.

Capricorn, being an Earth sign, may be prominent in horoscopes of real-estate men, farmers, geologists, coal merchants, and in those who work under the earth—miners. The restrictive nature of the planets is expressed in men who follow the occupation of jailers, and limit the freedom of others. Its caution is expressed in such occupations as watchmen.

Capricorn people may succeed as:

architects	engravers	miners
agricultural workers	executives	municipal employ-
and middlemen	farmers	ees
administrators	geologists	plumbers
brokers	governmental em-	politicians
bookbinders	ployees	potters
bricklayers	jailors	priests
contractors	land surveyors	printers
carpenters	labor union officials	real-estate men
civic employees	lawyers	religious recluses
day laborers	managers	watchmen

OCCUPATIONS OF URANUS AND AQUARIUS

Since Uranus governs what is new, it brings in occupations that are unusual, or not exactly conventional; for example, astrologers, metaphysicians, mesmerists, lecturers on New Thought, Christian Science, and occultism.

Being an electric planet, it governs electricians. Being scientific and original, it governs inventors, patent agents, radio and television operators, radar specialists, and advertising experts. Since Aquarius is a sign of distribution, distributors of all kinds come under the sign.

Aquarian people may succeed as:

advertising men	literary workers	surveyors
aviation officials	managers	social workers
astrologers	newspaper men	screen artists
astronomers	nurses	screen technicians
clerks	postal employees	salesmen
distributors	politicians	teachers
civil engineers	radio performers	violinists and pian-
electricians	reformers	ists
lecturers	railroad employees	watchmakers

OCCUPATIONS OF NEPTUNE AND PISCES

Neptune rules all spiritual matters; hence it can be associated with clergymen, and such as speak on spiritual matters. On its physical side it is connected with the sea, and with flight; hence, seafaring men and aviators come under its influence. Like Uranus, it is concerned with the wide distribution of ideas and commodities; so it rules propaganda, chain stores, etc. One might note that Uranus rules the actual airplane mechanism, whereas Neptune rules the ability to travel in the ether.

Neptune rules perfumers and distillers. It also rules those who work in oils, particularly volatile oils, and petroleum products. Ordinary oils and fats are under Venus.

Neptune seems to rule intangible influences; hence the

Neptunian can work on people's feelings and minds and fascinate them with his ideas, or his products.

Pisces people may succeed as:

agents of all kinds	detectives	oil and gas workers
acrobats	dyers	painters
actors	executives	perfumers
aviators	financial experts	poets
bankers	grocers	physicians
bookkeepers	hotel keepers	prophets
brewery workers	institutional workers	psychics
mass merchants	librarians	radar workers
cloth and wool men	literary men	shoe salesmen
cotton growers	mediums	singers
dancers	medical men	television workers
doctors	naval men	tobacco salesmen
druggists	nurses	translators

OCCUPATIONS OF PLUTO

Since Pluto rules subtle changes, one cannot be too definite about the occupations of the planet. Apart from the present atomic researchers, it is possible that many of Pluto's professions are not yet fully established. Probably the researchers on new plastics, nylons, and drugs, have strong Pluto aspects in their horoscopes. With the help of atomic byproducts, it is possible that in another fifty years the materials now used will be almost entirely replaced by others. Pluto does not necessarily rule gangsters and gangsterism. Every civilization from the Stone Age down has had such people and problems to face. The old astrologers assigned Mars and Mercury to them— Mercury giving the desire to steal, and Mars the brute force and murders involved.

Curiously enough, the discovery of Uranus heralded the knowledge and, later on, the use of electricity. The discovery of Neptune led to the widespread use of petroleum products, and to flight in the ether. Reasoning from the above, we know that the advent of Pluto will bring still greater changes.

MASS MEDIA - ADVERTISING - COMMERCIALS -

LESSON FOURTEEN

How to Erect an Accurate Horoscope

♈ ♉ ♊ ♋ ♌ ♍ ♎ ♏ ♐ ♑ ♒ ♓

INTRODUCTION: *With this final lesson, in which you will learn how to construct accurate charts—one for the eastern hemisphere, one for the western, and then one for southern latitudes—we leave you for the time being. We might have inserted this chapter earlier in the book, but if we had you might not know so readily, as you know now, how to read a chart.* **Astrology is a science in that it is based upon mathematical knowledge, but its greatest glory is as an art** *in which you encourage people to live and act according to their highest concepts. Remember that, when you read a chart for anyone, you* **reveal yourself** *to that person.*

Let us consider the data of Mohandas K. Gandhi, who was born October 2, 1869, 7:45 A.M. at Purbandur, near Bombay. Standard Time was not in effect in 1869. Purbandur is 19° N and 73° E.

In this precise map we shall calculate the Midheaven from the noon previous to birth. This will be October 1. We must add the time that is elapsed from this noon to the birth hour, which will be 19 hrs. 45′.

	Hrs.	Min.	Sec.
Sid. T. Oct. 1, 1869 is	12	41	01
Add time elapsed	19	45	00
	32	26	01
Subtract circle of 24 hrs.	24	00	00
Sidereal Time	8	26	01

This last figure is the one upon which we could base an approximate chart, but in an exact chart, two slight corrections have to be considered:

1. For Time
2. For Longitude

1. The correction for time is at the rate of 10″ per hour
   or 1″ for each 6′.

Correction for 19 hrs. is 19 × 10 = 190″, or 3′ 10″
Correction for 45′ is 45 ÷ 6 = 7½″ 7½
Total correction is 3′ 17½″
   or approximately 3′ 18″

This time correction must be added to the Sidereal Time found above:

	Hrs.	Min.	Sec.
	8	26	01
		3	18
Sidereal Time	8	29	19

2. The correction for longitude is at the rate of 10 seconds for every 15 degrees of longitude; hence we divide the longitude of the birthplace by fifteen, and multiply our result by ten (or, divide by three and multiply by two). Our given longitude is 73 E, so:

$$\frac{73 \times 10}{15} \text{ or } \frac{730}{15} \text{ or } \frac{146}{3} = 48\tfrac{2}{3} = 49'' \text{ correction}$$

When the longitude is east of Greenwich, subtract the correction for longitude.

When the longitude is west of Greenwich, add the correction for longitude.

Since Gandhi was born east of London (Greenwich), we subtract 49″.*

---

* Since the total of the corrections for the time and longitude never amounts to four minutes, that is, one degree on the Midheaven; and, as most people do not know their birth time within four minutes, we did not burden you with these corrections before.

	Hrs.	Min.	Sec.
	8	29	19
			49
Sid. T. of M.C.	8	28	30	(abbreviation S.T.M.C.)

Using latitude 19 degrees for Purbandur, the *A-P Table of Houses* shows:

Hrs.	Min.	Sec.	House Ten
8	25	19	4° Leo
8	29	26	5° Leo

Gandhi's Sidereal Time of 8 hours, 28 min. 30 sec. would lie about three-quarters of the way between these two Sidereal times; hence the Midheaven we need will lie about three quarters of a degree between 4° and 5° Leo. We have to calculate the exact figure. First subtract to obtain the Sidereal Time needed for one degree of travel upon the Midheaven:

Hrs.	Min.	Sec.	House Ten
8	29	26	5° Leo
8	25	19	4° Leo
	4	07	1° travel on M.C.

This difference of 4' 07" represents the Sidereal Time during which one degree (60' of arc) travels over the M.C. How much beyond the Sid. T. of 4° Leo is Gandhi's Sid. T.? It is:

Hrs.	Min.	Sec.	
8	28	30	Sid. T. for Gandhi's M.C.
8	25	19	Sid. T. of 4° Leo
	3	11	Difference

We know that 4' 07" yields one degree (60') on the Midheaven, hence 1' of Sid. T. will yield $\frac{60'}{4'\ 07''}$ arc on M.C. We must multiply this fraction by 3' 11":

$$\frac{60 \times 3'\ 11''}{4'\ 07''} = 46'\ \text{arc on M.C.}$$

We add this 46′ to 4° Leo giving us a Midheaven of 4° Leo 46′.

Such multiplications and divisions are tedious; hence Napier introduced logarithms.

THE USE OF LOGARITHMS

The use of logarithms enables us to simplify many calculations. At the back of all recent issues of *Raphael's Ephemerides*, is a page called "Proportional Logarithms for Finding the Planets' Places." We give you a similar table on page 296. Along the top are the words *Degrees or Hours*. In the left-hand column is the abbreviation *Min.* for Minutes.

Logarithms are merely fractions or proportions that are shown as decimal fractions. If you wish, you can study them in any good textbook on mathematics, but we show you how to use them without going deeply into the subject.

The Table of Logarithms gives logarithms for hours and minutes, but because there are as many seconds in a minute as there are minutes in a degree, we can use this table for working in minutes and seconds.

We can find our true Midheaven by means of this table. The figures along the top can represent minutes, and the figures down the columns can represent seconds.

The value of logarithms is that when one needs to multiply two sets of figures, one simply adds their logarithms.

When one needs to divide two sets of figures, one simply subtracts their logarithms.

We now work our last problem with the aid of logarithms. It was:

$$\frac{3' \, 11'' \times 1°}{4' \, 07''}$$

We need three logarithms:

1. Log. of 3′ 11″
2. Log. of 1°
3. Log. of 4′ 07″

We look along the top line of our Table of Logarithms and find the column marked 3. Then, keeping our finger on this column, we travel down the column until we find a cross column level with the number 11 on our left. This is the logarithm we need. We find the other logarithms in the same way:

1. Log. of 3' 11" is   .8773
2. Log. of 1°   is   1.3802
3. Log. of 4' 07" is   .7657

We merely add the first two logarithms and subtract the third:

Log. of 3' 11"   .8773
Log. of 1°   1.3802
Total of logs.   2.2575
Subtract log. of 4' 07"   .7657
Result   1.4918

We now have to turn this last result back into minutes. Look down the Logarithm Table and you will find that the figure nearest lies in the column marked 0. To the left you find 46'. We add 46' to 4° Leo making the Midheaven for Gandhi 4° Leo 46'. This is exactly the same figure we found by multiplication and division.

HOW TO FIND THE ASCENDANT

Next find the true Ascendant in much the same way. At latitude 19° N, the *A-P Table of Houses* shows:

1. Midheaven 5° Leo   Ascendant 5° Scorpio 00'
2. Midheaven 4° Leo   "   4°   "   04'

Subtracting #2 from #1, we find:

One degree of travel on the Midheaven is equivalent to 56' of travel on the Ascendant.

Our question is what will the Ascendant travel when the Midheaven travels only 46′.

The Ascendant will travel:

$$\frac{56′ \times 46′}{60′} = 43′$$

Adding this 43′ to 4° Scorpio 04′, gives us the wanted Ascendant, which will be 4° Scorpio 47′.

We could have used logarithms on this problem, adding the logarithms for 56′ and 46′, then subtracting the logarithm for 60′, or 1°, from our total:

Logarithm for 56′	1.4102
Logarithm for 46′	1.4956
Total	2.9058
Log. for 1° subtract	1.3802
Log. of Asc.	1.5256

Turning this last logarithm back into minutes, we find it is 43′, which we add to 4° Scorpio 04′, giving us 4° Scorpio 47′ for our Ascendant, as we had before.

Since most *Tables of Houses* do not give the cusps correct to minutes, except for the ascendant, you need not apply exactitude to them. However, if you happen to have a *Dalton's Table of Houses*, which does give cusps correct to minutes, then refinements, similar to the above, can be calculated. It sometimes happens that when a planet is very close to a cusp, it is difficult to know whether it is in one house or another without calculating the cuspal degree. Still, we allow an orb of six degrees when considering a planet that is close to a cusp. The influence of a planet is always thrown forward into the following house, when it lies six degrees of longitude or less than the cuspal degree.

RULE TO OBTAIN THE MIDHEAVEN BY LOGARITHMS

After you have calculated the Sidereal Time for the Midheaven, look in the *Table of Houses* for this. If you do not find
a Sidereal Time that corresponds exactly with this:

a. Write down the nearest Sid. Time greater than your Sid. T.
b. Write down the nearest Sid. Time less than your Sid. T.
c. Subtract b from a.
d. Subtract b from the Sid. T. needed for your chart.
e. Your problem is now stated as:

$$\frac{d \times 1°}{c}$$

f. Fnd the logarithms for these three figures. Add the logarithms of d and 1°. Subtract logarithms of c.
g. Change result of f back into minutes.
h. Add g to Midheaven degree corresponding with b. The result will be the actual Midheaven for your chart.

RULE TO OBTAIN THE ASCENDANT BY LOGARITHMS

i. Write down Ascendant corresponding to a of previous
   exercise.
j. Write down Ascendant corresponding to b of previous
   exercise.
k. Subtract j from i.
l. Your problem is now stated:

$$\frac{g \times k}{1°}$$

m. Find logarithms for these three numbers. Add logarithms
   of g and k. Subtract Logarithm of 1°.
n. Change result of m back into minutes.
o. Add n to j. Result gives the Ascendant for the Sidereal
   Time required.

CORRECTION OF THE PLANETS BY MEANS OF LOGARITHMS

In order to calculate the planetary positions, you have first to change the Local Mean Time of birth into Greenwich Mean Time.

Bombay is 73 degrees East longitude.

Multiply 73 by 4, since there are 4′ of time for 1° longitude.

$$73 \times 4 = 292'$$

Divide 292′ by 60′ = 4 hours 52 mins.

Since Bombay is East longitude, we have to subtract this from the Local Mean Time:

L.M.T.	7 hours	45′	A.M.
subtract	4	52	
G.M.T.	2	53	A.M.

We now use logarithms to find the planetary positions.

Rule: 1. Find the interval of this G.M.T. to the nearest noon, which will be on October 2.
The interval is 9 hrs. 7′ before noon.

2. Find the logarithm for this interval:
Log. for 9 hrs. 7′ is .4204
This you call your Permanent Logarithm (P.L.), and, as it will be involved in all planetary calculations, write it down in a prominent position on your working paper.

3. Subtract the positions of all planets on October 1 from their positions on October 2, in order to get their rates of travel in 24 hours.

a.
Sun's position Oct. 2	9 Libra 18′	55″
Sun's position Oct. 1	8	19	48
Daily rate of travel		59	07

We shall approximate this to 59′

b.
Log of 59′	1.3875
Add P.L.	.4204
	1.8079

YEAR 1869		☉	☽	♇	♅	♄	♃	♂	♀	☿
1	Planetary Positions Oct. 2	9° ♎ 19'	25° ♌ 41'	18° ♈ 26' ℞	21° ♋ 46'	12° ♐ 23'	20° ♉ 08' ℞	18° ♍ 40'	16° ♍ 55'	4° ♍ 00'
2	Planetary Positions Oct. 1	8° ♎ 20'	11° ♌ 18'	18° ♈ 27' ℞	21° ♋ 45'	12° ♐ 19'	20° ♉ 13' ℞	17° ♍ 59'	15° ♍ 43'	3° ♍ 23'
3	Subtract #2 from #1 Gives Rate of Travel	0° 59'	14° 23'	0° 01' ℞	0° 01'	0° 04'	0° 05' ℞	0° ♍ 41'	1° 12'	0° 37'
4	Logarithm of Rate of Travel	1.3875	.2223				2.4594	1.5456	1.3010	1.5902
5	Permanent Logarithm	.4204	.4204				.4204	.4204	.4204	.4204
6	Add #4 to #5	1.8079	.6427				2.8798	1.9660	1.7214	2.0106
7	Changing #6 from Logarithm	0° 22'	5° 28'				0° 02'	0° 16'	0° 27'	0° 14'
8	From #1, i.e., Nearest Moon, Subtract #7	9° ♎ 19' / 0 22	25° ♌ 41' / 5 28	18° ♈ 26' ℞	21° ♋ 46'	12° ♐ 21'	20° ♉ 08' ℞ / 0 02	18° ♍ 40' / 0 16	16° ♍ 55' / 0 27	4° ♍ 00' / 0 14
9	RESULT	8° ♎ 57'	20° ♌ 13'	18° ♈ 26' ℞	21° ♋ 46'	12° ♐ 21'	20° ♉ 10' ℞	18° ♍ 24'	16° ♍ 28'	3° ♍ 46'

DIAGRAM 55

Table of Planetary Corrections for Horoscope of Gandhi

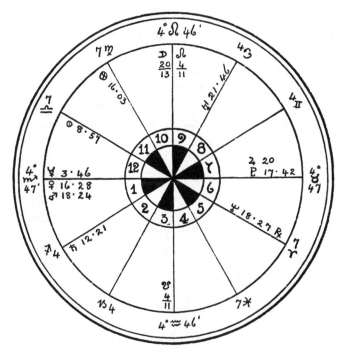

DIAGRAM 56
Horoscope of Mohandas K. Gandhi
October 2, 1869

c. Change this logarithm back to minutes. We find it
nearest to 22'. Hence we subtract 22' from the Sun's
position on Oct. 2:

Sun's position Oct. 2	9 Libra 18'	55"
Subtract		22	00
Sun at 2:53 A.M., G.M.T.	8	56	55

or, approximately, 8° Libra 57'

Having calculated the Sun's position, we must apply this
method to all the planets. You will, however, find it easier to
make all the calculations in some kind of tabular system, as per
Diagram 55.

Neptune, Uranus, and Pluto move so slowly that it is rarely necessary to make any corrections for them. In this case we note that they are nearer to Gandhi's G.M.T. on October 2 than on October 1.

Regarding the retrograde movement of Jupiter, we add our correction, because the farther back from the noon position, the greater will be the degrees and minutes of a retrograding planet.

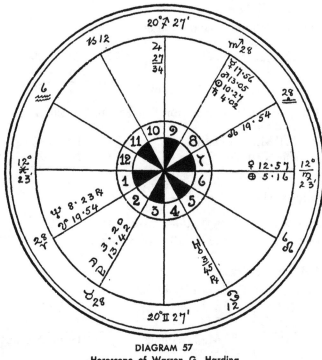

DIAGRAM 57
Horoscope of Warren G. Harding
November 2, 1865

Let us next take the chart of President Harding, who was born at Brooming Grove, Ohio (Lat. 40° N., Long. 83° W.) on November 2, 1865, at 2:30 P.M. Since the date is before 1883, we can call this time Local Mean Time.

	Hrs.	Min.	Sec.
1. Sid. T. Nov. 2, 1865	14	47	05
2. Add Local Mean Time of birth	2	30	00
3. Add correction for time			25
4. Add correction of long. 83° W.			55
Sidereal Time of M.C. for Harding	17	18	25

To Find the Midheaven:

From the Dalton Table of Houses
for 40° N., we have:

21° Sag. on M.C.	17	20	49
20° Sag. on M.C.	17	16	29
1° difference for Sid. T. of		04	20

Let us find the difference from 20° Sag. to the Sid. T. of M.C.
for Harding.

S.T.M.C. of Harding	17	18	25
Sid. T. of 20° Sag.	17	16	29
Difference		1	56

Harding's M.C. will be: $\dfrac{1' \, 56'' \times 1°}{4' \, 20''}$

or, 1.0939 plus 1.3802 minus .7434 = 27'
This 27' must be added to 20° Sag. giving M.C. 20° Sag. 27'.

To Find the Ascendant:

From *Dalton's Table of Houses* for 40° N.

21° Sag. on M.C. gives Asc.	13° 23' Pisces
20° Sag. " M.C. " "	11° 35' "
1° " M.C. requires	1° 48' on Ascendant

Our Asc. is $\dfrac{1' \, 48'' \times 27'}{1°}$

or, 1.1249 plus 1.7270 minus 1.3802 = 48'
This must be added to 11° 35' Pisces, giving the Asc. 12° 23'
Pisces.

Greenwich Mean Time for calculation of Harding's planets:

The longitude is 83° W.
Multiply this by 4' = 83 × 4 = 332'
Divide by 60 to get hours   =   5 hours 32'
Add the above result to the birth hour:

	Hrs.	Min.
	2	30
	5	32
G.M.T. is	8	02 P.M.

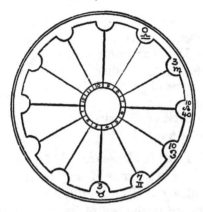

DIAGRAM 58
House Cusps for Southern Latitudes

TO ERECT A HOROSCOPE FOR A LATITUDE SOUTH
OF THE EQUATOR

The Tables of Houses are all calculated for places north of the equator, but they can be used for places south of it, if we proceed as in the example below:

Let us take the chart of Sir Hubert Wilkins, the famous aviator and Arctic explorer. He was born October 31, 1888, at 11:36 A.M., Standard Time, Australia, 139° E., and 34° S.

South Australia is standardized on 142° E 30', that is, 9½ hours fast of G.M.T. We must first correct our Standard Time into Local Mean Time. The birthplace (139° E.) is 3° 30' west of the meridian that sets the time (142° E 30'), hence subtract 14' from Standard Time to get L.M.T. This will be 11:22 A.M., or, 38' before noon.

In order not to weary you with details while you are engaged in a new problem, we first find the M.C. (as for North Latitude) in the simple way shown in earlier lessons, not using corrections:

	Hrs.	Min.	Sec.
1. Sid. T. Oct. 31, 1888	14	41	00
2. Subtract 38′ (time before noon)		38	00
Sid. T. for North Latitude	14	03	00
3. Add 12 hours to get South Lat.	12	00	00
	26	03	00
4. Subtract circle of 24 hours	24	00	00
Sid. T. of 4th cusp is	2	03	00

Look in your *Table of Houses* for 34° N. and find the nearest Sidereal Time for 2 hrs. 3 min. It is 3° Taurus.

Instead of putting 3° Taurus on the tenth cusp, place it on the fourth, then fill in the rest of the data from the *Table of Houses* as per Diagram 58.

To find the Greenwich Mean Time: This will be the Standard Time less 9½ hours, and from this you can calculate the planetary positions. (See Diagram 59.)

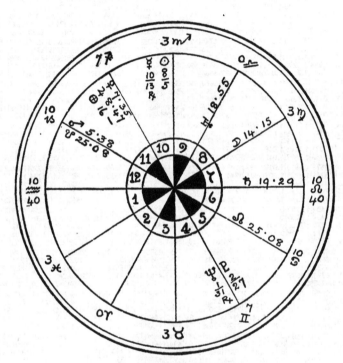

DIAGRAM 59
Horoscope of Sir Hubert Wilkins
October 31, 1888
11:36 A.M., 139° E., 34° S.
Southern Australia

TABLE OF PROPORTIONAL LOGARITHMS

Min.	0	1	2	3	4	5	6	7	8	9	10	11	12	13	14	15	Min.
0	3.1584	1.3802	1.0792	9031	7781	6812	6021	5351	4771	4260	3802	3388	3010	2663	2341	2041	0
1	3.1584	1.3730	1.0756	9007	7763	6798	6009	5341	4762	4252	3795	3382	3004	2657	2336	2036	1
2	2.8573	1.3660	1.0720	8983	7745	6784	5997	5330	4753	4244	3788	3375	2998	2652	2330	2032	2
3	2.6812	1.3590	1.0685	8959	7728	6769	5985	5320	4744	4236	3780	3368	2992	2646	2325	2027	3
4	2.5563	1.3522	1.0649	8935	7710	6755	5973	5310	4735	4228	3773	3362	2986	2640	2320	2022	4
5	2.4594	1.3454	1.0614	8912	7692	6741	5961	5300	4726	4220	3766	3355	2980	2635	2315	2017	5
6	2.3802	1.3388	1.0580	8888	7674	6726	5949	5289	4717	4212	3759	3349	2974	2629	2310	2012	6
7	2.3133	1.3323	1.0546	8865	7657	6712	5937	5279	4708	4204	3752	3342	2968	2624	2305	2008	7
8	2.2553	1.3258	1.0511	8842	7639	6698	5925	5269	4699	4196	3745	3336	2962	2618	2300	2003	8
9	2.2041	1.3195	1.0478	8819	7622	6684	5913	5259	4690	4188	3737	3329	2956	2613	2295	1998	9
10	2.1584	1.3133	1.0444	8796	7604	6670	5902	5249	4682	4180	3730	3323	2950	2607	2289	1993	10
11	2.1170	1.3071	1.0411	8773	7587	6656	5890	5239	4673	4172	3723	3316	2944	2602	2284	1989	11
12	2.0792	1.3010	1.0378	8751	7570	6642	5878	5229	4664	4164	3716	3310	2938	2596	2279	1984	12
13	2.0444	1.2950	1.0345	8728	7552	6628	5866	5219	4655	4156	3709	3303	2933	2591	2274	1979	13
14	2.0122	1.2891	1.0313	8706	7535	6614	5855	5209	4646	4148	3702	3297	2927	2585	2269	1974	14
15	1.9823	1.2833	1.0280	8683	7518	6600	5843	5199	4638	4141	3695	3291	2921	2580	2264	1969	15
16	1.9542	1.2775	1.0248	8661	7501	6587	5832	5189	4629	4133	3688	3284	2915	2574	2259	1965	16
17	1.9279	1.2719	1.0216	8639	7484	6573	5820	5179	4620	4125	3681	3278	2909	2569	2254	1960	17
18	1.9031	1.2663	1.0185	8617	7467	6559	5809	5169	4611	4117	3674	3271	2903	2564	2249	1955	18
19	1.8796	1.2607	1.0153	8595	7451	6546	5797	5159	4603	4109	3667	3265	2897	2558	2244	1950	19
20	1.8573	1.2553	1.0122	8573	7434	6532	5786	5149	4594	4102	3660	3258	2891	2553	2239	1946	20
21	1.8361	1.2499	1.0091	8552	7417	6519	5774	5139	4585	4094	3653	3252	2885	2547	2234	1941	21
22	1.8159	1.2445	1.0061	8530	7401	6505	5763	5129	4577	4086	3646	3246	2880	2542	2229	1936	22
23	1.7966	1.2393	1.0030	8509	7384	6492	5752	5120	4568	4079	3639	3239	2874	2536	2223	1932	23
24	1.7781	1.2341	1.0000	8487	7368	6478	5740	5110	4559	4071	3632	3233	2868	2531	2218	1927	24
25	1.7604	1.2289	0.9970	8466	7351	6465	5729	5100	4551	4063	3625	3227	2862	2526	2213	1922	25
26	1.7434	1.2239	0.9940	8445	7335	6451	5718	5090	4542	4055	3618	3220	2856	2520	2208	1917	26
27	1.7270	1.2188	0.9910	8424	7318	6438	5706	5081	4534	4048	3611	3214	2850	2515	2203	1913	27
28	1.7112	1.2139	0.9881	8403	7302	6425	5695	5071	4525	4040	3604	3208	2845	2509	2198	1908	28
29	1.6960	1.2090	0.9852	8382	7286	6412	5684	5061	4516	4032	3597	3201	2839	2504	2193	1903	29
30	1.6812	1.2041	0.9823	8361	7270	6398	5673	5051	4508	4025	3590	3195	2833	2499	2188	1899	30
31	1.6670	1.1993	0.9794	8341	7254	6385	5662	5042	4499	4017	3583	3189	2827	2493	2183	1894	31
32	1.6532	1.1946	0.9765	8320	7238	6372	5651	5032	4491	4010	3576	3183	2821	2488	2178	1889	32
33	1.6398	1.1899	0.9737	8300	7222	6359	5640	5023	4482	4002	3570	3176	2816	2483	2173	1885	33
34	1.6269	1.1852	0.9708	8279	7206	6346	5629	5013	4474	3994	3563	3170	2810	2477	2168	1880	34
35	1.6143	1.1806	0.9680	8259	7190	6333	5618	5003	4466	3987	3556	3164	2804	2472	2164	1875	35
36	1.6021	1.1761	0.9652	8239	7174	6320	5607	4994	4457	3979	3549	3157	2798	2467	2159	1871	36
37	1.5902	1.1716	0.9625	8219	7159	6307	5596	4984	4449	3972	3542	3151	2793	2461	2154	1866	37
38	1.5786	1.1671	0.9597	8199	7143	6294	5585	4975	4440	3964	3535	3145	2787	2456	2149	1862	38
39	1.5673	1.1627	0.9570	8179	7128	6282	5574	4965	4432	3957	3529	3139	2781	2451	2144	1857	39
40	1.5563	1.1584	0.9542	8159	7112	6269	5563	4956	4424	3949	3522	3133	2775	2445	2139	1852	40
41	1.5456	1.1540	0.9515	8140	7097	6256	5552	4947	4415	3942	3515	3126	2770	2440	2134	1848	41
42	1.5351	1.1498	0.9488	8120	7081	6243	5541	4937	4407	3934	3508	3120	2764	2435	2129	1843	42
43	1.5249	1.1455	0.9462	8101	7066	6231	5531	4928	4399	3927	3501	3114	2758	2430	2124	1838	43
44	1.5149	1.1413	0.9435	8081	7050	6218	5520	4918	4390	3919	3495	3108	2753	2424	2119	1834	44
45	1.5051	1.1372	0.9409	8062	7035	6205	5509	4909	4382	3912	3488	3102	2747	2419	2114	1829	45
46	1.4956	1.1331	0.9383	8043	7020	6193	5498	4900	4374	3905	3481	3096	2741	2414	2109	1825	46
47	1.4863	1.1290	0.9356	8023	7005	6180	5488	4890	4365	3897	3475	3089	2736	2409	2104	1820	47
48	1.4771	1.1249	0.9330	8004	6990	6168	5477	4881	4357	3890	3468	3083	2730	2403	2099	1816	48
49	1.4682	1.1209	0.9305	7985	6975	6155	5466	4872	4349	3882	3461	3077	2724	2398	2095	1811	49
50	1.4594	1.1170	0.9279	7966	6960	6143	5456	4863	4341	3875	3454	3071	2719	2393	2090	1806	50
51	1.4508	1.1130	0.9254	7947	6945	6131	5445	4853	4333	3868	3448	3065	2713	2388	2085	1802	51
52	1.4424	1.1091	0.9228	7929	6930	6118	5435	4844	4324	3860	3441	3059	2707	2382	2080	1797	52
53	1.4341	1.1053	0.9203	7910	6915	6106	5424	4835	4316	3853	3434	3053	2702	2377	2075	1793	53
54	1.4260	1.1015	0.9178	7891	6900	6094	5414	4826	4308	3846	3428	3047	2696	2372	2070	1788	54
55	1.4180	1.0977	0.9153	7873	6885	6081	5403	4817	4300	3838	3421	3041	2691	2367	2065	1784	55
56	1.4102	1.0939	0.9128	7854	6871	6069	5393	4808	4292	3831	3415	3034	2685	2362	2061	1779	56
57	1.4025	1.0902	0.9104	7836	6856	6057	5382	4798	4284	3824	3408	3028	2679	2356	2056	1774	57
58	1.3949	1.0865	0.9079	7818	6841	6045	5372	4789	4276	3817	3401	3022	2674	2351	2051	1770	58
59	1.3875	1.0828	0.9055	7800	6827	6033	5361	4780	4268	3809	3395	3016	2668	2346	2046	1765	59
	0	1	2	3	4	5	6	7	8	9	10	11	12	13	14	15	

DIAGRAM 60

Notes

LESSON ONE

1. **Mayans,** or Mayan Indians—name of a civilized people who lived in Central America.
2. **Gaston Maspero** (1846–1916), French authority on Egypt, Assyria, and Babylon. Wrote *The Dawn of Civilization*, and *The Struggle of the Nations*. translated and published by the S.P.C.K.
3. **Aristotle** (384–322 B.C.), one of the major Greek philosophers.
4. **Cicero** (106–143 B.C.), Roman lawyer, orator, and writer.
5. **Sennacherib** (705–681 B.C.), King of Assyria, a great conqueror. The story of how he tried to conquer Jerusalem is told in the Bible.
6. **Druids**—the priests and early lawgivers of early Britain and parts of Europe. The training for their duties is said to have taken twenty-five years.
7. **Geoffrey Chaucer** (1340–1400), "the father of English poetry."
8. **St. Thomas Aquinas** (1226–1274), of noble descent; renowned theologian of the Middle Ages. He is regarded as the patron saint of Roman Catholic educational institutions.
9. **Tacitus** (55–120 A.D.), Roman historian.
10. **Galien** (about 130–200 A.D.), the greatest physician of his time. Was taught astrology by his father, and used it in his profession of medicine. (Sometimes known as Galen, or Galenus.)
11. **Pierre d'Ailly** (1350–1420), theologian and cardinal. Chancellor of Notre Dame. Paris.
12. **Dante** (1265–1321), Italian poet. Author of *The Divine Comedy*. This poem is in three parts—Hell, Purgatory, and Paradise.
13. **Virgil** (70–19 B.C.), Roman poet, author of *The Aeneid*, the national epic of Rome. Dante admired him so much that he made him act as guide in his book.
14. **Copernicus** (1473–1543), a native of Poland, considered the founder of modern astronomy. His works developed the theory known, and hinted at, by ancient scientists that the sun is the center of the solar system, and that the earth revolves around the sun. He learned astrology at the University of Cracow.

LESSON TWO

1. **The eagle.** In medieval pictures, and in modern ones based on medieval thought, we find St. John the Gospeller is assigned the emblem of the eagle. The four gospellers can even be portrayed as the four fixed signs:

St. Matthew	as an angel	(Aquarius)
St. Luke	as an ox	(Taurus)
St. Mark	as a lion	(Leo)
St. John	as an eagle	(Scorpio)

In Babylonian art, however, the eagle was sometimes attached to Aquarius, largely because the constellation Aquila (the eagle) is not too

far distant from Aquarius. The Greeks believed that Ganymede, the most
handsome of young men, was carried off to Olympus by Jove's eagle in
order that he might become cupbearer to the god. Apparently, cupbearers
came under Aquarius.

LESSON FIVE

1. **Albrecht Dürer** (1471–1528), artist, considered the inventor of the art
of etching. His pictures are packed full of symbolic meaning. How wonderful if artists today knew enough of the inner meaning of astrology to
take any of the planets in a sign and interpret it in art!

If we study the details of this etching, we shall discover very clearly
what Dürer intended to convey. Under the scales of Libra sits a pensive
little figure of Cupid, son of Venus. At his feet, the sacrificial lamb of
Aries sleeps peacefully, indicating the day with all its problems has come
to its rest. Close to the lamb is the golden ball or apple of Venus, sym-
bolizing the earth.

The spirit of melancholia, winged, and crowned with the myrtle leaves
of Venus, sits in deep thought. She carries the compass of Saturn, indicating that the circle of days has been measured. Hanging on the wall are
the hourglass of Saturn and a magic square. Above the latter is the curfew
bell of departing day. In the background is the ladder of Saturn by means
of which, according to Dante and the mystics, the soul might climb
through the planets and enter the Seventh Heaven, which is that of
Saturn. At the extreme top left of the picture, we see the setting Sun of
Libra, and upon the face of the Sun is written *Melencolia*. At the extreme right of the foreground, we see the nails of the crucifixion because
Libra, like Aries, is a sign in which the ecliptic, or pathway of the Sun,
cuts the equator.

We gather from the details of this picture that Saturn (Death) has
struck down a loved one. It is the hour of sunset, the change from the
brightness of day to the darkness of the night of the soul. The hour-glass
of Saturn shows that the sands of life have run. The curfew bell of Saturn
indicates that the knell of life has sounded. A carpenter's tools lie idle
near the apple of Venus. Neither work nor pleasure is necessary any more.
Cupid, representing careless lighthearted love, has no smile upon his face,
but the great majestic-winged figure of the spirit of Saturn exalted in Libra
dominates the whole scene, counselling a patience that will mean the
triumph of the soul over sorrow through a penetration of the meaning of
life and death. How does Dürer portray this final triumph?

First, by the ladder of the planets, which provides a means of mounting
to the heaven of contemplation (Saturn):

> 'Tis sorrow builds the shining ladder up,
> *W*hose golden rounds are our calamities,
> *W*hereon our firm feet planeting, nearer God
> The spirit climbs, and hath its eyes unsealed.

Second, by the great faceted stone behind the lamb. This stone, cut
and shaped, was called by the Greeks Potent Father Saturn, for Saturn's
work is to cut and polish the crude stone. This cutting and polishing of
the soul is a painful process. Upon this earth Saturn is the planet of duty

Dürer portrays Saturn exalted in Libra

MELENCOLIA—DÜRER

and discipline, but in the Seventh Heaven it bestows the blissful joy of perfect understanding and inward peace.

Third, by the magic square. This is a series of numbers placed in a pattern, and therefore in harmonious (Venusian) relationship, such that each line, vertical or horizontal, adds up to the same number.

16	3	2	13
5	10	11	8
9	6	7	12
4	15	14	1

ILLUSTRATION 28
Dürer's Magic Square Enlarged

In the above square, each line adds up to thirty-four, as also do the diagonal lines. The digits add up to seven, hence this square becomes a symbol of the seventh planet, Saturn. We might also note that the highest number in the square is sixteen, whose digits again add to seven. Sixteen is four times four, whence we have a magic square of four, the number of the Sun when it is regarded as the power which brings the things of the earth into manifestation.

Various amulet makers of the Middle Ages wrongly assigned this particular magic square to Jupiter, but Jupiter is only the sixth planet. The magic square of Saturn clearly reveals Saturn as bringing earthly life to a close, but, because there is a Sun base, a means is provided for a new life.

How does the magic square indicate Libran or Venusian characteristics? It does so by its internal harmony—every digit must be in its right place to maintain equipoise. At the same time, Saturn necessitates the right relationship of the digit to the whole.

Saturn, lord of matter and of manifestation, has as one of his symbols the compass, by means of which he makes circles in space. But space is not altered, either when a circle is drawn, or when it is effaced. The lesson of Saturn, therefore, is that when the body of outer manifestation is withdrawn, nothing but the body is affected. The root of the square is the Sun, or eternal life.

Finally, the august contemplative Melencolia, who in the etching assumes some of the attributes of Saturn, wears the crown of Venus, the crown of myrtle leaves. To the Greeks this crown was not merely a symbol of the sweetness, sympathy, and love of Venus, but it was also, when dipped in gold, symbolic of heavenly wisdom and understanding. In this case it became the Golden Bough by means of which man could penetrate into the mysteries of the new life after death.

So Melancholia, or Saturn exalted in Libra, finds her place in the Sun! Below the sun lies the ocean or Great Sea from whose foam Venus was said to have been sprung into being:

> Hence, in a season of calm weather
> Though inland far we be,
> Our souls have sight of that immortal sea
> Which brought us hither. . . .

The above lines are from William Wordsworth's Ode to Immortality. He was a poet more modern than Dante, and he knew no astrology, but in meditation he seems to have caught intuitively the ideas of Saturn exalted in Libra, both in the above lines and also in his Ode to Duty:

> Stern Lawgiver! yet thou dost wear
> The Godhead's most benignant grace;
> Nor know we anything so fair
> As is the smile upon thy face:
> Flowers laugh before thee on their beds,
> And fragrance in thy footing treads;
> Thou dost preserve the stars from wrong;
> And the most ancient heavens, through Thee, are fresh
>   and strong.

INDEX

♈ ♉ ♊ ♋ ♌ ♍ ♎ ♏ ♐ ♑ ♒ ♓

301

CPSIA information can be obtained
at www.ICGtesting.com
Printed in the USA
BVHW061434130620
581340BV00004B/78